Child Abuse in Schools

About the Author

Dr. Sushma Pandey is Professor and Head, Department of Psychology, D.D.U. Gorakhpur University, Gorakhpur. She is serving in this university since the last 35 years. Earlier, she has worked in the Department of Population Studies, S.V. University, Tirupati, Andhra Pradesh.

Dr. Pandey has a total of 39 years of research experience. During this tenure she has immensely contributed to subject by publishing 85 research papers in national and International Journals and books of repute. Moreover, she has completed 12 research projects; three major research projects funded by U.G.C., N.C.W. and ICSSR, and nine minor research projects under D.S.A. programme. Dr. Pandey has published books on, "Psychological Consequences of Child Abuse", "Psycho-social Aspects of Domestic Violence", "Positive Psychology: Emerging Issues" (Edited, Vol. 1 & 2) and also published text-book in Hindi on "Manav Vikas Ka Manovigyan" in two volumes. Prof. Pandey has supervised/ supervising a total of 25 Ph.D. students. She is the member of many academic bodies and organizations of national and international repute.

Recently, Prof. Pandey has received National Award of Excellence, 2018 by Global Management Council, Ahmedabad for the best teacher. Presently, she is associated with GRRI international collaborative research project. Despite this, she is working on developmental problems in learning disabled children, elder abuse and intervention strategies to prevent child abuse/bullying in school context. Her major areas of interest include: Human Development, Cognitive and Social Psychology and Organizational Behaviour.

Child Abuse in Schools

Psychological Impacts

Dr. (Mrs.) Sushma Pandey
Professor & Head
Department of Psychology
D.D.U. Gorakhpur University
Gorakhpur-273009

CONCEPT PUBLISHING COMPANY PVT. LTD.
NEW DELHI-110059

ISBN-13: 978-93-5439-024-1

First Published 2021

Published and Printed by

Since 1974

Concept Publishing Company Pvt. Ltd.
A/15-16, Commercial Block, Mohan Garden,
New Delhi-110059 (INDIA)
T : 91 11 25351460, 91 11 25351794
E : publishing@conceptpub.com; *W* : www.conceptpub.com

Cataloging in Publication Data--Courtesy: D.K. Agencies (P) Ltd. <docinfo@dkagencies.com>

Pandey, Sushma, author.
Child abuse in schools : psychological impacts / Dr. (Mrs.) Sushma Pandey.
pages cm
Includes bibliographical references and index.
ISBN 9789354390241

1. Child abuse—India—Uttar Pradesh—Psychological aspects. 2. Abused children—India—Uttar Pradesh—Psychology. 3. Students—Crimes against—India—Uttar Pradesh. I. Title.

LCC HV6626.54.I5P36 2021 | DDC 362.7609542 23

Dedication

This Book is dedicated to my Mother
Late (Smt.) Janaki Tiwari who was my role model
and will always inspire me throughout my Life.

—**Sushma Pandey**

Preface

Over the last few decades, the incidence of child abuse in the family and outside the family have increased dramatically at epidemic proportion. Numerous social scientists including psychologists have endeavoured to investigate its various forms, dynamics and consequences on children. Although, majority of research studies is based on cases of child abuse by parents or family members, but little focus is given by researchers on issues related to abuses outside the family in the forms of institutional abuses, ritualistic abuses, organized child sexual abuse and child pornography. Apart from this, numerous cases of abuse are witnessed at workplace and schools. School bullying is one of the most epidemic forms of abuses. Unfortunately, when cases of abuse are observed in schools, it is left unreported. Students do not report to other teachers or school authority as well as their parents because they believe that nothing will be done. As a result, such abusive activities by school personnel or bullies gradually take ugly shape and exert detrimental outcomes on the development and career of a large number of children.

This problem struck to my mind a few years ago, when I was engaged with fieldwork, for my earlier research project on "Social Dynamics of Child Abuse and its Psychological Consequences in Eastern Districts of Uttar Pradesh". I observed that children are not only abused in the family but also they are victims of abuses outside the family by neighbours, classmates, gang of children/ students (Bullies) or school personnel (teacher etc.).

Such events were eye-opener and oriented me to plan for this study entitled, "Child Abuse in Schools: Psychological Impacts". Present study was conducted in schools of seven districts (Gorakhpur, Ballia, Deoria, Basti, Gonda, Lucknow and Kanpur) as these districts are densely populated and sensitive to occurrence of abuses in many forms (as identified from secondary resources). This study investigated the role of environmental, socio-demographic and psychological factors in the origin of child abuse in school setting. Moreover, the researcher tried to explore the psychological consequences of school abuse on cognitive, motivational, affective and behavioural functioning as well as personality and health status of students.

This book titled "Child Abuse in Schools: Psychological Impacts" consists of four major chapters. In chapter 1, the conceptualization of child abuse, its incidence rate in India and around the globe, predictors and consequences of abuse on children have been systematically reported. Further, the objective and hypotheses have been derived on the basis of sound review of literature. Chapter 2 focuses on research strategy, measures and procedure of the study. Further, in Chapter 3, statistical treatment of data (both Quantitative and Qualitative) and obtained results have been displayed and reported. Lastly, in Chapter 4, findings of present study have been interpreted and discussed on the basis of numerous empirical and theoretical evidences. Moreover, on the basis of present findings some recommendation/remediation for prevention of child abuse in schools are reported.

Although, the author is aware of the limitations of this piece of research and does not claim that this phenomenon has been thoroughly explored, yet, undoubtedly, she can assert that this research is a pioneering effort to investigate the roles of environmental, socio-cultural and psychological factors in the origin, prevalence and outcomes of child abuse and neglect in schools. Results of the study suggest the need for preventive interventions to both, abusive teachers/school personnel as well as children, who are victims of various forms of abuse. This research sincerely suggests the need for developing innovative intervention programmes to aware school teachers, and other employees of the school about the adverse consequences of abusive acts on the development of students. Thus, the present piece of research has raised many more issues, which are still unresolved. However, this study will provide sound base for designing other research studies and projects on issues in school setting.

—Prof. (Mrs.) Sushma Pandey

Acknowledgements

It is with a great sense of gratitude that I acknowledge the guidance and support, which I received from inception to completion of this research study. Since this investigation was carried out with the financial assistance provided by the Indian Council of Social Science Research (ICSSR), New Delhi, thus, I express my sincere gratitude to the organization for timely support to complete the project without difficulty.

During the conduction of this study, I consulted and received guidance, support and encouragement from a number of renowned senior psychologists. I express my sincere gratitude to Prof. Anand Prakash, Head, Dept. of Psychology and Dean, International Relations, Delhi University for his support, invaluable suggestions and guidance throughout the period.

I am grateful to Prof. Adesh Agarwal, Former Head, Dept. of Psychology and Dean, Faculty of Arts, Prof. Anupam Nath Tripathi, and Prof. P.S.N. Tiwari, former Heads, Dept. of Psychology, D.D.U. Gorakhpur University, Gorakhpur for their suggestions, support and encouragement.

I also consulted and received suggestions and support from many academicians of other universities amongst whom the names of Prof. R.C. Tripathi, ICSSR, National Fellow and Former Head, Dept. of Psychology, Allahabad University, Prof. Girishwar Misra, Former Vice-Chancellor, Mahatma Gandhi Antarrashtriya Hindi Vishwavidyalaya, Vardha and Former Head, Delhi University and Prof. R.C. Mishra, Former Head, Dept. of Psychology, B.H.U., Varanasi need special gratitude for their invaluable suggestions and encouragement.

I extend my heartfelt thanks to my husband Prof. R.N. Pandey, Principal, National P.G. College, Barhalganj, Gorakhpur, to my mother Smt. Janaki Tiwari, brothers and both sons Avanish Dev Pandey and Rishabh Dev Pandey. They have been constant sources of motivation and pillars of support throughout the period.

I express my sincere gratitude to my Brother Late Dr. Saurabh Kumar Tiwari for his unending co-operation and support. I extend thanks to my students Dr. Abhay Pratap Singh, Nimisha Tripathi, Astha Shukla, Pratibha Singh, Niharika Tripathi, Nidhi Gupta and Annu Prasad who worked silently with great devotion, throughout the period. Last but not the least, I must be thankful to all teachers and students who participated in this investigation as participants.

—Dr. (Mrs.) Sushma Pandey

Contents

1
Introduction

Child abuse as a serious psycho-social problem is present at epidemic threshold around the globe. The problems emanating from child abuse and neglect are indeed complex and multifaceted. Majority of child population is maltreated within and outside the family (in schools or workplace) in many forms. In fact, child abuse (maltreatment) is neither a recent phenomenon, nor it is emerged with any historical period or cultural practice. It is as old as history of humankind. Primarily, the child abuse emerged as a social issue in developed countries. Later on, it was realized that it is present in developing countries like India and has achieved alarming volume. First of all, this problem inflamed social scientists, psychologists, medical scientists and practitioners, following a seminal paper on the "Battered Child Syndrome" in early 1960s, presented by Henry Kempe *et al.* (1962). Afterwards researchers, practitioners and Government organizations started working on this issue and U.S. government called it national emergency. In 1974, the first National Incidence Survey (NIS) was conducted in United States of America and 60,000 cases of child abuse were recognized. Again second NIS survey conducted in 1980, reported 1.1 million cases of abuse whereas, the 1989 survey (NIS III) presented 2.4 million figure of abuse and the 1997 NIS survey identified 9,69,000 cases of child maltreatment. This statistics and many other reports indicate the epidemic growth rate of child abuse and neglect (maltreatment) in our society. Multifarious approaches have been exercised by researchers and professionals to explore incidence, causative factors and consequences of child maltreatment in the family and outside the family.

Though, majority of researches on child abuse have focused on the cases of abuse within the family however; less emphasis is given by investigators in studying child abuse outside the family. Some forms of abuses outside the family are; ritualistic abuses, organized child sexual abuse, child pornography and institutional/ school abuses and such types of child maltreatment are witnessed in high proportion. Some children experience their first incidence of abuse by teachers in schools. When abuse is observed in schools, it is sometimes left unreported by teachers and principals as well as other school personnel. Children often do not report experiences of abuses to teachers or other school professionals because they believe that nothing will be done about it. When they do report, they will disclose to peers or family members. In most states, educators who fail to report incidence or suspicions of abuse are subject to fines or other legal consequences, so professional development training for teachers and other school personnel is essential to help them understand signs and symptoms of abuse reporting guidelines and interventions.

There is no specific profile of abusers, although various characteristics have been identified over time. Perpetrators of child abuse are identified as Parents, Teachers or other care givers such as relatives, neighbours, principals and senior students (Bullies). According to NCANDS's report, *Child Maltreatment 2004,* of the 8,72,000 child abuse victims, parents were the abusers in 78.5 per cent of the cases; 6.5 per cent were relatives; 4.1 per cent were teachers and the remaining were residential facility staff, legal guardians, and foster parents. More than half (50%+) of these perpetrators neglected their children, 10 per cent physically abused them, and 6 per cent sexually abused them, and 15 per cent committed more than one type of abuse. Over the last few decades, as the magnitude and severity of the problem have become apparent, the preventive intervention programmes have proliferated in developed countries. Recently, the international organizations have started launching programmes to generate international awareness about the root causes and consequences of child abuse on overall development of children (Finkelhor and Korbin, 1988; Korbin, 1987; Rohner and Rohner, 1980; Taylor, 1991). Unfortunately, little preventive efforts are made in developing countries like India so far.

Child maltreatment is a global problem which occurs in a

variety of forms and settings, and in some countries it is rooted in social, economic and cultural practices (Butchart, Harvey, Milan, Eurniss and Kahane, 2006; Pinheiro, 2006). The problem is multi-faceted in some developing countries such as India in which there is little information about the magnitude, trends and socio-economic correlates of child maltreatment. The growing complexities of life and socio-economic transition increase the vulnerability of children. Certain forms of child abuse are particularly prevalent in India and recognition of child rights as primary and inviolable is still deficient. Compared with affluent countries, the prioritization of problems in a low-income country such as India is different because malnutrition, infectious diseases, chronic disabilities, poverty, housing and shelter, population explosion and illiteracy abound. Understandably, a large proportion of the country's resources are directed towards these more immediate problems. In developed countries, where other causes of childhood morbidity and mortality are relatively rare, child maltreatment ranks high in importance among services for children. Although India's National Policy for Children (1974) declared children to be a "supreme national asset", the total budget allocated to Indian children for health, education, development and protection together amounted to a mere 3.8 per cent in 2005-2006, rising to 4.9 per cent in 2006-2007, with an abysmally low allocation to child protection at 0.034 per cent. With recent reports of increasing crimes including rape of females, especially minor (under-age) girls, the problem of child maltreatment seems all the more evident. Unfortunately, in India, the cases of child abuse and neglect in the family, in hospitals, schools or institutions are present at alarming threshold, but no significant effort is made to understand the multifarious causes and consequences of child abuse within and outside the family.

Therefore, this research endeavoured to explore psycho-social correlates of child abuse in schools and consequences on children. The introductory section includes concept of child abuse, its epidemiology, contributing factors and consequences on victimized children.

Conceptualization of Child Abuse

Child abuse as a socio-psychological construct in social sciences is fraught with ubiquity. A number of social scientists including psychologists have investigated its forms, dynamics and psychological consequences. Some of them have developed preventive interventions. Yet, the empirical referents of child abuse are still not systematized as a result the term 'child abuse' has been neither comprehensively characterized nor some suitable theory has been developed (Pandey, 2007). Apart from this, controversy exists in defining child abuse (maltreatment) because of multiple reasons. Since the nature and forms of child maltreatment vary from culture to culture and nation to nation. Thus, defining child maltreatment is obviously problematic because these definitions are subjective and constantly changing. Despite several disagreements, definitions are the essential part of any research. Apart from this, child protection programmes or schemes largely depend on understanding of definitions. Yet, attempts to define and clarify the concept of child abuse runs into several difficulties. Firstly, the concept has largely been clarified in western context where it has been extensively studied. Secondly, there is lack of clarity and specificity in use of the term. To some extent, this issue is multidisciplinary; consequently medical researchers refer to "child battering" who focus on the need for intervention whereas; psychiatrist/psychologists to "child abuse" which emphasizes emotional aspect of the situation. Quite often, the term "child battering", "child neglect", "child abuse", "child maltreatment" and "physical abuse", are used by different authors to refer to the same situation.

In fact, 'Child maltreatment' is a generic phrase that covers a wide range of behaviours. It covers all behaviour patterns, whether or not sanctioned by law and custom, which are in some way injurious to the child's health or social, economic, emotional and moral well being. It comprises a wide range of behaviour distinguished conceptually as well as operationally. For analytical purpose, such behaviours have been grouped under broad categories. It is to be noted that these are not mutually exclusive categories. Social scientists, psychologists, child advocates and professionals, sincerely working in the areas of child maltreatment have defined this issue in different manner.

Legally based definition heavily focuses on evidentiary criteria in an effort to prove or disprove an act of abuse. Therefore, the Child Abuse Prevention and Treatment Act, passed in 1974, defined

Child Abuse as, **"The physical or mental injury, sexual abuse, negligence or maltreatment of the child under the age of 18, by person who is responsible for the child's welfare under the circumstances which indicate that the child' health and welfare is threatened thereby" (Child Abuse Prevention and Treatment Act, P.L.93-247, 1974).** However to identify the nature of child abuse a widely accepted definition of child abuse and neglect is barely essential, involving two main objectives: Firstly, it should distinguish child abuse from other social, economic and health problems of international concerns and secondly, it should be sufficiently flexible to apply to wide range of child abuse situation in a variety of social and cultural context. Taking these perspectives into consideration, Finkelhor and Korbin (1988) defined Child Abuse, **"As the portion of harm to children that results from human action which is proscribed, proximate and preventable".** The term 'proscribed' refers to any human action concerning harm, if it is evaluated negatively with its deviance, harmful intent, violation of law and social expectation. Such action has to be 'proximate' which refers to the action of immediate caretakers closer to child's immediate environment and the term 'preventable' denotes that if some alternative course of action is potentially available in the setting but the caretakers to check harm do not exercise it, such actions are also considered abuse.

Later, **The World Health Organization (WHO) defines child maltreatment as "All forms of physical and/or emotional ill-treatment, sexual abuse, neglect or negligent treatment or exploitation, resulting in actual or potential harm to the child's health, survival, development or dignity in the context of a relationship of responsibility, trust or power."** (WHO, 1999). There are four types of child maltreatment: physical, sexual, emotional/psychological abuse and neglect. Very often, they occur in different combinations. In fact, any universal definition of child abuse in the Indian context is not yet available. However, in 2007, a working definition was proposed by the Ministry of Women and Child Development (MWCD), Government of India as "Child abuse is intended, unintended and perceived maltreatment of the child, whether habitual or not and including psychological and physical abuse, sexual and emotional maltreatment; any act which debases the intrinsic worth and dignity of a child as a human being; unreasonable deprivation of his/her basic needs for survival; and physical, educational, emotional or psychological neglect" (Govt. of India, 2007).

An overview of definitions of child abuse denotes lack of consensus in the definitions of child abuse. Legal professionals have focused on documentation of abuse and proof of the occurrence of abusive act by perpetrators. Contrary to this, researchers imply variety of definitions depending on their theoretical perspectives of research requirements. However, professionals have given relatively broader definition and focus on injuries and sufferings that result from child maltreatment.

Forms and Pattern of Abuse

Researchers and professionals working sincerely in the field of child abuse opined that the forms of abuse and neglect differ nation to nation yet there is consensus on some forms or patterns of abuse, which are found throughout the world (Finkelhor, 1996; Korbin, 1987; Pandey; 2007; Strauss and Steinmetz, 1980; Wolfe, 1988). Generally, child abuse is classified into four major types, viz. Physical Abuse, Neglect, Sexual Abuse and Psychological or Emotional Abuse (Straus, 1980; Wolfe, 1999). On the basis of three National Incidences Studies (NIS) conducted by the U.S. Department of Health and Human Services in 1981, 1988 and 1993, the definitions are framed following two different sets of definitional standards: (i) the harm standard, whereby child has suffered from apparent harm as a result of maltreatment as sign of cuts, belts or broken bones, and (ii) the endangerment standard, which includes entire forms of harm, adding those maltreatment experiences, put them in danger of being harmed, such as witnessing violence in the family or outside the family.

1. Child Physical Abuse (CPA)

Child physical abuse refers to the inflection or endangerment of physical injury due to beating, kicking, hitting, burning or otherwise harming a child. Sometimes, injuries are intentional (parents'/teachers' intention to control the child), but nonetheless corporal punishment and harsh disciplinary tactics can result in child injuries. The nature of injuries, resulting from physical abuse may range from minor (bruises) to moderate (scars) to severe (burns, sprains or broken bones etc.). However, physical injury denotes only the visible scars of abuse due to harsh and insensitive treatment. Physically abused children have many emotional and cognitive problems (Aber and Cicchetti, 1984; Pandey, 2007).

2. *Child Neglect (CN)*

Physical and emotional neglects are characterized by inability of caregivers to provide children's basic physical, educational or emotional needs:

(i) **Child Physical Neglect (CPN):** Physical neglect covers refusal of or delay in seeking health care, abandonment, expulsion from the home/classroom or refusal to allow a runway to return home and inadequate supervision.

(ii) **Child Educational Neglect (C Edu. N):** Practices such as allowing chronic truancy, failure to admit a child at appropriate school age in the school and failure to provide special educational requirements or sending child for wages instead of attending the school etc. are considered educational neglect.

(iii) **Child Emotional Neglect (CEN):** It includes actions such as marked inattention to the child's needs for attachment, or affection, failure or refusal to give psychological care, spousal abuse in front of the child and permission of drug or alcohol use by the child. However, the determination of neglect requires the consideration of cultural values and contextual factors embedded in poverty and deprivations.

3. *Child Sexual Abuse (CSA)*

This form of child abuse involves fondling a child's genitals, intercourse, incest, rape, sodomy, exhibition and commercial exploitation through prostitution or the production of pornographic materials etc. Sexual abuse may be underreported because of the secrecy or conspiracy of silence that so often characterizes these cases. The behaviour and development of sexually abused children may be affected significantly, especially in relation to longer duration/greater frequency of abuse, the use of force, penetration and a closer relationship to the perpetrator

(Finkelhor and Brown, 1988; Kendall-Tackett, Williams and Finkelhor, 1993)

Unlike physical abuse and neglect, sexual abuse has no connection to child rearing, discipline, or inattention to developmental needs. Rather, it constitutes a breach of trust, deception, intrusion and exploitation of a child's innocence and status (Finkelhor, 1995). Whereas, all types of maltreatment share a common ground in relation to the abuse of power by an adult over a child. Sexual abuse stands out from physical abuse and neglect in term of these specific dynamics.

4. Child Psychological/Emotional Abuse

Psychological maltreatment of children consists of acts of omission and commission, which are judged on the basis of combination of community standards and professional expertise to be psychologically damaging. Individuals commit such acts singly or collectively, who are in a position of differential power (e.g., age, status, knowledge and organizational form) that render a child vulnerable to abusive practices. Such acts damage immediately or ultimately the behavioural, cognitive, affective or physical functioning of the child. Examples of "psychological maltreatment includes acts of rejecting, terrorizing, isolating, exploiting and miss socializing."

O' Hagan (1995) has argued that psychological abuse and emotional abuse are not the same, although they are not entirely separate experiences and has made the distinction that emotional abuse affects emotional life and development, whereas, psychological abuse affects mental (i.e. cognitive) life and development. The APSAC Guidelines (1995) include the following widely accepted broad conceptual statement and psychological maltreatment categories. Psychological Maltreatment means "a repeated pattern of caregiver behaviour or extreme incident(s) that conveys to children that they are worthless, flawed, unwanted, endangered, or only of value in meeting another's needs." Psychological maltreatment includes (a) spurning, (b) terrorizing, (c) isolating, (d) exploiting/corrupting, (e) denying emotional responsiveness, and (f) mental health, medical and educational neglect (APSAC, 1995).

Epidemiology of Child Abuse (Worldwide)

Child maltreatment is widely studied problem in developed countries thus, accurate figure is nearly known. National incidence study (NIS) reports that almost 3 million children are harmed or endangered by abuse or neglect each year in United States amounting to a total yearly incidence rate 42 of every 1,000 children (Sedlak and Broadhurst, 1996). This rate is derived from estimates of National Incidence Study (I, II, III and IV) based on official reports of all four types of maltreatment as well as from a nationally representative sample of professionals who came in contact with maltreated children in a verity of settings (Fig. 1.1).

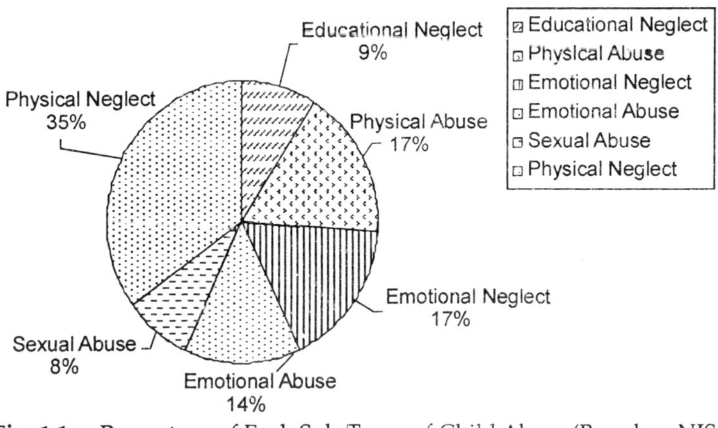

Fig. 1.1: Percentage of Each Sub-Types of Child Abuse (Based on NIS-III Report).

It is clear from Figure 1.1, the percentage of reported cases of abuses broken down according to each sub-types, proportions that has remained fairly constant over the past decade. Child abuse continues to hold the title as the most commonly reported form of maltreatment, affecting almost 30 children of every 1000 in United States and accounting for 70 per cent of all reported incidents. Physical, sexual and emotional abuses affect another 18 children per 1000, or 43 per cent of the total (these percentages exceed 100 per cent due to overlap). Specifically, physical abuse accounts for 22 per cent, sexual abuse for 11 per cent and emotional abuse for 18 per cent of maltreatment incidents (again, with overlap in reports and substantiated case rose dramatically in the 1980s but have since leveled off) (Sedlak and Broadhurst, 1996).

Further, official incidence rates provide a useful comparison of reported rates of child abuse over time, but they likely underestimate the actual prevalence of abuse by parents throughout the country (Straus and Kantor, 1994). Apart from this, population-based estimate, which is also subject to reporting bias, presents the incidence of physical abuse 5 times higher than the NIS-based rate of physical, sexual and emotional abuses combined. A third approach to estimating the extent of the problem uses lifetime prevalence estimates of maltreatment as a child. Males (32.2%) reported more child physical abuse than females (21.1%), while sexual abuse during childhood was more commonly reported by females (12.8%) than males (4.3%). Retrospective reports of childhood maltreatment are also imperfect but current evidence suggests valid and reliable estimates of significant past events (Bernstein *et al.*, 1994).

Therefore, it is difficult to ignore the findings that the total number of abused and neglected children reported to authorities has nearly doubled since 1986. Physical abuse nearly doubled, sexual abuse more than doubled, emotional abuse, physical neglect and emotional neglect reports are almost more than 2.5 times greater. Moreover, the total number of children seriously injured and the total of those endangered by maltreatment have quadrupled since 1986. These dramatic increases in estimated number of maltreated children prompt the question as to whether the estimates detect an actual increase in maltreatment or merely reflect a greater awareness and reporting than previous generations. NIS investigators believe that both awareness and actual prevalence have increased.

Incidence of Child Abuse and Neglect in India

In India, the incidence of child abuse is prevalent. It is increasing day by day and has achieved to alarming threshold in many forms. India is home to one-fifth of the total world child population (Kacker, Varadan, Kumar, 2007; UNICEF, 2012). The number of children, 18 years rose from 428 million in 2001 to 430 million in 2006. The total number of children aged 0-6 years is 158 million; constituting 13 per cent of the country's total population in 2011

(Government of India Census, 2011). The five states of Uttar Pradesh, Bihar, Maharashtra, Madhya Pradesh and Rajasthan constitute one-half of this population. Boys (51.5%) slightly outnumber girls.

According to a report released by the Ministry of Women and Child Development (MWCD) in 2007, more than two-thirds (69%) of children, particularly in the age-group 5-12 years, face physical abuse, mostly (89%) by parents. Sexual abuse occurs in over half of them (53%) and is severe in one-fifth (22%), and half of the abusers are known to the child or in a position of trust and responsibility. Every second child faces emotional abuse; mostly by parents (83%). This is different from high-income countries where the annual prevalence of all forms of abuse are much lower. In developed countries, for example, physical abuse ranges from 4 to 16 per cent, sexual abuse from 2 to 62 per cent and approximately 10 per cent are abused emotionally (Gilbert, Widom, Browne, Fergusson, Webb and Burden, 2012; National Center for Injury Prevention and Control, Division of Violence Prevention, 2012).

In a study of 51 children suspected to be victims of child abuse referred to Childline Chandigarh (a 24-hour emergency outreach service for children in need of care and protection), physical abuse was the most common (84%), followed by emotional abuse (76%) and neglect (47%) (Malhi and Dhillon, 2006). Girls were significantly more affected than boys; neglect was more common in the younger age-group whereas physical and emotional abuse increased with age. Parents or close family members were the commonest perpetrators of child maltreatment (Malhi and Dhillon, 2006). Similarly, high prevalence of physical abuse have been reported from other settings such as child observation homes (77%) and in child domestic workers (70%) (Ray and Lyer, 2006, Pagare, Meena, Singh and Sahu, 2004).

India has the dubious distinction of having the world's largest number of sexually abused children: a child under 16 years is raped every 155th minute, a child under 10 every 13th hour and one in every ten children is sexually abused at any point of time (Child line, 2007). Community-based studies have revealed that sexual abuse of children in India crosses all barriers of socio-economic classes and is widespread in both rural and urban areas and among boys and girls (National Commission for Women, 1997).

Sexual abuse in adolescent school-children has been noted in at least one-third and is associated with poorer health and greater prevalence of risky behaviour (Patel and Andrew, 2001). A higher prevalence of sexually transmitted diseases in younger children has been a surrogate indicator of probable sexual abuse/assault (Chopra, Mittal, Chander and Kanta 1990; Pandhi, Khanna and Sekhri, 1995). A researcher studied 100 child abuse cases handled by Childline Chandigarh over a 2-year period and found that 12 per cent involved protection or rescue from sexual abuse, 9 per cent were subjected to severe forms of sexual abuse and half of them (50%) had serious psychosocial sequelae. Most children belonged to socio-economically disadvantaged families, were aged 7-15 years, and the majority (10 out of 12) were girls (unpublished data) and a large number of cases are not reported because of a lack of awareness of the services available, inadequate knowledge about what comprises sexual abuse, and the associated shame and secrecy. Likewise, earlier studies also confirm high incidence of child maltreatment around the country. According to an estimate of the Juvenile court (1980-81), the largest number of maltreated children was reported from Maharashtra (8016), Karnataka (1572) and Delhi (1246). Mehta (1979) reported that in Bombay, among the 150 cases of rape victims studied, the youngest was a six month old child. Despite this, the available official statistics on maltreatment (in India) do not indicate the actual extent of the criminal victimization of children owing to large number of cases remaining unreported or unregistered. These statistics, however, provide us with a peep into nature of crimes, which come to the knowledge of the police.

A report (1997) of crime against children in India tells us that amongst the 10 types of crime against children, the child sexual maltreatment tops the list followed in descending order by kidnapping and abduction, procreations of minor girls, selling of girls for prostitution, buying of girls for prostitution; abetment of suicide, exposure and abandonment, infanticide, feticide and marriage of minor children. Child rape (up to 16 years) has shown noticeable figure in its reported incidence from 1993 to 1997 and percentage variation has been 8.1 per cent over 1993 figure. Almost similar increase was noticed in other crime heads. A further probe into the rising incidence of child rape revealed that (i) of all victims in rape cases during 1997, children alone accounted for 28.8 per cent. (ii) Since 1993, the cases of rape of children below the age 10 years were on a rise every year in the country except in 1996. (iii) for the first time in the last 5 years, the year 1997 witnessed a sharp rise of 26.6 per cent, a rise of 4 per cent in victims in the age group of 10-16 years; and (iv) the child rape victims below 10 years reported still increase in 1997 over 1996. Pandey (2005; 2007) identified a large number of various types of abused cases in eastern districts of Uttar Pradesh and no family/community was found immune of child victimization. Still cases of child abuse are witnessed at epidemic rate in the family, at workplace (as child labour) in orphan homes, institutions or in schools. Unfortunately, such cases are either unreported or unnoticed, and perpetrators are freely committing such dirty acts and ruining a large number of child population.

Research Done in India

Child abuse is a multidimensional concept, thus multidisciplinary research efforts are needed to understand the root causes and consequences of child abuse and strategies for prevention. Earlier, social scientists identified that child abuse occurs more frequently during rapid socio-economic changes, urban migration and family disorganization (Chattoraj and Saxena, 1990; Korbin, 1987; Mehta, 1979). Later, psychological researches identified some of the deep-rooted reasons of child abuse and neglect in India. These factors are: population density, poverty, unemployment, lack of education, social isolation, high mobility, distorted family relationship, poor bond between parents and children, negative parenting style, high anxiety and stress, poor coping ability, traumatic disastrous experiences, childhood abusive experiences and so on (Baruah, 2003; Pandey, 2005; 2007). Mehta (1979) identified that motive behind kidnapping of children was mainly prostitution, selling, sexual gratification, unemployment, extreme poverty, broken homes, anti-social surrounding, ignorance and illiteracy. In another study, Bhattacharya (1979) showed that children are generally the victims of prolonged and severe malnutrition, undernutrition resulting impairment and underdevelopment or growth. Whereas, Faller (1981) indicated that the environmental, familial and individual parental factors and their interplays are often the causes of abuse and neglect of children. On the basis of an extensive study,

Gil (1971) reported that stress and frustration are the major causal factors of child abuse. Stress caused by deprivation or poverty, high density in overcrowded housing, large number of children, single parent families, the absence of child caregivers and poor education were found to be associated with abuse and neglect.

In a comprehensive study, Pandey (2007) reported that child abuse is present at high proportion in eastern districts of Uttar Pradesh and no community was found immune of child maltreatment. Various psychosocial factors like low SES and caste, unemployment, low education, high anxiety, stress, poor coping ability, disorganized family environment and negative parenting styles were found positively associated with child abuse and neglect. Moreover, she identified the adverse consequences of child abuse by parents on cognitive, motivational and behavioural functioning and personality of victimized children. In a further study, Pandey (2010) explored that abused children displayed poor behavioural functioning in schools. Despite this, there is a bare need to study child abuse outside the family and its impact on children.

CHILD ABUSE OUTSIDE THE FAMILY

The concept of the child abuse, as discussed earlier, however, has been extended include additional conditions and circumstances occurring both within the family (e.g., children maltreated by parents or exposed to marital violence) and outside the family (e.g., children exposed to community violence). In this section, other forms of child maltreatment are described that primarily occur extra familially, such as abuse in institution/schools, and day care setting, ritualistic abuse, sex rings, and the exploitation of children through pornography and prostitution, and sex rings has often contributed to the public's misperception about the extent of such child maltreatment. In general, this type of child exploitation occurs less commonly than those discussed previously. Yet frequency of occurrence, alone, should not determine social concern about a problem. The negative impact on children's lives resulting from such experience can be just as significant as other forms of child maltreatment.

Ritualistic Abuse

Through the late 1980s and early 1990s, many social scientists became interested in a form of abuse that was reportedly quite insidious and shockingly common: ritualistic abuse. Ritualistic abuse has been defined as, "Abuse that occurs in a context linked to some symbols or group activities that have a religious, magical, or supernatural connotation and where the invocation of these symbols or activities are (sic) repeated over time, and used to frighten and intimidate the children". (Finkelhor *et al.*, 1988)

Debates about ritualistic abuse have produced some of the most heated exchanges seen within the field of child maltreatment. These debates have centred on question about the actual existence of this form of abuse (Jones, 1991; Putnam, 1991). Some of the most controversial claims involve cases of sexual abuse that are associated with forced drug use, cannibalism; impregnation; witnessing and receiving physical abuse or torture (e.g.; biting, burning, whipping, and animal mutilation); being buried alive; death threats; witnessing or forced participation in infant "sacrifice" and adult murder; "marriage" to Satan; and acts involving feces, urine, and blood. Many issues remain unresolved. Several experts have questioned the foundation on which ritualistic abuse research is based, namely the claims of victims reporting such experiences.

Information about ritualistic abuse comes primarily from reports of children attending day care centres and from the memories of adults reporting a history of childhood abuse. Research studies investing the parameters of ritualistic abuse have focused on the prevalence of reported cases, the impact of this form of abuse on victims, and the characteristic of victims and perpetrators (for a review, see Kelly, 1996). Estimates of ritualistic abuse are difficult to determine not only because of disagreement about definitional issues but also because child protection and law enforcement agencies do not uniformly recognize ritualistic abuse as specific and separate form of child maltreatment. Most studies attempting to determine estimates of ritualistic abuse either examine samples of children in day care centres, collect clinical sample, or survey mental health professional about the number of cases they have encountered (Bottoms, Shaver, and Goodman, 1996; Goodman, Bottom and Shaver, 1994; Kelly, 1989; Snow and

Sorenson, 1990). Although some of these reports indicate that as many as 13 per cent of sexual abuse cases include ritualistic elements, most reports that ritualistic abuse is relatively infrequent (Bottoms *et al.*, 1996; Finkelhor *et al.*, 1988 Goodman *et al.*, 1994).

To fully understand the controversy surrounding ritualistic abuse, we must consider the historical context in which these claims have appeared. Beginning in the 1980s more and more adults began reporting recovered satanic memories of devil worship, human and animal sacrifices, and sexual torment. Children also reported abuse that included ritualistic elements. The term Satanic Ritual Abuse (SRA) was introduced to describe this new form of child abuse. Although the term ritualistic abuse appeared later, it is a broader term that includes SRA as one of several forms of ritualistic abuse and de-emphasized in early definitions. Proponents of the reality of SRA have argued that thousands of children each year are victimized in satanic rituals involving cannibalism, sexual torture, incest, and murder. Critics, however, are skeptical and wonder whether large number of Satanist actually are preying on children, or whether the so-called Satanism scare is merely rumour and mass hysteria.

Today the social hysteria that characterized the Satanism scare of the 1980s appears to have subsided (Mulhern, 1994). Although some observers remain true believers, it seems that most probably agree with Susan Kelley (1996), who reached the following conclusion after reviewing the literature: "The existence of a large scale network of satanic cults whose primary interest is the sexual abuse of children is clearly not supported by empirical finding or law enforcement findings". At the same time, however, the sexual abuse of children involving some ritualistic elements has been documented. It seems clear that child maltreatment, at times, does included abuse by adults who claim some allegiance to Satan, use satanic symbols, or invoke the name of Satan as a terrorizing tactic (Kelley, 1996: Waterman *et al.*, 1993). Examples, survey of clinical members of the American Psychological Association about their experiences with ritualistic abuse indicate that out of 2,722 respondents, 803 indicated that they had encountered one or more ritualistic or religion-related cases. Reports of ritualistic abuse indicate that these cases tend to involve male and female victims to an equal degree (Snow and Sorenson, 1990; Wateman *et al.*, (1993). With regard to perpetrator characteristic, however, gender discrepancies have been observed. Compared with no ritualistic abuse cases, ritualistic abuse is more likely to involve female perpetrators, multiple perpetrators, and multiple victims (Finkelhor *et al.*, 1988; Jonker and Jonker-Bakker, 1991; Kelly, 1989; Snow and Sorenson, 1990; Waterman *et al.*, 1993). Initial studies on psychological impact of ritualistic abuse have found symptoms similar to those observed in sexually abused children, although several studies suggest that ritualistic abuse victims exhibit a greater degree of symptomatology compared with sexually abused children (Kelley, 1989; Waterman *et al.*, 1993).

Organized Exploitation

Of all the major forms of child maltreatment, child sexual abuse is most likely to occur between a child and an adult who is not a family member. Organized exploitation is one form of child sexual abuse that typically occurs outside the family, although recent reports suggest that some elements of organized exploitation also occur intrafamilially (Itzin, 1997). Organized exploitation typically refers to the sexual maltreatment of groups of children for the sexual stimulation of one or more perpetrators, for commercial gain, or both. Although the research on organized sexual exploitation is limited, this form of child maltreatment includes these activities, which are often interrelated: sex rings, pornography, and prostitution.

Child Sex Rings: Child sex rings consist of number of children sexually abused by one or more perpetrators. Sexual demands are required for acceptance into the group, and various modes of deception, enticement, and manipulation ensure the cooperation of the children (Burgess, Groth, and McCausland, 1981; Lannig and Burgess, 1984). Burgess and her colleagues have distinguished between the following three types of sex rings (Burgess and Hartman, 1987; Burgess, Hartman, McCausland and Power, 1984):

(i) Solo rings consist of single adults involved with small groups of children.
(ii) Syndicated rings consist of multiple adults who create a well-structured organization for the purpose of requiting children, producing pornography, delivering direct sexual service, and establishing a group of customers.

(iii) Transitional rings can be described as functioning between solo and syndicated rings. The transitional ring consists of one or more adults and several children do not include organizational aspects. This type of ring may eventually move toward an organizational status (e.g.; photographs may be sold).

(iv) One core element of sex rings as noted in the above description is the inclusion of pornographic activities. Pornography is sometimes used to stimulate and instruct children in the groups (Burgess *et al.*, 1984). In addition, the similar activities of children in the rings are often photographed or videotaped, and believed that such rings may be the first phase of an organization leading and prostitution and pornography (Creighton, 1993; Hunt and Baird, 1990).

Child Pornography: Child pornography has been defined as "photograph, films, videotapes, magazines, and books that depict children of either gender in sexually explicit (Burgess and Hartman, 1987). Child pornography, by definition, is a form of child maltreatment. Child pornography, however, was legal in most U.S. states until the 1970s. In 1978, the Protection of Children against Sexual Exploitation enacted in the United States to halt the production and dissemination of graphic materials involving children. Soon thereafter, several other organizations adopted prohibition against child pornography as well (Doek, 1985; Taylor and Stone, 1985). In addition, the Child Sexual Abuse and Pornography Act of 1986 provided for federal prosecution of individuals engaged in child pornography, including parents who permit their children to engage in such activities (Otto and Melton, 1990). Legislation within the United States has also been passed in several states mandating that commercial film and photo processors inform authorities about suspected child pornography that is discovered during the processing of film (Wurtele and Miller-Perrin, 1992).

Determining the number of children involved in child pornography is an extremely difficult task, given that the production, distribution, and sale of child pornography are often clocked in secrecy because such activities are illegal. Government subcommittees investigating the problem of child pornography in America, however, determined that a significant number of children are sexually exploited, with an estimated 7 per cent of the pornographic industry in the United States involving children in sexual activities (Pierce, 1984). Youth who are runaways constitute the majority of children involved in child pornography (Pierce, 1984).

Child pornography not only is abusive in and of itself but also may contribute to the problem of child maltreatment by stimulating adults' sexual interest in children (Rrush, 1980; Russell, 1988). Results of studies evaluating the role of pornography in affecting a perpetrator's likelihood of offending a child are equivocal. Some studies have found that CSA perpetrators do use pornography more than comparison groups, whereas others have found no relationship between sexual perpetration and pornography (Carter, Prentky, Knight, Vanderveer, Boucher, 1987; Howe, 1995; Malamuth and Briere, 1986). There is no doubt, however, that child pornography contributes to the exploitation of children by creating a market for the victimization of children and by serving as a tool for perpetrators to educate and stimulate victims or to blackmail victims into maintaining secrecy in abusive activities (Burgess and Hartmma, 1987; Hunt and Baired, 1990; Tyler and Stone, 1985).

Little has been recorded about addressing the problem of child pornography outside the enactment of federal and state legislation that prohibits the use of minors in the production of pornographic material. Although such laws have been somewhat successful in curtailing the problem within the United States, world-wide prohibition will be necessary to completely eliminate the problem of child pornography (Tyler and Stone, 1985). With the advent of the computer, the problem has become increasingly complex because access to and trading of child pornography have become a worldwide problem of considerable magnitude (Durkin and Bryant, 1995; Hughes, 1996; Ireland, 1993).

Child Prostitution

Over the last decade, child prostitution has received the greatest empirical attention. Official estimates of child prostitution are not currently available. Surveys of adult prostitutes, however, suggest that a significant number began work as prostitutes when they were children. Sibert and Pines (1983) found that 70 per cent of the 200 San Francisco street prostitutes they surveyed reported that they were less than 21 years of age at the time they began prostitution. Of these 60 per cent reported they were under age 16 when they started work as prostitutes. Other studies report on child prostitutes as young as 10 years of age, with a median age for entry into prostitution at age 14 (e.g., Nadon, Koverola, and Schludermann, 1998). A considerable number of investigations have explored possible antecedents to child documented in the literature include a history of childhood maltreatment including physical and sexual abuse and exposure to inter-parental violence, personal and parental alcohol or drug abuse, and poor family functioning (Bagley and Young, 1987; Bracey, 1979; Earls and David, 1990; Sibert, 1982). One of the most predictive factors is because of death of a parent, being kicked out of the family, home, or running away from home because of alcoholism or abuse in the home (Nadon *et al.*, 1998).

Like child sex rings, child prostitution is also associated with child pornography. Silbert and Pines (1983) found that 38 per cent of their sample of San Fransisco adult prostitutes described the talking of sexually explicit photograph of themselves for commercial purposes when they were children. Ten per cent described being used in pornographic films and magazines when they were children. Children pornography and prostitution have also been linked in reports of international trafficking of women and children, a trade sometimes referred to as sex tourism. Sex tourism involves the purchase of women or children as part of a package that includes sexual privileges (Itzin, 1997; Joseph, 1995).

Institutional or School Abuse

Institutional abuse can occur in various settings but not limited to, foster homes, group home, residential treatment centres, and licensed child care facilities. It is present at high level in schools, colleges and other institutions. In 1984, the issue of child abuse perpetrated by institutional personnel was dramatically brought into public view through the attention focused on the McMARTIN Preschool CASE in Manhattan Beach, California. Although there were no convictions, the publicity surrounding this case brought institutional abuse into public focus and left many with the impression that children are at increased risk of abuse in child care settings.

Studies evaluating the extent of abuse and neglect in institutional settings suggest that child maltreatment in these out-of-homes setting is less common than other forms of child maltreatment. Wang and Daro (1998) reported on data from the Annual Fifty Survey and found that only 3 per cent of confirmed abuse cases in 1997 occurred in day care centres, foster care, or other institutional care setting. Wang and Daro further asserted that this pattern has remained consistent during the past 11 years. Finkelhor *et al.* (1988) conducted a national survey of day care centres and this pattern was: 5.5 per 10,000 children, compared with 8.9 per 10,000 children in private households. These researchers concluded that children are at greater risk of being sexually abused at home than in child care centres and that child care centres are not a particularly high risk of maltreatment situation for children.

Although less common than other forms of child maltreatment, many children suffer sexual and physical abuse at the hands of individuals licensed to provide quality care for children. The majority of studies addressing child abuse and neglect in institutional settings have focused on physical and sexual abuse in child care centres. The characteristics of child maltreatment occurring in child care facilities differ in significant ways from abuse perpetrated in other circumstances (Faller, 1988b; Finkelhor *et al.*, 1988; Kelley, Brant, and Waterman, 1993; Waterman, Kelly, Olivery, and McCord, 1993). The proportion of women involved as perpetrators in child care centres, for example, is higher than in other cases of child maltreatment (Faller, 1988b; Finkelhor *et al.*, 1988).

The types of sexual activity that occur in day care setting are similar to activities in other setting (e.g., activities ranging from fondling to sexual intercourse). But fondling appears to the most commonly reported form of the abuse in day care setting (e.g.; Bybee and Mowbray, 1993a; Finkelhor *et al.*, 1988). Aspects of physical abuse have also been described, including hitting physical restraint, and food deprivation (Kelley *et al.*, 1993). Other forms of sexual abuse described in day care setting include group sex situation in which three or more people are involved, pornography (e.g., taking picture of children or of children and adults in various sexual activities), and more controversial claims such as bestiality and ritualistic elements of abuse (Bybee and Mowbray, 1993a; Faller, 1988b; Finkelhor *et al.*, 1988; Kelley *et al.*, 1993).

Studies examining the psychological impact of abuse in child care centres suggest that children abused in child care setting exhibit symptoms similar to children abused within their homes. A comprehensive study of sexual abuse in preschool setting described in '*Behind the Playground Walls: Sexual Abuse in Preschool*' (Waterman *et al.*, 1993), for example, found that children who reported experiencing sexual abuse in preschool exhibited more social incompetence, cognitive problems, emotional difficulties, sexualized behaviour, and behaviour problems than a control group of children attending preschool. There is also evidence that abuse circumstances involving multiple perpetrators, multiple victims, pornography, and ritualistic elements are associated with more psychological difficulties for victims (Finkelhor *et al.*, 1988; Kelley, 1989; Waterman *et al.*, 1993).

In response to concern about the problem of institutional abuse, a number of policy and legislative changes have been initiated. Recommendations have been made for change and reform in the provision of institutional care service and requirements providing for independent investigations into institutional maltreatment and state definitions of abuse and neglect that include person providing out of home care have been established (Rindfleisch and Nunno, 1992). In addition, the U.S. Congress enacted a law in 1984 that required states to provide the employment history, background, and criminal checks to be made on out of home care employees.

In addition to the various forms of child maltreatment discussed earlier, conception of child maltreatment has broadened to include the circumstances that are associated with negative developmental outcomes on children. Some of these forms of child maltreatment, such as exposure treatment and community or school violence, are common and have been increasingly recognized threats to the development and well-being of children.

Legal Efforts to Control Child Maltreatment

Review of researches conducted worldwide reveals that prolific cases of child maltreatment are witnessed in the family and outside the family but no single legislation deals exclusively with the problem of child abuse and neglect in India. However, there are numerous central and state laws, which have been enacted with a consideration on child exploitation, cruelty and neglect.

Article 39 provides that children at a minor age are not to be abused but protected against exploitation and against moral and material abandonment. Article 25 prevents the employment of children in hazardous occupations. The National Policy for Children (1974) made efforts to provide protection and care for them. Similarly, the Indian Penal Code (Sec. 363A) deplores acts like kidnapping or maiming the child for the sake of begging, selling or for the purpose of prostitution (Sec. 372-373), exposure and abandonment of the child under 12 years by parents (Sec. 317), is viewed as serious offences. The Juvenile Justice Act (1986) provides for the "care, protection, treatment, development and rehabilitation of neglected or delinquent Juveniles (Juvenile Justice Act, 1986).

Cruelty and willful neglect of children by their parents or caretakers in any form is punishable, under sub-section (1) of Section 41, imprisonment up to six months or with fine or both. In Section 42, employment of juveniles for the purpose of begging is also a punishable offence. Under Section 43 of the Juvenile Justice Act, giving intoxicating of juvenile employees, Section 50 provides authority to a police officer to take charge without warrant of a juvenile who has escaped from a special home to send him back there. Despite constitutional guarantee and legislative measures, it is found that a large number of children are still the victims of various forms of maltreatment.

A cursory glance at the welfare statistics on children, however, denotes only a part of the reality, which is quite different. Socio-psychological researches show that the children have been admitted to the institution due to abandonment, parental neglect, broken homes, undesirable home environment, and delinquency, running away from home or due to their being lost.

The cases in which children are abused and neglected are grouped under two broad sections: (i) Crimes committed against children who are punishable under Indian Penal Code (IPC), and (ii) Crimes committed against children who are punishable under special and local laws:

(1) The crimes which are punishable under the Indian Penal

Code include: (i) foeticide (crime against unborn child), Sections 315 and 316 IPC; (ii) infanticide (crime against newly born child), Section 315 IPC; (iii) exposure and abandonment (crime against children by parents or others to expose or leave them with the intension of abandonment), Section 317 IPC; (iv) Kidnapping or abduction for exporting, Section 360 IPC; kidnapping for ransom, Section 363 read with Section 360 IPC; kidnapping for ransom, Section 363 read with Section 384 IPC; for camel racing, Section 363 IPC; for begging, section 363-A IPC; to compel for marriage, Section 366 IPC and for slavery, Section 367 IPC; (v) procurement of minor girls (for inducement to force or seduce to elicit intercourse), Section 366-A IPC; (vi) selling of girls for prostitution, Section 372 IPC; (vii) buying of girls for prostitution, Section 373, IPC and so on.

(2) Crimes against children, which are punishable under special and local laws, fall under the ambit of: (i) Immoral Trafficking Prevention Act, 1956; (ii) Child Marriage Restraint Act, 1979; (iii) Child Labour Prohibition and Regulation Act, 1986; and (iv) Juvenile Justice Act, 1986. Apart from numerous legal efforts at national and international levels, the number of abusers and abused victim are dramatically increasing day by day.

Contributing Factors of Child Maltreatment

A bulk of researches has proved the numerous potential causative factors of child maltreatment. Although earlier 1960s studies indicated that this problem is rooted in adult's psychological disturbances. Abusive adults were found abused in their own childhood, having unrealistic expectation that children would satisfy their own unmet emotional needs, and poor aggression control (Spinetta and Rigler, 1972; Kempe, *et al.*, 1962) yet, recent studies did not confirm "abusive personality type" variable. Certain other parental and child characteristics of parents include: disturbance, substance abuse, history of abuse as a child, belief in harsh physical discipline, desire to satisfy unmet emotional needs through the child, unreasonable child behaviour, young age (below 30 years) and low educational level. Close associations between child abuse and parental factors i.e., poor parenting skills, mentally disturbed parents, parental stress and drug abuse have been identified. Certain child characteristics prone to being target of abuse are: premature or very sick baby; children who are inattentive and overactive and having difficult temperament and other developmental problems. Current approaches to understanding child abuse and neglect emphasize an interlinked cluster of individual, family, environmental and socio-cultural risk factors that can result in increased risk of maltreatment, as well as the possible protective mechanisms that disrupt this etiological process (National Research Council, 1993). Societal and cultural factors that influence the formation of a healthy parent-child relationship play prominent roles in child abuse, in addition to specific psychological processes affecting the dynamics of the relationship. Belsky (1980) propounded a conceptual framework for integrating diverse theories on etiology of child maltreatment (Table 1.1).

Table 1.1: Conceptual Framework of the Causes of Child Maltreatment

Ontogenetic Factors	*Micro System Factors*	*Exo-system Factors*	*Macro System Factors*
History of abuse	Marital discord	Inadequate health care facilities	Economic recession
Alcohol abuse	Single parenthood	social isolation	Cultural acceptance of corporal punishment
Stressful experience. Psychiatric and Physical illnesses	Premature or unhealthy child	unsafe neighbourhood	View of children as possession

The framework (Table 1.1) includes psychological disturbances in parents, abuse eliciting characteristics of children, dysfunctional patterns of family interaction, stress—including social, and abuse—promoting cultural values. This model is mainly based on Bronfenbrenner's (1977, 1979) work related to the ecology of human development which conceptualized child maltreatment as a "Social Psychological Phenomenon" and multiple forces determine it across four different levels: the individual (Ontogenetic development), the family (the micro-system), the community (the exo-system), and the culture (the macro-system), in which both the individual and family are embedded. In fact, Belsky combined Tinbergen's concern for ontogenetic development with Bronfenbrenner's concern for the ecology (on the context) for developing his conceptual model of child maltreatment. He assumed that forces within the individual determine child maltreatment; the family, the culture and these determinants are nested ecologically with one another. Thus, causes of child maltreatment cannot be explained on the basis of single factor. It is the product of multiple factors interlocked with each other. Despite the parent characteristics, several interaction variables at the family, community, society and culture play prominent roles.

Table 1.2: Predictors of Child Abuse and Neglect

	Factor	*Description*
(i)	Adult Characteristics	Psychological disturbance; Substance abuse; History of abuse as a child; Belief in harsh physical discipline; Desire to satisfy unmet emotional needs through the child; Unreasonable expectations for child behaviour; Young age (Under 30); Low educational level, Cognitive deficits in abuser, Negative affect etc.
(ii)	Child Characteristics	Premature or very sick baby; difficult temperament; Inattentiveness and overactivity; other developmental problems, child behaviour etc.
(iii)	Family Characteristics	Low income; poverty; homelessness; marital instability; social isolation; physical abuse of mother by husband, frequent moves; large closely spaced families; overcrowded living condition; disorganized household, lack of steady employment; other signs of high life stress etc.
(iv)	Community	Characterized by social isolation, few parks, day-care centres, preschool programmes, recreation centres and churches to serve as family supports etc.
(v)	Culture	Approval of physical force and violence as ways to solve problems, social-cultural influences, poverty and social disadvantage and corporal punishment as disciplinary practices etc.

1. Adult (Perpetrators) Characteristics

Major adult characteristics associated with child abuse and neglect are: role of parenting, childhood experiences, stress and poor coping abilities, distorted beliefs, child rearing abilities and resources, and emotional reactivity. Belsky (1984) suggested that the quality of parenting is multiply determined by characteristics of parent, the child and social context.

(i) Early Maltreatment Experiences as a Child

Researchers endeavoured to identify relationship between childhood experiences of abuse and abusive treatment (Kempe and Helfer, 1972). Since prior abuse and family violence in childhood may perpetuate a cycle of violence across generation, this issue remains an important, yet not fully resolved concern. Abusive background significantly increases the likelihood that an individual will become subsequently involved in coercive relationship with peers (Dodge, Bates and Pettit, 1990), dating partners (Malamulh *et al.*, 1991; Wolfe *et al.*, 1998), and their own children (Gaines *et al.*, 1978; Straus, Gelles and Steinmetz, 1980).

Maltreating adults usually have experienced psychological deprivation or maltreatment as children and suffer persisting conflicts about care and control. In adult life, they form relationship in which these conflicts are re-enacted through excessive, but often ambivalent, dependency. They often look to their children for emotional comfort, giving priority to their own need instead of their children. Demands for care taking from adults or infants readily provoke the parent's anxiety and knowledge. Other studies evinced that teacher who reported abused as child was found more abusive (Holland and Roisman, 2008; Pandey, 2017).

(ii) Cognitive Deficits

Child abuse seldom involves isolated or premeditated events but rather occurs in the context of child rearing. Studies of the everyday interactions between abusive parents and their children, accompanied by knowledge of what abusive parents are thinking and feeling during these interactions have afforded a useful understanding of the nature of these overt and covert processes. Numerous studies identified a strong association between knowledge of child development and potential for abuse (Larrance and Twentyman, 1983). Milner and Wimberley (1980) underscored the excessive rigidity in expectations of parents who are high in child abuse potential. Other study (Newberger and Cook, 1983) argues that abusive parents were less able to assess the developmental needs of their children. Furthermore, researchers (Larrance and Twentymen, 1983) reported that abusive mothers were less knowledgeable about the capabilities of their children. Whereas, other studies suggest that abusive parents tend to have a limited repertoire of parenting skills as well as inappropriate expectation for child behaviour. Trickett and Susman (1988) reported that abusive parents were found less satisfied with their children and perceived child rearing to be more difficult than the control parents. Researches thus indicate a strong link between parenting skill, knowledge of child development and potential for maltreatment. Wolfe (1985) concluded that abusive parents express significantly less positive behaviour during interactions with their children and other family members. Relative to other families, abusive family members interact less often with each other. When they do interact, the interaction tends to be more negative and involve excessive forms of verbal and physical control that exceed demands of the situation. Earlier researches (Hurlock, 1984, Hollowitz and Stulberg, 1959) present a vicious cycle of bad-parent child relationship that becomes increasingly worse as time passes. The deterioration in parent-child relationship continues as it weakens emotional bond between family members.

Cognitive deficits refer to an absence of thinking whether it would be beneficial, whereas cognitive distortion refers to persons who typically do not lack the ability to organize or process information, but their thinking is described as biased, dysfunctional, or misguided (Kendall, 1993). Distorted or negative perceptions that relate specifically to the parent's own experiences noticed among sample of abusive parents (Kempe and Helfer, 1972), which reflects the extent to which they accurately recognize the demands and responsibilities that accompany child rearing. Deficits and distortions both may play role in the process of perceptions and judgment of their child's behaviour. Abusive parents may misperceive child behaviour in way that lead to inappropriate responses and increased aggression (Azar, 1997; Milner, 1995; Crittenden, 1993; Larrance and Twentyman, 1983).

(iii) Negative Effects (Anger and Arousal)

Researchers have consistently described abusive parents/adults as impulsive and exhibiting low frustration tolerance. The act of interpersonal aggression is highly attributable to situational cues and characteristics of the individual (Averill, 1983; Berkowitz, 1983; Zillman, 1979). Certain situational cues often involve aversive behaviour or child features and individual characteristics include factors such as oversensitivity (Knutson, 1978), disinhibition of aggression (Zillman, 1979) and limited interpersonal skill (Burgess, 1985). Physiological arousal (i.e., increased respiration, pulse rate, muscular tension) can lead to aggression; especially if the person labels the source of such arousal as anger provoking (Berkowitz, 1983). Moreover, negative arousal interferes with rational problem solving. This association between arousal and child behaviour may occur gradually during everyday parent-child interaction during highly stressful episodes (Berkowitz, 1983). Emotional arousal by itself, however, is normal and adaptive reaction to many situation, hence, the development of an abnormal pattern requires a multidimensional explanation. Deviant arousal patterns most likely emerge as a function of an individual's predispositions, such as overreactivity and sensitivity to emotional cues and prior experiences (Bower, 1981).

(iv) Coping with Stress

Stress is found in many forms for different individuals and it can be understood as demands that create an acute or chronic imbalance for the individual or the family system. This imbalance, in turn, is typically met by counter-pressure from the persons' coping efforts to return him/her to a more comfortable state of equilibrium. Since, coping is considered an important resource, which may help individual to maintain psychological adaptation during stressful situation. Researchers have conceptualized coping under three distinct approaches, viz. trait or disposition, contextual approach and transactional approach. In recent researches, the last approach is widely exercised. With this view, Lazarus and Folkman (1984) have defined coping, "as an individual's constantly changing cognitive and behavioural efforts to manage specific external and/or internal demands which is appraised as taxing or exceeding the resources of the person". Lazarus (1981) indicated four main functions of coping, viz. (i) to reduce harmful environmental conditions and enhance prospects of recovery, (ii) to tolerate or adjust to negative events and realities, (iii) to maintain a positive self-image, and (iv) to maintain emotional satisfying relationship with others. The moderating role of coping in stress-health relationship has been thoroughly investigated by a sizeable number of researchers (Mishra, 1999; Pandey and Srivastava, 2004). Pandey (2007) evinced that abusive parents showed poor coping ability than non-abusive counterparts.

2. *Child Characteristics*

Research issues concerning the child's role in increasing the risk of child abuse have received careful scrutiny because abusive parents often attribute their anger to their child's behaviour (Herrenkohl, Herrenkohl and Egolf, 1983). Children's behaviour, physical feature or developmental limitations may increase the potential for abuse. Child characteristics (age, gender, temperament, low birth weight, hyperactivity, conduct problems or handicapping condition) have been associated with risk of maltreatment once environmental and adult factors are controlled (National Research Council, 1993; Whitmore, Kramer and Knustson, 1993). Importantly, children are not responsible for their own abuse in any manner; child abuse is an adult action that is never justified. Unintentionally, however, the child's behaviour may still play a role in the continuation or escalation of an abusive or neglectful relationship. Children are emotionally and practically dependent on their parents and therefore, very young children are the most at risk of abuse and neglect. Children born permanently with physical or intellectual defects, who are poor feeders, suffer illnesses or experience early separation also make extra-stressful, emotional demands on their parents.

3. *Demographic Characteristics and Child Maltreatment*

Apart from psychological characteristics, certain demographic characteristics are also found significantly associated with differential report of child maltreatment (Sedlak and Broadhurst, 1996).

(i) Age Differences

Toddlers, preschoolers and younger adolescents are the most common victims of physical and emotional abuse, which corresponds to the emergence of greater independence and parent-child conflict at both of these developmental periods. Neglect is most often reported when children are quite young. Declining with age, sexual abuse, in contrast, is relatively constant from age 3 onward, which assist to children's vulnerability from early pre-school years throughout childhood (Sedlak and Broadhurst, 1996). Although child physical abuse affects a sizeable proportion of all age group, the highest rate of physical injury is found among older children (12-17 year of age) probably because of increasing parent-teen conflict.

(ii) Gender Differences

There are few significant gender differences in maltreatment rates with the important exception of sexual abuse. Although, girls are 25 per cent more likely to be victims of any form of abuse than boys, this essentially reflects the fact that they account for about 80 per cent of the victims of sexual abuse (Finkelhor, 1993). Moreover, the dynamics of sexual abuse differ considerably for boys and girls. Although, boys as well as girls are likely to be abused by someone they know and trust, boys are more likely to be abused by male non-family members whereas girls are more likely to be sexually abused by male family members (Finkelhor, 1995; Pandey, 2007). These findings suggest different patterns of vulnerability for boys and girls, which have implications for safety and prevention.

4. *Family Characteristics*

Apart from parental factors, family dynamics are important for explaining the range of psychological sequels of abuse, because it often occurs in the context of multiple functional factors whereas poverty, parental psychopathology, alcoholism and family dysfunction are prevalent (National Research Council, 1993). Family context is generally described as one of insensitive, marginal parenting and harsh interactions (Friedrich, 1990), even though abusive parents and their children may sometimes behave appropriately under limited or superficial conditions (Crittenden, 1988).

(i) Marital Conflict and Violence

In a study, Straus *et al.* (1980) identified that marital conflict and violence are often associated with child abuse. They estimated that approximately 40 per cent of the families where the adults were violent towards one another; there was also violence towards a child at some point during a 12 month period. Other investigators have reported that in fact marital conflicts and violence most often arise during disagreements over child rearing, discipline and each partner's responsibility in child care (Hilton, 1992; Edleson, Eisikovits, Guttman and Sela-Amit, 1991). Tragically, marital violence and family turmoil not only frighten and disturb children in a direct manner, but the resulting fallout from such events ranging from changes in financial status, loss of family unity and safety, prolongs the stress and harmful impact on children's development and behaviour (Pandey, 2008; Wolfe *et al.*, 1985).

(ii) Family and Perpetrator

Family demographic characteristics reflect the cultural and social forces that shape child-rearing method at a broad level. Child abuse and neglect appear to be mediated by several major environmental conditions of which social status (SES; family income below the poverty mark, underemployment and less education) plays a significant role.

Child maltreatment was found more common among the poor and disadvantaged (Gelles, 1983). It is striking that the incidence rate for all forms of maltreatment rises from 42 per 1,000 (averaged across all SES level) to 99 per 1,000 children among those from the poorest families (earning less than $ 15000/year) this rate is three times greater than that of children from moderate income families ($ 15,000-30,000/year) and 25 times higher compared with children in families in the highest income bracket (>$ 30,000/year). This finding is not likely due to a reporting bias, because it has remained unchanged for the last 20 years, despite increased awareness and reporting (Pelton, 1978). What does it imply; however, is that the economically based context of maltreatment, viz., restricted childcare opportunities, crowded and unsafe housing, and lack of healthcare and so forth, is powerful contributor to the high incidence rates (Pandey, 2005; 2007).

The significance of low SES is felt not only on rates of maltreatment but also growing up with poverty has a substantial effect on the wellbeing of children and adolescents, especially in terms of impairment in learning disability and school achievements (Brooks-Gunn and Duncan, 1997; Schteingart *et al.*, 1995). Moreover, low income is tied to many other forms of disadvantage such as less education, poor paying jobs, inadequate healthcare, single parent status, limited resources, poor nutrition and greater exposure to violence, any of which can impair children's developmental progress significantly (Brooks-Gunn and Duncan, 1997). Poverty has a significant, yet indirect effect on children's adjustment, most likely because of its association with such negative influences, particularly harassment, inconsistent parenting and elevated exposure to acute and chronic stressor that define the day to day experience of children in poverty (Mcloyd, 1998). Thus, it is widely accepted that lower SES can serve as a significant risk factor to child development and maltreatment, whereas higher SES can serve as an ameliorating protective factor (Masten and Garmezy, 1985; Pandey, 2007).

(iii) Family Structure

Family structure is also connected to the probability of child maltreatment. Children living with single parent are significantly at greater risk of both physical abuse and neglect most likely because of added stress, fewer resources and opportunities to share child rearing burden and lower SES than two parent homes. Children living factors in particular are almost twice as likely to be physically abused as those living with mothers alone (Sedlak and Broadhust, 1996). Similarly, maltreatment—especially physical and educational neglect—is more common in large families where additional children in the household mean additional tasks, responsibilities and demands.

Perpetrators of child maltreatment are the child's birth—parents about 80 per cent of the time although there are important exception and key gender differences in relation to different forms of maltreatment. Nearly one half sexually abused children are abused by persons other than parents of caretakers, compared with only a fraction in other categories. Child neglect is committed predominantly about 90 per cent of the time-by mothers, which fits with the fact that mothers and mother substitutes tend to be primary caretakers and the head of single-parent home. In contrast, sexual abuse is committed more often—about 90 per cent of the time—by males about half of whom are the child's father or father figure. Males are also the offenders in the majority of emotional (63%) and physical abuse (58%) incidents as well (Sedlak and Broadhust, 1996). Moreover, in 30 per cent to 60 per cent of families where either child maltreatment or woman battering is occurring, one will find that the other forms of violence are also being perpetrated (Edleson, 1999). Studies report that Straus and Gelles (1990) found that men who reported beating their wives were also more likely to report abusing their children (Pandey, 2008; Straus and Gelles, 1990).

5. *Socio-cultural Factors*

(i) Social Isolation

Social isolation is one of the commonly noted features of abusive families, coupled with stressful living conditions, such as lack of adequate day care, peer groups or close friends, and adequate housing (Thompson, 1994; Grabarino, 1976). Abusive parents/ adults often lack significant social contacts to others in the extended family, the neighbourhood, the community, and to the social agencies most likely to provide need assistance (Korbin, 1994). These factors play an indirect, yet significant role in the early formation and healthy establishment of a positive versus abusive parent-child relationship. As a result, abuse and neglect are difficult to detect and community agents who could promote healthy parent-child relationship are less likely to be influential. Apart from this, some cultural factors, such as child rearing practices, geographical distinctions, and kinship systems might serve as risk-enhancing or risk-reducing factors in abuse and neglect. Social isolation, however, is not a singular factor but rather a set of variables linked to the parent's perception of support and their networks (Coohey, 1996).

Many contemporary societies face high rates of child maltreatment in relation to social condition at the community and cultural level (Garbarino, 1997). Researchers have identified a sizeable number of socio-cultural factors, directly associated with child maltreatment.

(ii) Poverty and Social Disadvantage

Poverty and social disadvantage are associated with severe restrictions in the child's expectable environment such as lack of adequate day care, safety and housing, which often impair the development of healthy parent-child relationship collectively, structural determinants of a community's social organization such as economic and family resources, residential instability, household structure, neighbourhood and poverty influence rates of child maltreatment more than any individual of family factor alone (Pelton, 1978; Gil, 1970; Coulton, Korbin, Su and Chow, 1995). Although child maltreatment occurs across all the social strata, there is no doubt that adverse social circumstances, such as poverty, poor housing, and ill health, intensify the risk. In addition, maltreating parents are commonly socially isolated, having least contact with their family of origin through geographical mobility, or make little use of social support network. Despite socio-economic forces, maltreatment appears to have significant impact on child development above and beyond the influence of stressful socio-economic circumstances alone (Kurtz *et al.*, 1993).

(iii) Cross-cultural Comparisons

Although, it is difficult to draw comparisons between countries because of differences in defining and reporting child maltreatment, what little is known about the prevalence of maltreatment worldwide suggests that unfortunately all forms of child maltreatment are at epidemic proportion in both developed and developing countries. Child abuse is found in all societies and is almost always a highly guarded secret wherever it occurs (World Health Organization, 1997). Studies in which children or younger adults were interviewed about their childhood experiences further confirm that prevalence rates of sexual abuse in other western societies around the world are comparable with north American rates, clustering about 20 per cent for females and between 3 per cent and 11 per cent for male sexual abuse prior to the age of 18 years (Finkelhor, 1994).

The U.N. also estimates that nearly 2 million children worldwide are being sexually abused, including many who are forced into prostitution and pornography. Similar estimates of physical abuse and neglect unfortunately are not available. A comparison of incidence rates of child abuse and neglect in the United States, Canada and Australia indicates how the broader social context may influence the incidence and reporting of maltreatment. Canadian estimates extrapolated from the province of Ontario suggest that the U.S. has about double than overall rate of maltreatment in Canada (42/1,000 *vs.* 21/1,000). Similar differences are reported for Australia (16/1000) (Brodbent and Bently, 1997).

(iv) Changing Attitude Towards Child Rearing and Corporal Punishment

Child rearing practices have been changing dramatically over the past 50 years. Today's parents are expected to appreciate their child's developmental strengths and limitations and to move away from total reliance on disciplinary control methods towards ones that encourage the child emerging independence and self-control (Maccoby and Martin, 1983). Differentiating child abuse from child discipline remains difficult, because cultural norms in many societies accept corporal punishment as a primary, even necessary component of discipline. Many parents spank their children even though they question its effectiveness (Gallup Organization, 1995). Cultural values, historical precedence and community standards therefore may set the stage for one person's abuse being another person's discipline (Korbin, 1994).

An overview of studies on child abuse revealed that child abuse-outcome relationships are mediated/moderated by certain factors. However, it does not affect each victim in a consistent manner. Some of the identified moderating factors are: Severity and duration of abuse, stress and psychopathology, age at onset of abuse, gender of the child, abuser-abused relationship, abuse with violence, response to abuse, and the role of protective factors.

PSYCHOLOGICAL CONSEQUENCES OF CHILD ABUSE

A cursory glance at examining the available literature on child abuse denotes the short-term and long-term detrimental consequences of child maltreatment on overall development of children, yet, some psychological factors need in-depth investigation in relation to child abuse and neglect outside the family. Therefore, in the present study the researcher endeavoured to explore the impact of child abuse in schools on Cognitive, Motivational, Affective and Behavioural functioning of Students. Apart from this, the consequences of child abuse on personality development and health status of students have also been investigated. A brief review of researches on child abuse impacts is presented in the following section.

Cognitive Processes and Child Abuse

This section focuses on the consequences of child abuse and neglect on cognitive functioning of children. Since cognitive processes are the extensively studied area of psychological researches and over the last few decades, cognitive processes have represented one of the important topics of empirical investigations in developed as well as in developing countries. Since 1971, Indian researchers have contributed a lot in the area of cognitive processes; thus, this area has achieved prestigious status in the realm of psychological investigation (Gupta, G.C., 1980; Mishra, R.C., 1992; Tripathi, L.B., 1988). Now this area has rich theoretical and empirical foundation (Mishra, R.C., 1992).

Psychologists endeavoured to define the term "cognition" and "cognitive processes". Cognition refers to any and all forms of various modes of knowing and understanding the world around us. It contrasts with the affective, volitional, viz. feeling and 'will' aspects of conscious life. It is a meditational process. According to Neisser (1967), "cognitive process refers to all the processes by which the sensory input is transformed, reduced, elaborated, stored, recovered and used". It includes a cluster of processes through which we get knowledge about our environment and apply this knowledge to the solution of day-to-day problems. The continuum of cognitive processes ranges from the simple perceptual to more complex thinking and reasoning processes. In other words, sensation, perception imagery, retention, recall, language, problem-solving and thinking are the various aspects of cognition. Apart from this, recognition, labeling, analysis, planning and categorization are also some of the cognitive processes and viewed as intellective processes through which individuals try to comprehend their environment and solve numerous problems that they encounter with environment.

1. *Cognitive Functioning in Relation to Child Abuse*

A sizable number of researchers have proved the impact of child abuse on various forms of cognitive processes. Some of the classical researches are reviewed and presented here.

(i) Impact of Child Abuse on Cognitive/Intellectual/Academic Functioning

Several studies have documented that physically abused children (PAC) show lower intellectual and cognitive functioning relative to a comparison group of children on general intellectual functioning as well as specific measures of verbal facility, memory, verbal language, communication abilities, problem-solving, and perceptual motor skills (Fantuzzo, 1990; Friedrich, Einbender and Luecke, 1983; Haskett, 1990; Hoffman-Plotnik and Twentyman, 1984). Academic performance is another area of substantiated difficulty in physically abused children. It is evident from a sizeable number of studies that physically abused children as compared with non-abused children, display poor school achievement and adjustment, receive more special education services, score lower on reading and math test, exhibit more learning disabilities and are more likely to repeat a grade (De Paul and Arruabarrena, 1995).

(ii) Intellectual/Academic Deficiencies in Abused and Neglected Children

A large number of studies comparing neglected children and adolescents to non-neglected groups indicated that neglected victims show deficits in language abilities, academic skills, intelligence and problem-solving skills (Egeland *et al.*, 1983; Hoffman-Plotkin and Twentyman, 1984; Wodarski *et al.*, 1990). Child maltreatment damages the school performance of children.

Wodarski *et al.* (1990) evaluated 139 school-age adolescents physically abused, neglected and non-maltreated children and found that both neglected and abused children were significantly poorer on overall school performance and math skills. However, the neglected children expressed poor language and reading skills than the group of non-maltreated children. These intellectual deficits continued even after the researchers controlled the influence of socio-economic disadvantages.

Exposure to severe child physical abuse may produce cognitive or intellectual deficits or other related problem in academic achievement. Certain early studies showed reduced task intimation and motivation (Aber and Allen, 1987; Allen and Tranowski, 1989), limited intellectual functioning among maltreated youngsters (Alessandri, 1991; Erickson *et al.*, 1989) and school children (Salzinger *et al.*, 1984) whereas, other studies have failed to find differences in these areas (Augoustions, 1987; Azar, 1997; Fantuzzo, 1990; Slade *et al.*, 1984). Language deficits have also been found in both receptive and expressive areas, including more limited syntactic expression, functional communication, and self-related language (Coster *et al.*, 1989; Mc Fayden and Kitson, 1996).

Problems with academic performance also include low scores on school discipline, referral and suspensions (Eckenrode, Laird and Doris, 1993). Overall maltreated children were 2.5 times more likely to repeat a grade. These effects were not attributable to socio-economic status (SES), gender or age. As suggested by researchers, the academic careers of maltreated children may be marked by considerable discontinuity due to frequent moves, school transfer and tardiness. In contrast, no relation between child physical abuse and school grades or receptive language was found in a large community study (Fisher *et al.*, 1997).

The varied outcomes in this area may be attributable to several background factors such as the failure to distinguish among types (severity) of maltreatment or to use objective measure (Augoustions, 1987). Cognitive functioning may be closely related to the quality of the care taking environment, as shown in one study that found that young victims of physical abuse had more receptive language problems than non-abused children but did not differ from children residing in low SES families (Vondra, Barnett and Cicchetti, 1990). Given that the degree of enrichment in the home environment influences a child's cognitive abilities

(Aber *et al.*, 1989), the impact of family environmental variables may be considerable. The impact of physical injuries on children's cognitive abilities and their level of academic achievement merits further evaluation.

(iii) Perceptual and Attribution Problems in Physically Abused Children

Certain perceptions or attributions related to the experience of physical violence have been reported among children with a history of child physical abuse. Relative to controls, abused children have reported a greater willingness to use physical punishment (Carlson, 1986, 1991), were more likely to assimilate aggressive stimuli (Reider and Cicchetti, 1989). These few studies provide some understanding of the cognitive deficits or distortion evinced by abused children, there is a need to more carefully examine the cognitive repertoires of physically abused children. Potential cognitive problems include their belief in the appropriateness of violent behaviour as a coping skill and their difficulties identifying non-aggressive solutions to interpersonal problems. It would be instructive to learn, for example, whether victims to child physical abuse show negative attribution biases comparable to those of aggressive children (Dodge, Bates and Pettit, 1990) or the types of cognitive distortions commonly seen in depressed children (Kendall, Stark and Adam, 1990). If so, then specific method designed to enhance children's use pro-social, verbal mediation skill would be likely to affect these cognitive processes.

(iv) Cognitive Difficulties and Distortions in Sexually Abused Children

Cognitive functioning may be affected by sexual abuse experiences. Einbender and Friedrich (1989) reported greater cognitive impairment in sexually abused girls whereas Rust Troupe (1991) reported sexually abused children have deficits in school achievement. Negative or distorted attribution and perception have also been frequently observed (Hunter *et al.*, 1992). Sexually abused children exhibit numerous cognitive problems: like (1) Academic problem, (2) Intellectual delay, (3) Lower level of overall intelligence, (4) Receptive and excessive language deficits, (5) Less creative and flexible in problem-solving, and (6) Deficits in language comprehension/and verbal abilities, etc.

(v) *Cognitive Deficiencies in Psychologically Abused Children*

Child characteristics likely to interfere with cognitive function have been found to be associated with psychological maltreatment in many of the studies. The conditions identified include: decline in mental competence, lower intelligence, non-compliance, lack of impulse control, impaired learning, academic problems and lower achievement level and impaired development of moral reasoning (Claussen and Crittenden 1991; Crittenden *et al.*, 1994; Egeland and Erickson, 1987; Huges and Graham-Bermann, 1998; Main and Goldwyn, 1984; Main and George, 1985; Pandey, 2007; Rohner and Rohner, 1980).

Several other studies have found that rejected children perform less well than comparison group, on achievement and intelligence test, perform poor in school (Chan, 1981; Manley, 1977; Sheintuch and Lewin, 1981; Strakey, 1980) and exhibited impaired development of moral reasoning (Bilbro, Boni, Johnson and Roe, 1979; Hoffman, 1970). Brassard, Hart and Hardy (1993) found that psychologically maltreated children from a disadvantaged group were more likely to show school-related problems in ability and academic achievement. Pandey (2007) explored that abused children exhibited poor perceptual differentiation, lower levels of creativity and intellect.

2. *Consequences of Child Abuse on Motivational Process*

Motivation refers to a process which initiates, directs and maintains progress towards the goal. A goal is a mental representation of something we need (National Advisory M.H. Council, 1995). It can be general or specific. Psychologists, trying to understand the motivation behind behaviour, focus their researches in one or two ways. From an individualist perspective, they study the person as independent entity. Whereas, from the collectivists perspectives, they view the person as inseparable from his or her relationship with the other and both perspectives have different ways of conceptualizing a person (Triandis, 1995). Mostly, psychological studies on motivation, based on individualistic perspective, have tried to identify the personal need and thoughts that produce goal oriented behaviour. The biological conceptualizations of motivation come first and behaviours as eating, protecting, aggression etc., have biological roots whereas psychological motives are learned or acquired and therefore are known as Psycho-Sociogenic motives. These motives are mainly acquired through experiences of socio-interaction at various levels and once learned, the motives influence the way in which person evaluate the demands and challenges raised by social motive, since the development of several psycho-sociogenic motives are largely determined by opportunities and experiences available to the person, it is not unrealistic to believe that individuals having varying levels of experiences would show differences in the motivational patterns. It was therefore, planned to investigate the level of academic achievement motivation and aspiration level in relation to child maltreatment.

(i) Impact of Child Abuse on Achievement Motivation

Researchers have made effort to investigate the role of child abuse and neglect in academic achievement motivation and level of aspiration in children. Empirical studies indicated negative linkages between child maltreatment and achievement levels of children. Brassard, Hart and Hardy (1991) found that psychologically maltreated children from disadvantaged group expressed school related problems in ability and academic achievement. Similarly, neglected children performed less well than comparison group on achievement test (Sheintuch and Lewin, 1981, Strakey, 1980). Pandey (2005; 2007) found that highly abused children displayed low achievement level and academic performance. Thus, in the present study it was considered pertinent to investigate the impact of child abuse in schools on academic achievement and aspiration level of children.

(ii) Impact on Level of Aspiration

Kurt Lewin developed a variant of expectancy value theory, known as Resultant Valence theory, within the context of the study of level of aspiration typically is defined as "the level of future performance in a familiar task which an individual knowing his level of post-performance in the task, explicitly undertakes to reach" (Frank, 1935). Level of aspiration thus, pertains to goal striving and perceived difficulty of the goals that one wishes to attain.

Numerous empirical findings have emerged from level of aspiration research. It has been demonstrated that feeling of success and failure are determined primarily by the attainment or non-attainment of the goal for which one is striving, as opposed to the absolute level of performance. For example, a student with a very high aspiration level might be unhappy upon receiving grade B while an equally bright student with lesser aspiration would be satisfied with this grade. Perception of success and failure involves subjective, rather than objective levels of attainment. William James stated that feeling of success or self-esteem is direct function of actual success and an inverse function of pretentions. Further, the subsequent aspiration level is, in part dependent upon the prior attainment discrepancy (subjective success or failure). In most instances, the goal level increases after success and decreases following failure. However, "atypical" reactions are sometimes observed; that is, sometimes an individual lower his or her aspiration level after goal attainment or raises it after failure.

The concept of level of aspiration has also been modified and used for the analysis of social interaction and interdependence. Thibaut and Kelley (1959) assumed that individuals can assess their degree of satisfaction with a relationship, just as one can determine the valence of an achievement related success or failure. They introduced the concept of "comparison level" (CL) to define "a neutral point on a scale of satisfaction-dissatisfaction". If the average of "outcomes from a relationship" is above the comparison level (CL), the relationship is "rewarding"; however, if the outcome average is below the CL, the relationship is relatively punishing. However, even if the relationship is negative, individuals may remain interdependent. The continuations depend, in part, on the alternatives that are available or the potential satisfaction from equivalent relationship or opportunities.

In sum, Thibaut and Kelley assume a rational person striving to maximize gains, capable of comparing a number of potential satisfiers and deciding which "goal" (relationship) to pursue. This is clearly a direct extension of aspiration work into the sphere of interpersonal relations. Individual differences, group standards, and cultural factors influence level of aspiration. For example, individuals with high ability, or those classified as ambitious, tend to set higher aspiration levels (Hoppe, 1930). In addition, the level that is set tends to be guided by, and conforms to group goals and performance (Festinger, 1942). Mishra and Tripathi (1980) found negative association between prolonged deprivation and level of aspiration than their low deprived counterparts. Pandey (2005; 2007) proved that parental abusive treatment caused adverse impact on aspiration level of children. Abused children expressed lower level of aspiration than their non-abused counterparts.

Therefore, it was assumed that abusive treatment by school teachers or other school personnel would cause negative impact on aspiration level of students.

3. Behavioural Process

The impact of child abuse on behavioural functioning of children is widely investigated area. Several behavioural consequences of child physical abuse (CPA), child sexual abuse (CSA), child psychological abuse (CPsyA) and child neglect have been identified.

1. Impact on Negative Behaviours

Heightened Aggression in Abused Children

One of the most extensively documented consequences in child physical abuse victims is heightened aggression and related externalizing behaviours (National Academy of Sciences, 1993) including poor anger modulation (Beeghly and Cicchetti, 1994; Shields, Cicchetti and Ryan, 1994). Group differences have been reflected on adult ratings (Cummings, Hennessy, Radideau and Cicchetti, 1994; Dodge, Pettit and Bates, 1997; Feldman *et al.*, 1995; Hotaling, Straus, Lincolin, 1990; Manly, Cicchelli and Barnett, 1994; Okun, Parker and Levendosky, 1994), self-ratings (Pelcovitz, Kaplan, Goldenberg and Mandel, 1994; Wolfe, Werkele, Reitzel-Jaffe and Lefebvre, 1998) and observations in both the home (Bousha and Twentyman, 1984) and play or social setting (Alessanddri, 1991; Howes and Espinosa, 1985; Kaufman and Cicchetti, 1989). Dodge *et al.* (1997) pointed out that the experience of child physical abuse included aggressive behaviour and conveys its appropriateness as a problem-solving skill.

The level of externalizing dysfunction may be related to the experience of witnessing family violence and other adverse family environment factors, such as negative life events (Wolfe, 1999). Both heightened family conflict that included verbal and physical aggression (*vs.* verbal only) and shelter residence (*vs.*, home) have been found to be significantly related to the clinical severity of children's conduct and emotional problems and diminished social functioning (Fantuzzo *et al.*, 1991). Pandey (2005) investigated the influence of child abuse and neglect on aggression level in children. Results revealed that child abuse was found to be positively correlated with aggression. Aggression was found to be high in physically abused children particularly belonging to low socio-economic status. Physical aggression and anti-social behaviour are among the most common correlates of child physical abuse (CPA) (Wolfe, 1987). In most studies, abused children show more aggression, even after the poverty, family instability, and wife battering that often accompany abuse is statistically controlled (Fantuzzo, 1990; Pandey, 2007; 2008). Apart from this, certain other impacts of physical and sexual abuse are identified. These outcomes are:

(i) Aggression and Acting out

Running away from home, committing criminal acts or turning to prostitution are behaviours common to abused children. The majority of runaways are found from neglectful, abusive and violent families. Children who become involved in prostitution are overwhelmingly characterized as having a history of sexual abuse. Their low self-image combined with a belief that sex is their only valuable asset, makes them natural prey for exploitation through prostitution. A child's entry into delinquency is often a product of a dysfunctional family life and subsequent susceptibility to negative peer pressure. The violence or severities of criminal acts by young offenders seem to be correlated with the level of violence and neglect they experienced at home. Children who have been physically abused are prone to acts of aggression against younger children and animal, defiance against authority figures and exaggerated temper outburst.

(ii) Regression or Pseudo-maturity

The stress from physical or sexual abuse together with demands that exceed the child development capacity can result in regression. Children acting younger than their chronological age characterize regression under pressure to older than their age; some victims develop a preconscious adult-like behaviour.

(iii) Grooming Habits and Hygiene

Child's grooming habits and hygiene may sign body shame or fear of detection of the abuse. These changes may include dressing with clothing that hides the body, especially when it is out of season, refusal to bath or bathing excessively, or an abrupt increase in modesty. Sexually abused children may have the mistake belief that their bodies are somehow marked by their sexual experiences, while physically abused children may seek to hide obvious bruises and belts. Some sexual abuse victims become obsessive about their hygiene.

(iv) Eating Problem

Studies report that some sexual abuse victims may develop eating disorders such as anorexia (starving oneself) and bulimia (bingeing and purging). A child's wish to change his or her appearance to avoid being attractive to the perpetrator may result in the child refusing to eat. Neglected children may gorge or hoard food when it is available because they are uncertain when they will be fed next. Some psychologically maltreated youngsters are told they are fat or ugly and develop eating problem in response to these negative messages. Other abused children find food intake is the only aspect of their lives that they can control.

(v) Sexual Behaviour

Perhaps the strongest behavioural indictor of sexual abuse is developing inappropriate sexual behaviour and sexual knowledge. These children may be sexually preoccupied, make drawings and tell stories with sexual content or tell jokes. Their conversations may contain frequent or unusual sexual references and their activity may be focused around their sexualized interests. It is common for children to be curious about body parts, have a desire to look at another's body to ask questions about procreation.

However, research shows that there are a number of sexual behaviours that occur with such low frequency that they can be considered red flag sexual abuse. Some sexually abused children re-enact their experiences with siblings, pet and peers. If a child persists in sexual behaviour after being told that behaviour is essential to protect the child.

(vi) Post-Traumatic Responses

When physical or sexual abuse overwhelms the child's coping ability, leaving the child feeling helpless, terrified and over-stimulated, traumatic responses may follow. A child's response to events that appear traumatic is based upon the child's resilience and ability to cope during the trauma. The three most common post-traumatic reactions involve experiencing; avoidance and increased physiological arousal; re-experiencing involves repetition of the trauma in dreams, thoughts play or action. Flashbacks and re-enactments of the abuse are also form of experiencing. An avoidance reaction includes efforts not to be reminded of the abuse by avoiding thoughts, place and people.

(vii) Hostility and Aggression in Sexually Abused Children

Sexually abused children respond by directing aggression outwards. Such response is more common among adolescents. Gomes-Schwartz *et al.* (1990) identified such a response in between 45 per cent to 50 per cent of the 7 to 13 years old children in their sample. Friedrich *et al.* (1986) found that children aged from 6 to 12 years are more likely to externalize their feelings than younger children. They point out that there are problems associating aggressive reactions purely with sexual abuse because many of the children in their sample were also subjected to physical violence or the threat of it. Thus, the aggression they displayed could have been a result of this rather than of the sexual abuse they experienced.

(viii) Self-injurious Behaviour

Some abused children demonstrate self-inflicted acts such as burning, cutting, disfiguring or hair pulling. These behaviours may reflect a desire to punish them for not stopping the abuse or an attempt to gain some control over their own bodies or to feel alive through the infliction of pain when they feel dead inside.

2. Effect on Positive Behaviours

(i) Pro-social Behaviours

Altruistic behaviour and helping behaviour are two key concepts, which are highly rated in our society, however differ on some aspects. Altruism refers to an act performed voluntarily to help someone else when there is no expectation of receiving a reward in any form (except perhaps a feeling of having done a good deed). By this definition, whether or not an act is altruistic depends on the intentions of the helper. Helping Behaviour on the other hand, is much broader category. It includes any act that helps or is designed to help others, regardless of the helper's motive. Many pro-social acts are altruistic. Our everyday experiences provide many examples of pro-social behaviour. Even young children show the capacity to be helpful to others (Zahn-Waxler *et al.*, 1995). The type of relationship between people affects pro-social behaviour. Whether because of linking social obligation, self-interest or empathy, we are more helpful to those we don't know. Helping behaviour is determined by numerous personal and situational and psycho-social factors.

(ii) Impact of Child Abuse on other Behaviours

Researches indicate negative association between child abuse and positive behaviours. It is quite possible that helping tendency in abused children might be damaged due to poor modeling and unfavourable circumstances in the abusive families. Pandey (2005; 2007) showed that abused children belonging to low socio-economic status expressed poor helping behaviour than their non-abused counterparts. Other studies also reported diminished helping tendencies in maltreated children.

One of the most often-cited problems associated with child abuse and neglect is difficulty in social skill and adjustment. As evidence of social difficulties, a number of studies have revealed a relationship between neglect and distributed pattern of infant caretaker attachment (Crittenden, 1992; Bousha and Twentyman, 1984; Egeland and Sourfe, 1981).

Other indication of disturbed parent-child interaction have appeared demonstrating the deficits in communication, increased aggression and poor involvement characteristic of the interaction between neglecting mother and their children (Bousha and Twentyman, 1984; Crittenden, 1992; Christopoulos *et al.*, 1988). Additional research has also revealed the other area of social maladjustment in victim of child neglect such as socially withdrawn behaviour (Crittenden, 1992; Hoffman-Plotkin and Twentyman, 1984). They observed other social difficulties in the form of disturbed parent-child attachment and disturbed parent-child interaction. Apart from this, abused children were found:

(1) Passive, show deficits in pro-social behaviour and communication, and display physical aggression;
(2) Parent exhibits less sensitivity, appears more withdrawn and uninvolved, uses less general speech and phrases of acceptance, uses more direct imperative, has or displays low rates of social interaction and verbal instruction, and
(3) Disturbed peer interaction such as deficits in pro-social behaviour, social withdrawal and isolation.

Other researchers have also proved that abused children displayed poor study behaviour and discipline, lesser social interaction and low helping behaviour. Contrary to this, levels of aggression, non-compliance and bullying behaviour were found far high in abused children than comparison group (Pandey, 2007; 2010; Pandey *et al.*, 2015). Further, it was considered pertinent to investigate the consequences of school abuse on students' behaviour.

3. Impact on Personality

Psychologists have explored a set of causative factors, viz. intelligence, physique, attractiveness, childhood experience, feelings, emotions, motive of success and failure, cultural influences and family influences etc., exercising impacts on personality development. A sizeable number of researchers have extensively studied the roles of family dysfunctions, inadequate treatment by parents or caregivers and poor bond between parent-child relationships as predictors of child maltreatment, which in turn damage the personality development of children (Hurlock, 1984; Pandey, 2007).

Consequences of Child Abuse on Personality Development

Child physical abuse and personality disorders are found closely associated with several problems, viz. major depression, conduct disorder, oppositional defiant disorder, agro phobia, over-anxious disorder, and conduct disorder (Fisher *et al.*, 1997). Higher rates of depression and conduct disorder have been found in abused adolescents (Pelcovitz *et al.*, 1994). A history of maltreatment has also been associated with borderline personality disorder (Famularo, Kinscherff and Fenton, 1991), attention deficit, hyperactivity disorder and appositional disorder (Famularo *et al.*, 1992). This latter study is noteworthy for its finding that maltreated cases differed from controls in certain disorders depending on whether children (e.g., greater psychotic symptoms, personality/ adjustment disorders) or parents (conduct/mood disorders) were interviewed. Psychological abuse has been found to contribute the prediction of current diagnosis of several disorders, cigarette smoking, as well as other lifetime disorders and problems (e.g., conduct disorder, drug abuse), when added to other identified risk factors (Kaplan *et al.*, 1998). Finally, traumatic victimization (e.g., assault, mugging and sexual molestation) has also been found to contribute to the prediction of oppositional defiant disorder but not attention deficit/hyperactivity disorder in outpatient child psychiatry clinic referrals (Ford *et al.*, 1999).

Child Sexual Abuse and Personality Disorders

Researchers have identified various short-term and long-term consequences of child sexual abuse on personality development.

(i) Low Self-Esteem, Guilt and Shame

The findings with regard to low self-esteem as a short-term consequence of sexual abuse are rather equivocal. De Francis (1969) reported that 58 per cent of victims expressed feelings of inferiority. However, Gomes-Schwartz *et al.* (1990) found that pre-school sexually abused children exhibited a more positive self-concept than the normal population. This finding held true for the older age groups as well. Conte and Schuerman (1987) pointed out that victims of CSA develop guilt symptoms.

(ii) Depression, Withdrawal and Suicide

Friedrich *et al.* (1986) found from a sample of 61 sexually abused females that 46 per cent were experiencing a range of internalized emotions including depression. They also found that withdrawn reaction was more common in younger victims. Anderson *et al.* (1995) found that 25 per cent of females who had been sexually abused showed symptoms of depression afterwards. Other studies have also pointed out to an internalizing response by school age sexually abused victims (Glad Stone *et al.*, 1999: Kolko *et al.*, 1988). Lindberg and Distand (1985) evinced that one third of adolescent victims of sexual abuse had attempted suicide.

(iii) Fearfulness

Browne and Finkelhor (1986) revealed that the most common initial effect noted in empirical studies is fear. Gomes-Schwartz *et al.* (1990) found 45 per cent of their most vulnerable group of children (7-13 years old) was experiencing fearful reaction to what had happened to them within the first six months following the onset of abuse. However, Beitchman *et al.* (1991) pointed out that similar degrees of fear and depression are to be found in general psychiatric population and therefore the emotion attributed in the studies specifically to sexual abuse could be linked to other stress including factors. Apart from this, child sexual abuse has certain long-term consequences.

4. Consequences Associated with Psychological Maltreatment

Researchers and professionals have identified the potential short and long term consequences of psychological maltreatment, as depression, withdrawal and low self-esteem (e.g., Gross and Keller, 1992). In the interpersonal realm, researchers have documented maladjustment in psychologically maltreated children in the area of attachment, social adjustment and peer relationship. Psychologically maltreated children, for example, are significantly more likely than their non-maltreated peers to be insecurely attached to a parent (Egeland, 1991; Crittenden and Ainsworth, 1989). Many investigators have also found that psychologically maltreated children exhibit lower level of social competence and adjustment relative to their non-maltreated counterparts (e.g., Brassard, Hart and Hardy, 1991; Claussen and Crittenden, 1991; Vissing *et al.*, 1991). However, a limited number of studies have evaluated the potential long term effect of psychological maltreatment. The available information indicates that adults who report a childhood history of psychological maltreatment exhibit psychological difficulties. Gross and Keller (1992) evaluated 260 university students, identified as physically and psychologically abused. Respondents had lower self-esteem scores than non-abused respondents but did not differ significantly on measures of depression and attribution style. Respondents experiencing both physical and psychological abuse, however, exhibited higher level of depression than non-abused college students with a history of only one type of abuse (Kent and Waller, 1998). Regression analysis also revealed that psychological abuse was a more powerful predictor of depression, self-esteem and attribution style. Other studies have confirmed the presence of low self-esteem, anxiety, depression, disassociation and interpersonal sensitivity in adults with a history of psychological maltreatment as well as the central role of psychological maltreatment in predicting the effect of child maltreatment (e.g., Briere and Runtz, 1988; 1990; Downs and Miller, 1998; Hoglund and Nicholas, 1995; Kent and Waller, 1998). Present researcher thus, planned to study the outcome of child abuse and neglect by teachers on personality development of students.

5. Consequences of Child Abuse on Health Status of Children

The effects of child abuse on health status of children have been documented by a number of researchers. Some of the representative studies are cited in the following section. Research investigating the effect of child abuse and neglect on overall physical health has largely focused on outcomes in adulthood. However, data from the Longitudinal Studies of Child Abuse and Neglect (LONGSCAN) have indicated strong associations between abuse/neglect and health problems in children/adolescents (Flaherty *et al.*, 2006, 2009). Flaherty *et al.* (2006) found that exposure to one adverse experience doubled the odds of children having overall poor physical health at the age of 6 years, and tripled them if children had experienced four or more adverse experiences. A further study by Hussey, Chang, and Kotch (2006) found that all types of abuse and neglect were associated with 8 of 10 major adolescent health risks. A common form of abuse affecting the health of babies is shaken baby syndrome. Health problems resulting from shaken baby syndrome may include brain damage, spinal cord injuries, hearing loss, speech difficulties and even death (Child Welfare Information Gateway, 2008).

Trauma caused by experiences of child abuse and neglect can have serious effects on the developing brain, increasing the risk of psychological problems (Streeck-Fischer and Vander Kolk, 2000). Extensive research has identified a strong relationship between abuse/neglect and post-traumatic stress disorder (Gilbert *et al.*, 2009; Schore, 2003; Streeck-Fischer and Vander Kolk, 2000). Recent research suggests that diagnosing children with post-traumatic stress disorder does not capture the full developmental effects of chronic child abuse and neglect and many researchers now prefer the term "complex trauma" (Cook *et al.*, 2005). Exposure to complex and chronic trauma can result in persistent psychological problems. Complex trauma affects the developing brain and may interfere with a child's capacity to integrate sensory, emotional and cognitive information, which may lead to overreactive responses to subsequent stress (Streeck-Fischer and Van Der Kolk, 2000).

Mental health problems, such as depression and anxiety disorders, have consistently been linked with child abuse and neglect, particularly for adolescents (Brown, Cohen, Johnson, and Smailes, 1999; Gilbert *et al.*, 2009; Harkness and Lumley, 2008; Kaufman, 1991). Prevalence rates of major depression have been shown to be approximately four times higher in adolescents than younger children (Harkness and Lumley, 2008). In a review of large-scale studies, Harkness and Lumley (2008) showed a high association between child abuse/neglect and depression in adolescence. Further, in a longitudinal study by Brown, Cohen, Johnson and Smailes (1999) children and adolescents who reported a history of abuse or neglect were three times more likely to exhibit a depressive disorder than non-maltreated children. In a Victorian study of characteristics of children referred to a therapeutic health service for children who had been abused or neglected 62 per cent of children met the criteria for at least one mental health diagnosis (Frederico *et al.*, 2008). Review of studies suggests serious health consequences of child abuse. Therefore, it was also planned to assess the effect of child abuse in schools on health status of students.

The Present Study

Child abuse is a widely studied area of psychological investigation particularly in developed countries and findings of these studies have not only explored the deep-rooted causes of child maltreatment within the family but also have significance for preventive interventions. However, a large number of cases of child maltreatment outside the family are witnessed in many forms i.e., Institutional abuse, Ritualistic abuse, Organized exploitation in terms of Child sex rings, Child pornography and Child prostitution. Despite the limited scientific knowledge about these forms of exploitation, their sensationalistic nature has been made popular in the media. In general, such types of child exploitation occur less communal than abuses within the family. Yet frequency of occurrence alone, should not determine social concern about a problem. The adverse impacts on children's lives resulting from such experiences can be just as significant as other forms of child maltreatment. Unfortunately, very little attention is paid by academicians for investigating causative roots and consequences of such type of abuses outside the family. Secondly, in larger number of researches, the consequences of child abuse have been studied in relation to classificatory or structural factors and therefore, causal explanation becomes little difficult. Thirdly, certain methodological problems in these studies are also identified as most of the studies are based on secondary data (either registered or reported samples) and another noticeable point is, that these studies are mainly conducted in developed countries, where multifaceted preventive efforts at multiple levels have been proliferated since the last few decades. However, this picture is quite different in developing countries like India. Because of the cultural variations, the nature and forms of abuse differ among developing and developed countries thus, studies suffer from correct screening of abused cases and adequate research methodology.

In India, although the cases of child maltreatment are present at alarming volume, but correct statistics of cases are unknown due to lack of awareness, ignorance and fear of defame. Some forms of abuses also vary in Indian context as compared to western countries. Earlier some efforts by sociologists (Chattoraj, Saxena, 1990; Mehta, 1979) and medical professionals (Bhattacharya, 1979) were made to investigate the forms of maltreatment, however, these studies provide incomplete or little clue, to understand the socio-demographic and pathological causes of abuse and neglect. So, in order to understand the psychological causes and consequences of abuse and neglect, the role of process variables should be properly investigated. In a comprehensive study, Pandey (2007) investigated the antecedents and mediators of child abuse in the family and consequences on children. The researcher identified the significant roles of ecological, socio-demographic and psychological factors in occurrence of child abuse and its adverse consequences on children's cognitive, motivational and behavioural functioning as well as personality of children. Apart from this, a bulk of studies has explored the incidents of child abuse around the country and its damaging consequences on children (Baruah, 2003; Pandey, 2011; Pandey and Tamta, 2013; Pandey, *et al.*, 2015). These studies have mainly focused on cases of child abuse by parents or family members. Despite this, cases of child abuse in institutions, schools, playgrounds and many other organizations are witnessed in high proportion, but such cases are unnoticed or ignored, and little effort has been done by social scientists and psychologists sincerely working in the areas of child abuse. Therefore, present study has focused on issues related to child abuse in school setting.

The abusive treatment by teachers/educators in school setting is found in plenty. As study on Child Abuse-2007 in India by Ministry of Women and Child Development, Govt. of India provides a glimpse of the incidence of abuse in schools. In India, 65 per cent of school going children reported facing corporal punishment (physical abuse). Two out of every three children were victims of physical abuse. Of 65.11 per cent school children reported being beaten in school with boys making up 54.28 per cent of the victims. The study reported that 53.8 per cent of children faced corporal punishment in state schools while 22.3 per cent faced it in public school and 3.1 per cent in other forms of schools.

In Juvenile Justice Institutions, 70.2 per cent of children were found in conflict with law and 52.86 per cent of children were in need of care and protection. Children facing discrimination based on social, economic, linguistic and religious identified inside the school, as well as discrimination based on disability and illness have also been reported. Psychological abuse is found more pervasive than physical punishment in some schools.

Abusive treatment of school children, often misinterpreted as discipline or punishment is totally wrong and detrimental for the growth of children. Although, responsible educators have known for a long time that both physical and non-physical mistreatment of children by teachers is unprofessional behaviours; that it can destroy children's curiosity for learning and causes serious impact on overall development of children. Though, majority of teachers are competent and caring professionals who do not mistreat children physically or emotionally. Unfortunately there are teachers in some schools who are unsuited to their profession and they habitually hurt children, and some school administrators who lack ability to maintain high professional standards in their schools.

The Parents and Teachers Against Violence in Educators (PTAVE) group continuously receive complaints about abuse to school children, denotes variety of mistreatment of school children by teachers, coaches, bus drivers or other adults in school setting. These abuses are concerned with physical abuse, mental harassment, neglect, emotional (psychological) abuse and sexual abuse. Except a few efforts (The National Commission for Protection of Child Rights "NCPCR" and some international organizations), child abuse in school setting is a less researched issue. The number of abusers and abused victims are dramatically increasing day by day. Therefore, it is seriously felt that intensive role of psychologists is important to understand the causative factors and consequences of school abuses and then only preventive efforts can be made to check incidence and prevalence rate of abuses in schools and to control adverse consequences on students.

The specific research problems, to be studied in present research include the following:

(i) Child Abuse and Neglect in Relation to Contextual and Socio-Demographic Factors: Apart from extensive studies conducted on child abuse and neglect throughout the world, there are still numerous questions unanswered concerning the role of contextual and socio-demographic factors in the origin of child abuse and neglect in schools and their interplay in the development of children.

(ii) Adult Characteristics and Child Abuse: Researchers have established an exclusive relationship between certain adult characteristics and child maltreatment. Adults, who were abused as child, were found more abusive than control group (Kempe and Helfer, 1972). Besides this, maltreating parents/teachers exhibited cognitive deficiencies (Pandey, 2010; Wolfe, 1985), high anger and high arousal level (Averill, 1983) and other emotional imbalances (Bower, 1981) than non-abusive counterparts. However, many other evidences do not support this and suggest that there must be certain other factors adding to the origin of abuse and neglect. Researches revealed that negative mental states were found to be positively linked with child maltreatment. Stress may be the cause of maltreatment or *vice versa*. Certainly, child abuse causes overwhelming amount of stress, especially when the attack was unexpected. Thus, a sizeable number of researches attempted to determine the relationship between stress and health/outcome. Adults abused as children and personality of adults (Abusers) may also have link with child maltreatment of children. This issue is taken for investigation in the present study.

(iii) Impacts of Child abuse on Children: A bulk of researches conducted around the globe has proved negative consequences of child abuse on children as well as adults, who were abused in their childhood. Abused children showed lower intellectual and cognitive functioning relative to a comparison group of children on general intellectual functioning as well as specific measure of verbal facility, memory, verbal language, communication abilities, problem-solving, and perceptual motor skills (Fantuzzo, 1990; Hoffman *et al.* 1994; Pandey, 2007; Pandey and Tamta, 2013). De Paul and Arruabarrena (1995) reported that abused children display poor school achievement and adjustment, receive more special education services, score lower on reading and math test, exhibit more learning disability and are more likely repeat a grade. Other studies proved that abused children showed lower levels of aspiration and academic achievement (Brassard *et al.* 1991; Pandey 2007). Several behavioural problems in abused children have also been recorded by a number of researchers. The most extensively documented impact of physical abuse is heightened aggression and related externalizing behaviours in victims (National Academy of Sciences, 1993; Cummings *et al.*, 1994; Pandey, 2007; 2010). Researchers have also identified that sexually abused children exhibited personality disorders, i.e. low self-esteem, guilt and shame, depression, withdrawal and fearfulness (Anderson *et al.*, 1995; Pandey, 2007). Moreover, researchers have identified adverse impacts of child abuse on physical and mental health of children (Pandey, 2007; 2017).

Research Questions

Apart from extensive studies on child abuse and neglect, there are still numerous issues, concerning the etiological factors and consequences of child abuse and neglect in school setting and their interplay in the development of children, are to be answered. Some unexplored issues of child abuse in school setting are:

i. What are the roles of environmental, socio-demographic variables in the origin of child abuse in school setting?
ii. What are the psychological characteristics of abusers?
iii. What are the extent and specific forms of abuses in school setting?
iv. What are the detrimental consequences of abuse on cognitive, affective and behavioural functioning of children?
v. How and at what extent abusive treatment by school personnel damage personality and health status of children?

Objective and Hypotheses

Objectives of the Study

Based on the research questions raised above, this study was carried out with following objectives:

1. To find out the role of environmental factors in the origin of child abuse in schools.
2. To examine social and demographic factors which provide

germane grounds to abuse in schools.

3. To assess the psychological characteristics of abusers.
4. To explore specific forms of abuses in school setting.
5. To assess the consequences of abuse on cognitive, affective and behavioural functioning as well as personality and health status of children.

Hypotheses

On the basis of research objectives, following hypotheses were formulated. It was hypothesized that;

1. The environmental setting of schools and school environment would influence the nature, magnitude and forms of abuses in schools.
2. Certain socio-demographic factors (like, caste, education, socio-economic status, age and gender of respondents) would be associated with origin of child abuse in schools.
3. The personality characteristics of teachers and their childhood abusive experiences would be linked with abusive treatment of children.
4. The specific forms of abuse as reported by teachers/school personnel would differ across different types of school.
5. The type of school and grade level of students would also exert influence on child abuse and its consequences.
6. Child abuse would cause adverse impact on cognitive, affective and behavioural functioning of students.
7. Abusive treatment by teachers would cause detrimental consequence on personality and health status of students.

2
Method

In this chapter, despite the methodological issues involved in the study of child abuse in school setting, the plan and strategy (design) of present research have also been described. At the outset, a preliminary survey/study was done to finalize study setting, identification of cases and finalization of the measures. Apart from this, an attempt has also been made to present an overview of sample characteristics, research strategies and assessment techniques of antecedent, mediating and outcome variables, selected for the present study.

Research Design

This study is correlational in nature. Therefore, to assess the links among antecedent variables, mediating variables and outcome variables, correlations would be computed. Besides this, to assess the differential roles of predictors in criterion variables, regression analysis would also be done. Despite this, factorial design (2×3×2) has been used to make comparison among groups. Therefore, Univariate and Multivariate analyses would be exercised in the present study.

Screening of Study Setting and Participants

In order to identify the settings of study and selection of participants, a preliminary survey of schools situated in different districts of Uttar Pradesh was done. At the outset, information was collected from the secondary sources (i.e. registered/reported cases) from District Institution of Education and Training (DIET) Centres, Health Centres, Public library, Family, and District court as well as from Child Care Centres to determine the incidence/prevalence rate, pattern and form of abuses in schools of Uttar Pradesh.

Uttar Pradesh is one of the most populous states in India with total population of 19,95,81,477. It is also one of the biggest states in India with a geographical area encompassing 2,40,928 square kilometers and comprising of 75 districts, 820 development blocks and over a lakh inhabited villages.

Population Structure: As per census 2011 (Provisional data), total population of U.P. is—19,95,81,477 (**Males:** 10,45,96,415, **Females:** 94,985,062). Other population features are: **Decennial Growth rate (2001-2011):** 20.09 per cent, **Sex Ratio:** 908 per thousand, **Density (persons per sq. km.)** (As per census 2011): 828 per thousand, **Child Population (0-6 years):** 2,97,28,235, **Child sex ratio (0-6 years):** 899 per thousand, **Total Literacy rate—Persons:** 69.72%) **(a) Male Literacy:** 79.24 per cent **(b) Female Literacy:** 59.26 per cent. In actual numbers, total literates in Uttar Pradesh stands at 11,43,97,555 of which males are 6,82,34,964 and females are 4,61,62,591. Table 2.1 displays population characteristics of various districts of U.P., which were selected as settings of the Study.

Table 2.1: Population Characteristics of Various Districts of U.P. (Selected as Settings of the Study)

S. No.	*District*	*Population*	*Male*	*Female*	*Literacy*	*Density*
1.	Gorakhpur	4,440,895	2,277,777	2,163,118	70.83	1337
2.	Basti	2,464,464	1,255,272	1,209,192	67.22	917
3.	Ballia	3,239,774	1,672,902	1,566,872	70.94%	1087
4.	Gonda	3,433,919	1,787,146	1,646,773	58.71%	858
5.	Lucknow	4,589,838	2,394,476	2,195,362	77.29%	1816
6.	Meerut	3,443,689	1,825,743	1,617,946	72.84%	1346
7.	Kanpur	4,581,268	2,459,806	2,121,462	79.65%	1452

This survey provided base to finalize the appropriate setting for this research. Therefore, it was decided to conduct study in schools of seven districts of U.P. i.e., Gorakhpur, Ballia, Deoria, Basti, Gonda, Lucknow and Kanpur. The main purpose of this research is to investigate psycho-social dynamics of child abuse in schools and its consequences on children.

Child abuse and neglect may take place at multiple points and setting as a result of multi-causative factors. Belsky (1980) conceptualized child abuse as a "Social-Psychological Phenomena" and indicated that multiple forces determine it across four different levels; the individual (ontogenetic level), the family (micro-system), the community (the exo-system), and the culture (the macro-system), in which the individual and family/community are embedded.

The agents of child abuse (perpetrators) in school setting are found within and outside the school setting. Perpetrators may be school administrators/principals, school teachers, non-teaching staff, classmates or peer group (bullies), bus drivers, caretakers and any significant member for the child related to school. The child abuse by school personnel is witnessed in plenty; however, correct statistics of the abused cases are underestimated or unreported due to methodological problems in the study of child maltreatment (abuse). Therefore, for the screening of abused cases two criteria were adopted: **(i) Reported/registered cases of Child Abuse in schools:** First of all, survey based data were collected from various sources (reported/registered cases of school abuse, parent's reporting, counsellor reports or reporting by students etc.) and a rough idea about the incidence rate of abuse in schools of Uttar Pradesh was drawn on the basis of secondary data. This information provided base for the development of Child Abuse in School Checklist to identify actual cases of abuse from the study setting. **(ii) Child Abuse in School Checklist (CASC)**: The CASC, developed and standardized by Pandey (2015) was used to identify the abused cases in schools of Uttar Pradesh.

Participants: In the present study both students and teachers participated as respondents. A total of 1200 students of different schools and settings (Rural-Urban) were selected from seven districts (i.e. Gorakhpur, Basti, Gonda, Lucknow, Kanpur, Deoria and Ballia as these districts were found more sensitive) of Uttar Pradesh, by exercising stratified random sampling technique. On the basis of responses by students on Child Abuse in School checklist, median score was calculated (Mdn = 117) and level of abuse (High and Low) in students was determined and category of high and low abused children was chalked out. Again, to identify the cases of abusive and non-abusive teachers, Child Abuse

Interview Schedule for Teachers was administered on a total of 250 teachers to assess the level and forms of abusive behaviour towards their students. Apart from this, Teachers' childhood abusive experiences and their personality were also assessed.

Despite this, subject selection procedure was used by manipulating the level of abuse in rural and urban school settings and other characteristics like type of school, medium of education, students characteristics i.e., gender, age, grade, socio-economic status of respondents as well as characteristics of perpetrators (school personnel). Since the participants of present study were school children (10-18 yrs., grade 6-12th) and school personnel (teachers), thus some of the variables were studied on students, while certain variables were assessed on school personnel. The categorization of sample in accordance with environmental setting, type of school, medium of education, level of abuse, gender, age and grade is displayed in Table 2.2.

Measures

To investigate the social and psychological correlates of child abuse in school setting and consequences on cognitive, affective, behavioural functioning as well as personality and health status of students (children), a set of measuring tools were developed/ selected. Variables and concerned measures, administered on students are displayed in Table 2.2, and measures used on school personnel are displayed in Table 2.3. A brief description of these measures is reported in following section.

(A) Measures Used on Students

(1) Personal Data Sheet (PDS): To assess the socio-demographic characteristics of participants (students) personal data sheet was prepared and administered on students.

(2) Development of 'Child Abuse in School Checklist' (CASC): To ascertain the magnitude and various forms of abuse of students by school personnel, 'The Child Abuse in School Checklist' was developed. This checklist was constructed with the help of Child Abuse Checklist (S. Pandey, 2012). The checklist includes four sub-sections i.e. Physical abuse (18 items), Psychological abuse (20 items), Sexual abuse (13 items) and Child

Table 2.2: Variables along with Measures Administered on Students

S. No.	*Variables*	*Measures*
1.	Demographic/Background Information	Personal Data Sheet (S. Pandey, 2015)
2.	Child abuse in schools	Child Abuse in School Checklist (S. Pandey, 2015)
3.	School Environment *School setting:* (Rural-Urban), *Type of school:* (Government-Private), *Medium of education:* (Hindi-English)	School Environment Inventory (K.S. Mishra, 1984) Personal Data Sheet (S. Pandey, 2015)
4.	Cognitive Variables (i) Verbal Ability (ii) Memory Span (iii) Working Memory	Measures-Verbal Ability Test (S. Pandey, 2013) Memory Span Test (S. Pandey, 2007) Working Memory Task (S. Pandey, 2013)
5.	Motivational Factors (i) Academic Achievement (ii) Aspiration Level	Academic Achievement Motivation Test (T.R. Sharma, 1984) Aspiration Scale (S. Pandey, 2007)
6.	Affective Variables (i) Depression (ii) Anxiety	Depression Scale (S. Pandey, 2015) State Trait Anxiety Inventory for children (modified version by S. Pandey, 2015)
7.	Behavioural Process	Child Behaviour Questionnaire (S. Pandey, 2015)
8.	Personality	Children Personality Questionnaire (CPQ), (R.B. Cattell, 1972) High School Personality Questionnaire (HSPQ), (R.B. Cattell, 1973)
9.	Health status (Physical and Mental health)	P.G.I. Health Questionnaire (Verma, Wig and Prashad, 1985)

Neglect (total = 28 items; physical neglect—08; emotional neglect—08 and educational neglect—12). The CASC has five point scale ranging from Always (5), Very often (4), Sometimes (3), Rarely (2), to Never (1). For NOT Applicable, zero (0) score is provided. The Test-retest reliability of the checklist was found high (r = .83). The reliability alpha was also calculated which was found to be high and significant (r = .89).

Scoring: Responses of each item were scored following 5, 4, 3, 2, 1 scores. The score could range from 79 to 395. Total summated

Table 2.3: Variables along with Measuring Tools Administered on School Personnel (Teachers)

S. No.	Variables	Measures
1.	Background Information of School Personnel	Personal data sheet (S. Pandey, 2015)
2.	Socio-Economic Status, Caste Age, Gender, Education, Occupation, Income, Health Status, Marital Status etc.	Personal data sheet (S. Pandey, 2015)
3.	Child Abuse by School Personnel	Child Abuse Interview Schedule for Teachers
4.	Childhood Abuse and Neglect	Childhood Abuse questionnaire (Holland and Roisman, 2008)
5.	Personality Questionnaire	NEO PI-R (Costa and McCrae)

scores in each area denote the magnitude of abuse and neglect in specific area and on the basis of grand total, abuse as a whole was determined and median score (mdn = 117) was calculated. Further on the basis of median score the category of high and low abused children was determined.

(3) School Environment Inventory (SEI): In order to assess the psycho-social climate of schools as perceived by the students, School Environment Inventory (K.S. Mishra, 1984) was used. SEI includes 70 items related to six dimensions of school environment i.e., (i) Creative Stimulation (CRS), (ii) Cognitive Encouragement (COE), (iii) Acceptance (ACC), (iv) Permissiveness (PER), (v) Rejection (REJ) and (vi) Control (CON). Twenty items belong to CRS, while each of the remaining five dimensions have ten items belonging to it. Each item is rated on 5 point scale ranging from Always (4), Often (3), Sometimes (2), Rarely (1) to Never (0) marks respectively.

Measures of Outcomes Variables

Further, to assess the consequences of child abuse on cognitive, affective, behavioural functioning, as well as personality and health status of students, following measures were developed or devised. Each measure is briefly described below:

1. *Cognitive Measures*

(i) Verbal ability Test: In order to assess the level and forms of verbal ability in children, the Verbal Ability Test (VAT) (developed and standardized by S. Pandey and P. Tamta 2014) was used. This test includes a total of 40 items viz., Word Meaning (08 items), Opposite (05 items), Analogy (10 items), Word Classification (08 items) and Sentence Completion (Fill in the blank: 09 items) presented in a 4 alternative answer. The reliability alpha of the scale is fairly high (r = 0.82) and the item total correlation ranged between 0.17 to 0.46.

Scoring: The success responses on items were given a score of one (1) and failure, a zero (0) score. On the basis of total scores the level of verbal ability in children was determined.

(ii) Memory Span Test: To ascertain the immediate memory span of children, the memory span test was devised. A set of three lists for three trials (for each number span) varying 3 to 10 digits were developed. Each digit chunk was read out by researcher one by one and students were asked to repeat the same immediately. The experimenter noted down each item as responded by the subject. Correctly recalled items denoted the memory span of the children. This test is extensively used by researcher previously (Pandey, 2005; 2007).

(iii) Working Memory Task: Three sets of working memory task devised and used earlier (Pandey and Pandey, 2013) was exercised to assess the level and forms of working memory. A brief description of these measures is given below:

(a) Reading Span Task (RSPAN): Based on Reading Span Task (Chiappe, Hasher and Siegel, 2000), the RSPAN was designed in Indian context to measure the combined processing and storage capacity of working memory. Reading Span Task contains 30 sentences each one written on separate card. The length of each sentence given in card is 8 to 12 words.

Each card was shown for ½ second. After the presentation of each sentence, respondents were asked to recall the red word (as written with red colour on the card) of the sentence in correct order.

Scoring: Item scoring method was used. Correctly recalled items on each trial were added together to obtain their average scores. Finally, these average scores were added together to get Reading Span Score. These scores denoted the level of Reading Memory Span in children.

(b) Visual Pattern Recall (VSPAN): The Visual Pattern Recall Task includes 25 Geometric designs. The participants were instructed to look carefully at the pattern and try to remember where the blank part of design was. The design was printed on the card and there was half second delay before presentation of empty geometric design of the same size for recall. After the presentation of card assigned, immediate memory test was done.

Scoring: The total numbers of correct recalled geometric design were added together. Total summated score indicated the level of V Span memory.

(c) Operation Span Task (OSPAN): The construction of OSPAN was done on the basis of Operation Span Task (Turner and Eagle, 1989). OSPAN task consists of 30 Math Equations. Each card contains one word. These cards are categorized under five sets based on increasing the number of Math equation with words. Each card was shown for ½ second. After the presentation of each set, students were asked to recall the word in proper order.

Scoring: Item scorning method was used. Correctly recalled items on each trial were added together to obtain their average scores. Finally, these average scores were added together to get Operation Span Score. These scores denoted the level of Memory Span in children.

2. ***Measures of Motivational Process:*** Following measures were selected to assess motivational functioning in students.

(i) Academic Achievement Motivation Test: To assess the level of academic achievement motive in school children, Academic Achievement Test (by T.R. Sharma, 1984) was used. The test contains a total of 38 items. The reliability (test-retest = .795 for girls sample and .807 for boys sample) and validity (construct validity) of the test are reported fairly high.

Scoring: Each item was responded on 'Yes' 'No' alternative. If 'A' alternative was ticked by respondent for item Nos: 1, 3, 4, 6, 8, 10, 12, 13, 15, 16, 17, 18, 21, 25, 27, 31, 35, 36, (1) score was provided whereas, reverse pattern was followed for scoring the remaining items. If B was ticked (√) in case of items at serial No. 2, 5, 7, 9, 11, 14, 19, 20, 22, 23, 24, 26, 28, 29, 30, 32, 33, 34, and 38 (1) score was given. Scores were added together and further with the help of Norm Table, the level of academic achievement in children was determined.

(ii) Aspiration Scale: To assess aspiration level of students

related to education, career, self-enhancement etc. A ten point-ladder scale (previously used by Tromnsdroff, 1998, Pandey, 2007), would be used. Students would be asked to put (√) mark to indicate their level of aspirations on 10 point ladder scale. The first step or rung of the ladder indicates lowest status and 10th step or rung denotes highest status of aspirations. Earlier, ladders have been successfully used by sizeable number of researchers to study aspiration, hopes and fears in respondents (Tromnsdroff, 1998; Mishra and Tripathi, 1980).

3. *Measures of Affective Process*

(i) Depression Scale: To assess the level of depression in children, Depression scale was developed and standardized. The scale contains a total of 29 items and each item is responded on 3 point scale ranging from rarely to often. Total summated scores were used to determine the level of depression. Greater score denoted higher level of depression in children.

(ii) State-Trait Anxiety Inventory for Children (STAIC): To assess the level of anxiety in children, State-Trait Anxiety Inventory for Children (Spielberger, 1973; Modified by S. Pandey, 2015) was used. The test includes 25 items and each item is responded on 3 point scale ranging from rarely to often. Total summated scores were used to determine the level of anxiety. Greater score denoted higher level of anxiety in children.

4. *Behavioural Measure*

Development of Child Behaviour Scale (CBS): To assess the multiple behaviours of children, CBS was developed and standardized. This scale includes 58 items based on seven behaviour patterns related to positive and negative behaviours i.e. Interpersonal Relationship, Pro-social Behaviour, Study Behaviour, Disciplinary Behaviour, Aggressive Behaviour, Non-compliance and Bullying behaviour. The child behaviour scale has five point scale ranging from Highly Agree (5), Agree (4), Neutral (3), Disagree (2), and Highly Disagree (1). This scale is pilot tested and coefficient alpha has been determined (r = .89).

Scoring: Responses on each item were scored following 5, 4, 3, 2 and 1 order. Total summated scores in each area denote the forms of behaviour pattern in children.

5. Personality Questionnaire

To check the personality pattern of children, Cattell's Child Personality Questionnaire (CPQ) and High School Personality Questionnaire (HSPQ) were used to measure personality pattern of the different age group of children. The CPQ was applied on 8-12 years age group of children. The reliability (ranged from r = .42 to .75) and validity (r value ranged from .75 to .90) were found to be high. Further, HSPQ was administered on 13-18 years of children. The reliability (r value ranged from .51 to .80) and validity of this test (r values ranged from r = .57 to .74 respectively) are high. CPQ contains 140 items, 70 in each forms (B1 and B2) related to fourteen factors of personality. Children were asked to respond on one of the two alternatives.

Similarly, HSPQ includes 142 items and children were asked to put (0) mark on any one point of the three alternatives, i.e. a-b-c. Obtained scores, known as raw scores for each factors were transformed into Sten scores. Then, children's personality on each factor was identified and personality profile was determined.

6. P.G.I. Health Questionnaire

To assess the health condition of school children, P.G.I. Health Questionnaire N-1 (Verma, Wig and Pershad) was used. This questionnaire contains 38 items, divided into two sections i.e., A (physical distress) and B (psychological distress) with 16 and 22 items, respectively. Each item is responded on Yes/No alternatives.

(B) Measures to be used on Teachers/School Personnel

1. *Child Abuse Interview Schedule for Teachers:* To assess the perception and practice of child abuse by teachers/school personnel, this interview schedule was developed. The schedule contains free-ended questions and respondents would answer these questions in their own statements, hence, for such responses qualitative analyses would be exercised.

2. *Childhood Abuse Questionnaire (CAQ):* This scale was developed to assess childhood abusive experience of teachers. The CAQ, a self-report measure includes 30 items to determine 6 types of childhood abuse and neglect: Physical abuse (06, CPA),

psychological abuse (06 CPsyA), sexual abuse, (06 CSA, Neglect (12), physical neglect (04), emotional neglect (04) and educational neglect (04). However for the present study psychological abuse, emotional neglect, and educational neglect dimensions were used. This scale is pilot tested and alpha coefficient of the measures is fairly high (r = .92).

Scoring: Each item was rated on 5 points scale ranging from Never (1) to Very Often (5). Therefore, the scale has a minimum score of 30 with maximum score of 150. Higher score denotes high abusive experience of participants.

3: Personality Test (NEO PI-R): To assess the personality characteristics of Teachers/School Personnel, the NEO PI-R (Costa and McCrae 1978) was applied on teachers/school personnel. This test contains a total of 240 items which measures five personality domains i.e. Neuroticism, Extraversion, Openness, Agreeableness and Conscientiousness. This test has been translated in Hindi and now it is Pilot tested by S. Pandey (2015).

Procedure

The screening of geographical settings of the study and identification of cases were already done in preliminary phase of the study. On the basis of secondary data (reported/registered cases), the research team consisting of project director and field investigators approached to the respective areas of the study and tried to establish rapport with the School Personnel. This study was conducted in various districts of U.P. viz. Gorakhpur, Basti, Ballia, Lucknow, Meerut and Kanpur; thus research team visited these places one by one.

Prior to this, a brief orientation session, to introduce the nature and purpose of the study and detailed instruction about administration of measuring tools, was organized by project director to field investigators. High degree of skill and ingenuity on part of the investigators was essential to communicate the respondents in effective manner. The sample of this investigation consisted of children and school personnel (Principal, teachers and other employees), thus multiple phases of data collection were required. Since, availability of participants for the study was a difficult problem because sample characteristics differed on degree of environmental setting (rural-urban), type of school (private and government), medium of education (English/Hindi), age (6-10, 11-14 and 15-18 Yrs.), gender (boys-girls), socio-economic status (high, middle and low) and level of abuses. So, it was quite difficult to approach the respondents and schedule them for administration of measuring tools, yet, efforts were made to contact the students and school teachers etc. in school settings. Therefore, the study was conducted into two phases in multiple sessions.

First Phase of the Study

First of all, students were contacted for this investigation in schools. This phase required multiple sessions.

1st Session: The consent and permission for study from school authority (Principal) was required. They were explained about purpose of the study and its significance on the academic growth and development of students. After receiving consent from the authority of the school, first session of research started.

In this session, students were contacted in their schools in leisure time. They were explained about the nature and purpose of the study in effective manner and proper rapport was established, then, they were given a booklet containing Personal Data Sheet (PDS), School Environment Scale and Child Abuse in Schools Checklist (CASC). Children were requested to respond on these measures one by one. As they completed responses on said measures data were collected and they were thanked for participation and further, were requested to participate in 2nd session of the study. First session ended with administration of Child Abuse in Schools Checklist. Other tests and tasks were administered in 2nd and 3rd sessions.

2nd Session: In this session, participants were given experimental tasks, tests and questionnaires. First of all students were given cognitive measures i.e. Verbal Ability Test, Working Memory Task and Memory Span Test. They were requested to perform on these tasks one by one. As they completed their task, children were given measures of affective process i.e. Depression Scale and State trait Anxiety Inventory for Children. They were requested to perform on these measures one by one. As soon as, students completed responses on these measures, they were thanked for co-operation and again requested to participate in 3rd session of the study.

3rd Session: In this session, first of all, achievement and aspiration levels of children were assessed. They were given Academic Achievement Motivation Test and Aspiration Scale and were requested to respond on these measures. After this, to ascertain the behavioural functioning of children, participants were requested to respond on Child Behaviour Scale (S. Pandey, 2007, modified, 2015). Further students were asked to participate again in 4th session.

4th Session: In this session, students' personality and health status were assessed with appropriate measures. First of all, CPQ/ HSPQ was administered on different-age group of students and were asked to respond carefully. Lastly, physical and mental health status of children was assessed by Health Questionnaire. As they completed responses on above said measures, data were collected and students were thanked for co-operation.

(II) Second Phase of the Study

In this phase, school personnel (principals, teachers and school staff) were contacted in school settings and requested for their co-operation. After getting their consent, they were described about the nature and aim of the study. First of all School Personnel were given Personal Data Sheet and Child Abuse and Neglect Interview Schedule to obtain demographic/personal background information as well as their perception about type of abuses in schools. Further, to examine their childhood abusive experiences, childhood Abuse Questionnaire was given to teachers and they were requested to answer. Finally, to assess teachers' personality, NEO PI-R personality questionnaire was administered. They, were requested to respond on each measure one by one. As they completed their responses on above-mentioned measures, data were collected and they were thanked for participation.

Data obtained on various measures were then scored according to defined rules, given in manuals. Scores were analyzed using IBM SPSS 21 Version.

3
Results

This chapter contains the results obtained from the statistical treatment of data obtained on various measures used in the present research. At the outset, the scores for the analysis were obtained on the basis of responses given by school children and school personnel (Teachers), belonging to different setting and types of schools of Uttar Pradesh (U.P.). Data were collected on school children on a number of standardized measuring devices (as mentioned in methodology section). Apart from this, Unstructured Interview Schedule, Childhood Abuse Questionnaire and NEOPI R were used on school personnel (teachers) to assess their personal characteristics, childhood abusive experiences and personality. Responses on various measures were scored according to defined rules. The statistical treatments of scores were done in terms of Univariate, Bivariate, and Multivariate analyses respectively. Apart from this, qualitative analysis of data was also done to provide vivid picture of incidence rate, forms, process, contributing factors, and consequences of child abuse in school setting.

1: Epidemiology of Child Abuse in School Setting (Based on Reporting of Students): Forms of abuses reported by students were recorded and the number of cases were determined and transformed into percentage. Results are displayed in Table 3.1 and Fig. 3.1.

It is apparent from the Table 3.1 and Fig. 3.1; a sizable number of students were identified as victims of different forms of abuses by school personnel. However, child neglect emerged as most common form of child abuse. Specifically:

Table 3.1: Percentage of Sub-Types of Child Abuse in Schools as Reported by Students

S. No.	*Forms of Abuses*	*Percentage (%)*
1.	Physical Abuse	25
2.	Psychological Abuse	26
3.	Sexual Abuse	13
4.	**Total Neglect**	**36**
	(i) Physical Neglect	10
	(ii) Emotional Neglect	10
	(iii Educational Neglect	16

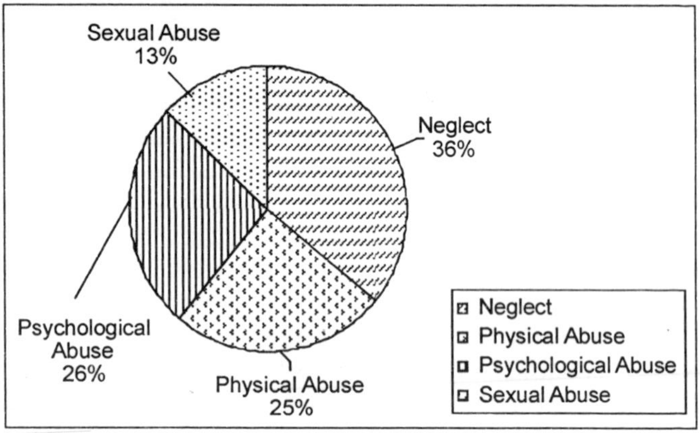

Fig 3.1: Percentage of Each Sub-Types of Child Abuse (Maltreatment).

1. A total of 25 per cent students reported as victims of physical abuse;
2. Whereas, 26 per cent students were found victims of psychological abuse;
3. 13 per cent students were found victims of sexual abuse; and
4. A total of 36 per cent students were identified as victims of child neglect. More specifically, the cases of educational neglect were found maximum (16%). Emotional neglect was found 10 per cent and again 10 per cent students were found physically neglected.

Above data indicate that child abuses in schools are present at high level in various forms. Abuses with children (in same or other forms) are present at high rate in schools of various districts of Uttar Pradesh and not a single school was found immune of abusive treatment with children.

Further, the causes and consequences of abuses in schools were assessed. In present study, a total of five objectives have been investigated and results are reported in accordance with objectives of the study in preferential order under five sections.

SECTION-1

First objective of the study includes the role of environmental and socio-demographic variables in the origin of child abuse in school setting. This section contains three types of statistical treatment of data i.e. comparative analysis, correlational analysis and step-wise multiple regression analysis (SRMA).

1: Comparative Analysis

(1) Child Abuse in Rural and Urban School Setting

In order to determine the extent of abuse and neglect in schools situated in urban and rural settings, Mean, S.D. and One Way Analysis of Variance (ANOVA) were calculated. Results displayed in Table 3.2 and Fig. 3.2 amd 3.3 evinced that children differed significantly on physical abuse, psychological abuse, emotional neglect, educational neglect and abuse as whole ($P<.01$). Child physical abuse differed significantly across urban and rural settings. Rural children were found more physically abused (M (Phy.) = 11.27) than urban children (M (Phy.) = 8.71). Whereas, urban children were found more psychologically abused (M (Psy.) = 14.08) than rural children (M (Psy.) = 7.96). Rural and urban children differed significantly on emotional neglect. Urban children were found more emotionally neglected (M = 5.75) than rural school children (M = 3.77). Whereas, educational neglect was found higher in rural school children (M = 9.53) than urban school children (M = 6.56). But child abuse as a whole, was found greater in urban school children (M = 43.04) as compared to rural school counterparts (M = 40.57). However, Rural and Urban school children did not differ significantly on physical neglect and sexual abuse.

(2) Type of School and Child Abuse

It is apparent from the results (Table 3.3, Fig. 3.4 and 3.5), various forms of abuse differed significantly in government and private schools.

Table 3.2: Mean, S.D. and F-values of Child Abuse by School Setting

School setting		Abuse			Neglect			Child abuse as a whole
		Physical Abuse	Psychological Abuse	Sexual abuse	Physical Neglect	Emotional Neglect	Educational Neglect	
Urban	Mean	8.71	14.08	3.62	4.34	5.75	6.56	43.04
	S.D.	(5.16)	(4.52)	(2.25)	(2.80)	(1.21)	(3.74)	(19.68)
Rural	Mean	11.27	7.96	3.24	4.80	3.77	9.53	40.57
	S.D.	(7.4)	(7.2)	(2.74)	(2.62)	(1.15)	(4.84)	(25.95)
	F-Values	21.92***	64.72***	1.08	2.05	26.82***	30.62***	41.60***

***P<.001, **P<.01, *P<.05.

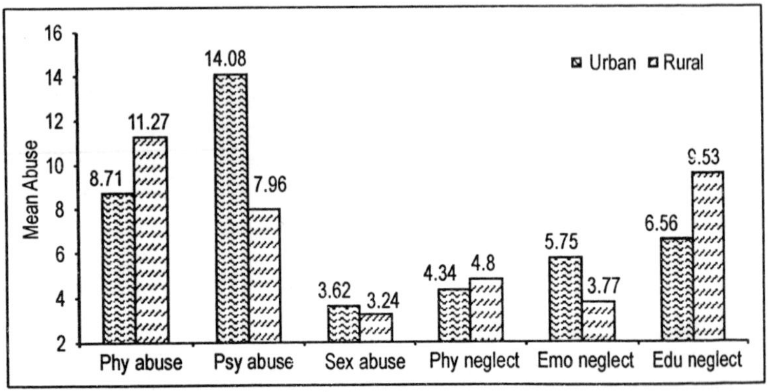

Fig. 3.2: Various Forms of Abuse as a Function of Urban-Rural Environmental Setting.

Government school children were found more physically abused (M = 12.80) than private school children (M = 8.99). Contrary to this, private school children (M = 17.26) as compared to government school children (M = 8.97) were found more psychologically abused. Results (Fig. 3.4) indicate that government school children were found little more sexually abused (M = 5.05) than private school children (M = 2.50). Students of Government and private schools differed significantly on physical neglect,

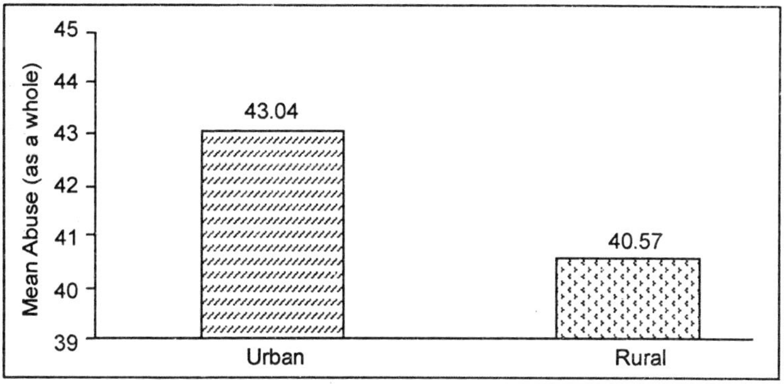

Fig. 3.3: Child Abuse (as a whole) as a Function of Urban-Rural Environmental Setting.

emotional neglect, educational neglect and abuse as a whole. More specifically, government school children were found more physically neglected (M = 6.07) than private school children (M = 3.75). Emotional neglect was also found higher in students of government school (M = 7.89) than private school counterparts (M = 3.37). Similarly, government school students were found more educationally neglected (M = 12.42) than private school children (M = 6.17), likewise, abuse as a whole, was found greater in government school students (M = 53.2) as compared to private school counterparts (M = 42.04), (Table 3.3, Figs. 3.4 and 3.5).

Table 3.3: Mean, S.D. and F-value of Child Abuse by Type of School

Type of School		*Abuse*			*Neglect*			*Child abuse as a whole*
		Physical Abuse	*Psycho-logical Abuse*	*Sexual abuse*	*Physical Neglect*	*Emotional Neglect*	*Educational Neglect*	
Government	Mean	12.80	8.97	5.05	6.07	7.89	12.42	53.2
	S.D.	(6.06)	(7.87)	(7.51)	(6.48)	(8.26)	(11.13)	(35.54)
Private	Mean	8.99	17.26	2.50	3.75	3.37	6.17	42.04
	S.D.	(6.23)	(9.10)	(1.34)	(2.87)	(2.99)	(4.53)	(25.83)
	F-Values	56.82**	141.26**	58.57**	62.64**	173.24**	167.72**	172.52**

** P<.01.

(3) Child Abuse in Schools of Hindi and English Medium

In order to ascertain the extent of abuse and neglect in Hindi and

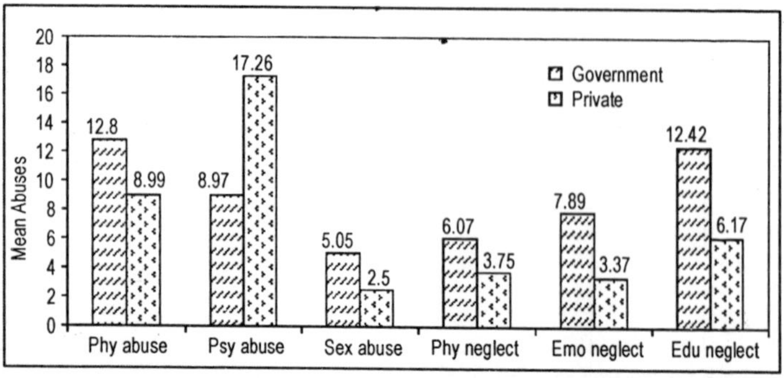

Fig. 3.4: Various Forms of Abuse as a Function of Type of School.

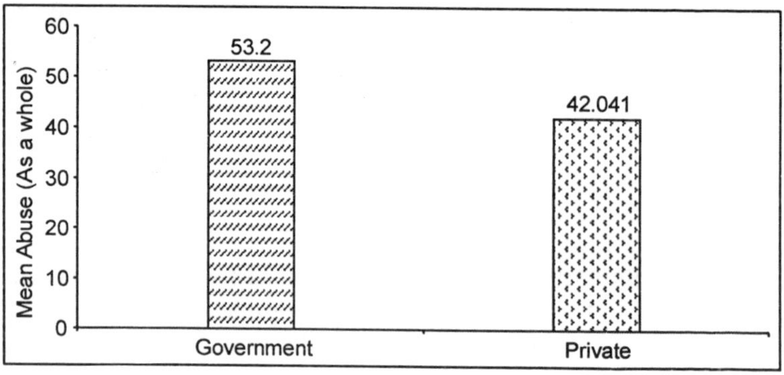

Fig. 3.5: Child Abuse (As a Whole) as a Function of Type of School.

English Medium schools, Mean, S.D. and analysis of variance were calculated for abuse and neglect scores. Results displayed in Table 3.4 and Fig. 3.6 revealed that on physical abuse, medium of education (Hindi and English), did not differ significantly, whereas, on child psychological abuse differed significantly. In English medium schools children were found more psychologically abused (M = 13.73) than Hindi medium children (M = 9.49). But, Hindi medium school children were found more sexually abused (M = 4.38) as compared to English medium students (M = 1.89). As Fig. 3.6 indicates, Hindi and English medium children differed significantly on physical neglect, emotional neglect, educational neglect, and abuse as a whole (Fig. 3.8). More specifically, Hindi medium children were found more physically neglected (M = 5.59) than English medium children (M = 2.95). Emotional neglect was higher in the Hindi medium children (M = 6.35) than English medium children (M = 2.93). Hindi medium children were found

Table 3.4: Mean S.D. and F-Value of Child Abuse by the Medium of Education

Type of Medium		Abuse			Neglect			Child abuse as a whole
		Physical Abuse	Psychological Abuse	Sexual abuse	Physical Neglect	Emotional Neglect	Educational Neglect	
Hindi	Mean	10.65	9.49	4.38	2.95	6.35	9.98	49.81
	S.D.	(9.70)	(6.28)	(3.16)	(2.11)	(4.46)	(5.27)	(37.52)
English	Mean	10.22	13.73	1.89	5.59	2.93	6.14	40.5
	S.D.	(9.82)	(10.76)	(0.26)	(4.17)	(2.79)	(4.69)	(25.95)
F-Values		.64	32.92**	53.12**	77.51**	90.24**	56.46**	57.39**

***P<.001, **P<.01, *P<.05

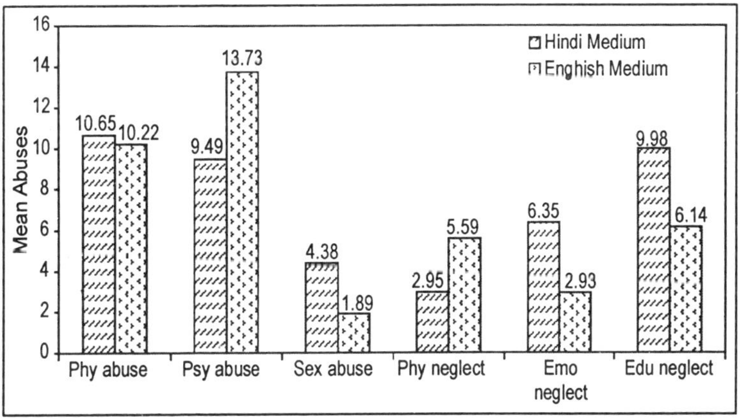

Fig. 3.6: Various Form of Abuse as a Function of Medium of Education.

more educationally neglected (M = 9.98) than English medium children (M = 6.14). Abuse as a whole was found more in Hindi medium students (M = 49.81) as compared to English medium schools counterparts (M = 40.5), (Fig. 3.7).

2. Social Structure and Child Abuse

Child Abuse by Socio-Demographic Characteristics of Students: Certain socio-demographic characteristics of children were found as potential factors, exerting influence on child abuse and neglect. Results are displayed in tables and figures and are reported below.

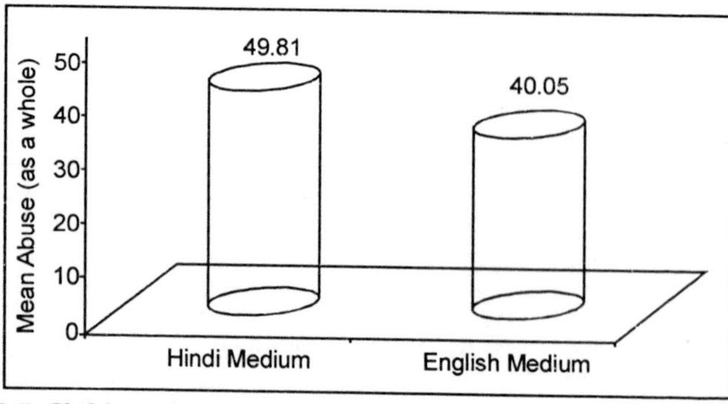

Fig. 3.7: Child Abuse as a Function of Medium of Education in Schools

(1) Gender and Child Abuse

It is apparent from the results (Table 3.5 and Fig. 3.8) boys and girls differed significantly on physical abuse. Boys were found more physically abused (M = 13.11) than girls (M = 9.65). However, on psychological and sexual abuse, boys and girls did not differ significantly. As Fig. 3.8 indicates boys and girls differed significantly on physical neglect, emotional neglect and educational neglect. More specifically, girls were found more physically neglected (M = 4.92) than boys (M = 3.87). Emotional neglect was also higher in girls (M = 5.45) than boys (M = 4.25). Similarly, Educational neglect was also found higher in girls (M = 8.98) as compared to boys (M = 7.57). But, Boys and girls did not differ significantly on sexual abuse and abuse as a whole.

Table 3.5: Mean, S.D. and F-value of Child Abuse by Gender of Students

Gender		*Forms of Abuses*						*Child abuse as a whole*
		Physical Abuse	*Psycho-logical Abuse*	*Sexual abuse*	*Physical Neglect*	*Emotional Neglect*	*Educat-ional Neglect*	
Boys	Mean	13.11	12.31	3.68	3.87	4.25	7.57	43.96
	S.D.	(10.34)	(10.06)	(2.97)	(2.95)	(3.39)	(5.98)	(35.69)
Girls	Mean	9.65	12.22	3.45	4.92	5.45	8.98	44.07
	S.D.	(9.39)	(10.02)	(2.54)	(3.87)	(3.23)	(5.82)	(34.87)
F-Values		35.69***	.011	.372	9.50***	8.55***	5.95**	.002

***P<.001, **P<.01, *P<.05.

(2) Caste and Child Abuse

It is apparent from the results (Table 3.6 and Fig. 3.10 and 3.11)

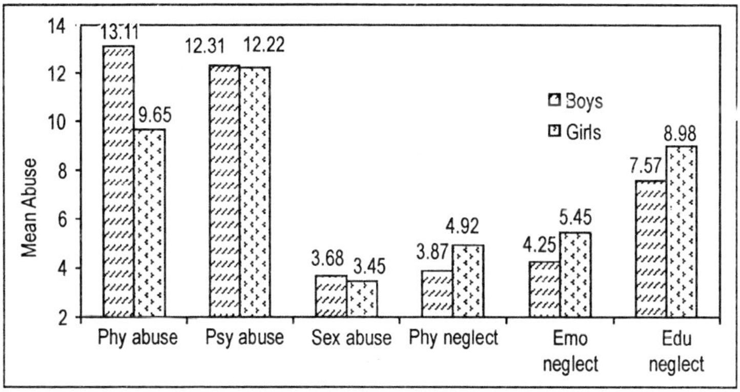

Fig. 3.8: Various Forms of Child Abuse as a Function of Gender.

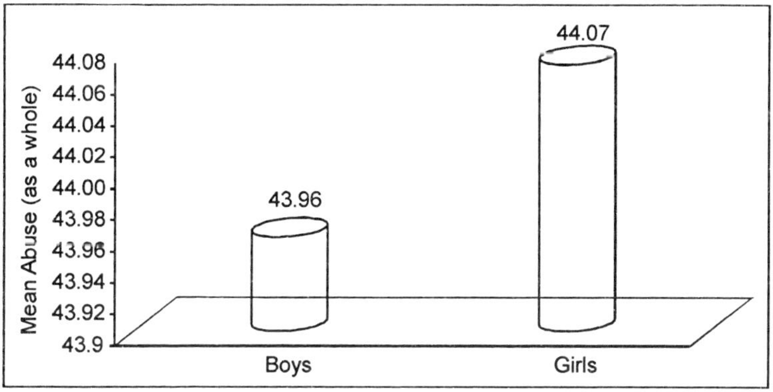

Fig. 3.9: Child Abuse (As a Whole) as a Function of Gender of Students.

that various forms of abuse and neglect varied across caste structure of respondents. Specifically, SC children were found more psychologically abused (M = 13.69) than OBC (M = 12.67) and general caste (GC) (M = 10.15) students. Similarly, sexual abuse was found more in SC students (M = 4.02) than OBC (M = 3.85) and general caste (GC) counterparts (M = 2.39). Students differed significantly on physical neglect, emotional neglect, educational neglect and abuse as a whole (Table 3.6). OBC children reported more physically neglected (M = 5.19) as compared to SC (M = 5.03) and general caste (GC) students (M = 3.30). Contrary to this, emotional neglect was found maximum in SC children (M = 6.07) than OBC (M = 5.52) and general caste (M = 3.63) respectively.

Table 3.6: Mean, S.D. and F-value of Child Abuse by the Different Castes

Children's Caste		*Abuse*			*Neglect*			*Child abuse as a whole*
		Physical Abuse	*Psychological Abuse*	*Sexual abuse*	*Physical Neglect*	*Emotional Neglect*	*Educational Neglect*	
General	Mean	10.06	10.15	2.39	3.30	3.63	7.23	36.05
	S.D.	(1.55)	(8.19)	(1.79)	(2.17)	(2.67)	(4.57)	(28.94)
OBC	Mean	10.85	12.67	3.85	5.19	5.52	8.82	46.32
	S.D.	(8.39)	(9.60)	(2.92)	(3.31)	(3.36)	(6.78)	(34.36)
SC	Mean	10.18	13.69	4.02	5.03	6.07	9.85	48.06
	S.D.	(8.25)	(13.34)	(3.64)	(4.36)	(4.57)	(6.21)	(40.37)
	F-Values	1.08	6.70**	8.11**	15.44**	13.86**	6.99**	9.72**

**P<.01.

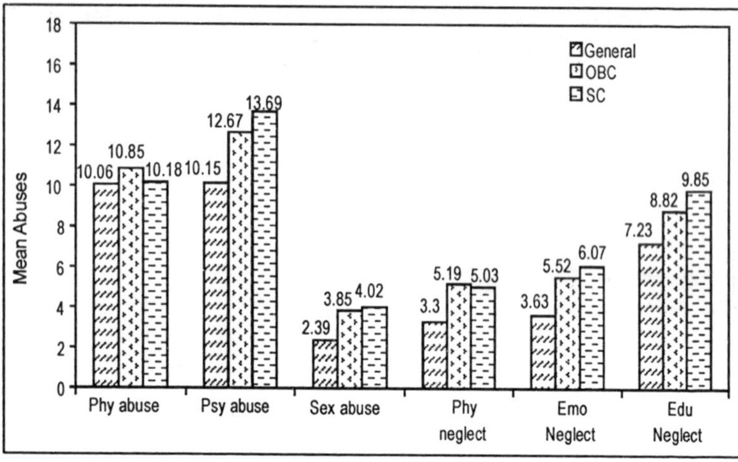

Fig. 3.10: Various Forms of Abuse as a Function of Caste Category.

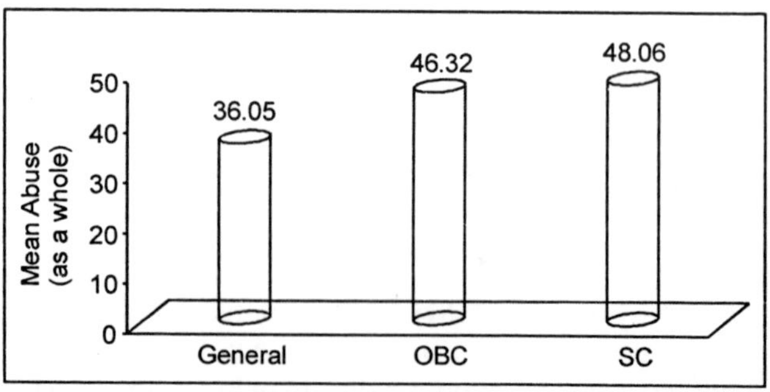

Fig. 3.11: Child Abuse (As a Whole) as a Function of Caste Category.

Educational neglect was also found higher in SC caste children (M = 9.85) than OBC (M = 8.82) and general caste (GC) counterparts (M = 7.23). Abuse as a whole, was also found greater in SC students (M = 48.06) as compared to OBC (M = 46.32) and general caste (M = 36.05) counterparts.

(3) Education and Child Abuse

Results (Table 3.7, Fig. 3.12 and 3.13) evidenced that various forms of abuse and neglect significantly varied across different level of education. ANOVA results indicate that junior high school (6-8th grade) students reported greater physical abuse (M = 12.68) than intermediate level students (11th-12th grade) (M = 10.86) and high school level students (9th-10th grade) counterparts (M = 8.01). Contrary to this, Intermediate level (11th-12th grade) students were found highly psychologically abused (M = 18.61) than Junior High school (6th-8th grade) (M = 11.22) and High School (9th-10th grade) (M = 7.98) level students. Sexual abuse was higher in Junior High School (6th-8th grade) (M = 4.24) than Intermediate level (11th-12th grade) children (M = 4.20), minimum in High School level (9th-10th grade) (M = 2.19) students. Similarly, students differed significantly on physical neglect, emotional neglect, educational neglect and abuse as a whole. Further Intermediate level students (11th-12th class) were found more physically neglected (M = 7.04) than junior high school students (6th-8th class) (M = 4.63) and high school students (9th-10th class) (M = 2.72). Emotional neglect was also higher in Intermediate level students (11th-12th grade) (M = 8.50) than Junior high school (6th-8th) students (M = 4.83) and High School (9th-10th) students (M = 2.69). Intermediate level students (11th-12th) were found more educationally neglected (M = 13.13) than Junior High School students (6th-8th class) (M = 8.02) and High School (9th-10th class) children (M = 5.51) and child abuse as a whole was also found greater in intermediate level students (11th-12th grade) (M = 61.84) as compared to junior high level students (6th-8th class) (M = 44.61) and high school students (9th-10th class) (M = 28.67). It is clear from the results that forms of abuses were found higher in Intermediate level (11th-12th) students than Junior High School (6th-8th) and High School (9th-10th) students.

Table 3.7: Mean, S.D. and F-value of Child Abuse by Educational Level (Grade) of Students

Student's grade		*Abuse*			*Neglect*			*Child abuse as a whole*
		Physical Abuse	*Psychological Abuse*	*Sexual abuse*	*Physical Neglect*	*Emotional Neglect*	*Educational Neglect*	
6-8th	Mean	12.68	11.22	4.24	4.63	4.83	8.02	44.61
Class	S.D.	(9.47)	(8.21)	(2.28)	(3.85)	(3.68)	(6.43)	(33.92)
9-10th	Mean	8.01	7.98	2.19	2.72	2.69	5.51	28.67
Class	S.D.	(6.13)	(5.45)	(1.58)	(1.82)	(1.14)	(3.94)	(19.52)
11-12th	Mean	10.86	18.61	4.20	7.04	8.50	13.13	61.84
Class	S.D.	(8.49)	(8.36)	(3.95)	(6.39)	(4.19)	(10.88)	(42.26)
F-Values		21.71**	54.13**	11.76**	51.02**	65.39**	56.91**	54.83**

**P<.01.

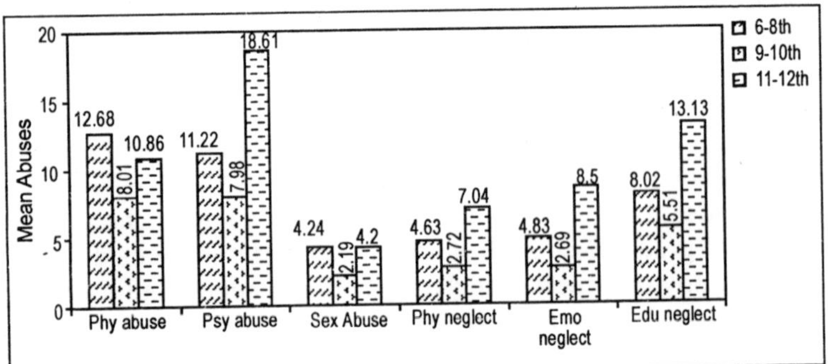

Fig. 3.12: Various Forms of Abuse as a Function of Educational (Grade) Level of Students

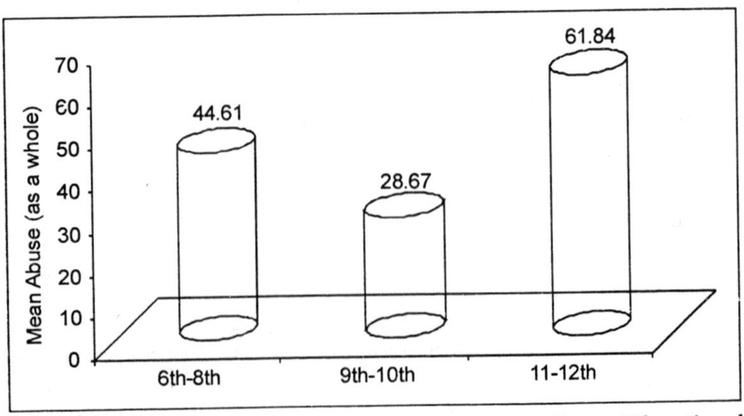

Fig. 3.13: Child Abuse (as a Whole) in Relation to Different Educational Level of Children.

It is clear from comparative analysis (ANOVA) that extent and forms of abuses in schools varied in accordance with environmental factors (setting, type and medium of education) and socio-demographic features of students.

2.1 Correlational Analysis

In order to determine the linkages between environmental factors and child abuse correlations were computed. Results are displayed in Table 3.8. Further, to establish association between socio-demographic factors and child abuse correlations were calculated. Obtained results are presented in Table 3.9.

(1) Relationship between Environmental Factors and Child Abuse

Correlations were computed between environmental factors (school setting, type of school and school environment) and child abuse. Results are displayed in Table 3.8 and reported below.

Table 3.8: Correlations between Environmental Factors (School Setting, Type of School, Dimensions of School Environment) and Child Abuse

Variables		*Physical Abuse*	*Psychological Abuse*	*Sexual Abuse*	*Physical Neglect*	*Emotional Neglect*	*Educational Neglect*	*Child Abuse (as a whole)*
School Setting (rural-urban)		-.143**	-.198**	-.050	-.031	-.127**	-.134**	-.167**
Type of School		-.119**	-.197**	-.173**	-.136**	-.239**	-.218**	-.228**
Dimensions of School Environment	Creative Stimulation	.001	-.018	-.072*	-.010	-.046	-.060	-.040
	Cognitive Encouragement	.024	.047	-.068*	.001	-.008	-.010	.007
	Permissiveness	.037	.021	-.011	.042	.010	-.012	.018
	Acceptance	-.065*	-.071*	-.067*	-.017	-.090**	-.127**	-.093**
	Rejection	.186**	.167**	.118**	.141**	.166**	.135**	.192**
	Control	-.024	-.020	-.045	.013	-.017	-.042	-.031

*P<0.05, **P<0.01.

(1) Relationship between School Setting and Child Abuse

Results displayed in Table 3.8 denote a negative relationship between school setting and child abuse. More specifically school setting was negatively related with physical abuse, psychological abuse, emotional neglect, educational neglect and abuse as a whole. Therefore, results suggest that some forms of abuses are found higher in urban school setting as compared to rural school setting.

(2) Type of School and Child Abuse

Results presented in Table 3.8 further indicate that types of school (Government and Private) and child abuse were found inversely related with each other. Specifically, physical abuse, psychological abuse, sexual abuse, physical neglect, emotional neglect, educational neglect and abuse as a whole were found negatively related with type of school. The results suggest that incidence of abuses are higher in government schools than private schools.

(3) School Environment and Child Abuse

Correlation results displayed in Table 3.8 denote that dimensions of school environment were found significantly associated with child abuse. Specifically, creative stimulation was found negatively related with sexual abuse. Similarly, cognitive encouragement was found negatively correlated with sexual abuse. Again negative but low correlations were found between permissiveness and child abuse. Acceptance was found negatively correlated with physical abuse, psychological abuse, sexual abuse, emotional neglect, educational neglect and abuse as a whole. Contrary to this, rejection dimension was found positively related physical abuse, psychological abuse, sexual abuse, physical neglect, emotional negelect, educational neglect and abuse as a whole. However, low and negative link between control and child abuse was found. This result indicates that positive dimensions of school environment were found as buffer to minimize incidents of child abuse whereas, negative dimensions were found as intensifier in maximizing the case of child abuse in schools.

(2) Relationship between Demographic Factors and Child Abuse

In order to determine the linkage between demographic characteristics of students and child abuse correlations were computed. Results are displayed in Table 3.9.

Table 3.9: Correlations between Socio-Demographic Factors and Child Abuse

Demographic variables	*Physical Abuse*	*Psychological Abuse*	*Sexual Abuse*	*Physical Neglect*	*Emotional Neglect*	*Educational Neglect*	*Child Abuse (as a whole)*
Age	.017	.179**	.080*	.163**	.195**	.165**	.166**
Gender	–.196**	–.088**	–.076*	.018	–.032	–.024	–.096**
Grade	–.044	.166**	.031	.127**	.171**	.154**	.131**
Caste	–.007	.055	.094**	.102**	.110**	.064	.078*

*P<0.05, **P<0.01.

(1) Linkage between Students' Age and Child Abuse

Correlation results displayed in Table 3.9 indicate positive association between age and child abuse. Specifically, age was found positively correlated with psychological abuse, sexual abuse, physical neglect, emotional neglect, educational neglect and abuse as a whole. This result suggests that with increasing age the incidence of abuses also increased.

(2) Relationship between Gender and Child Abuse

Results displayed in Table 3.9 indicate negative association between gender and child abuse. Specifically, gender was found negatively correlated with physical abuse, psychological abuse, sexual abuse and abuse as a whole. This result suggests that boys were found more abused than girls on some dimensions of child abuse.

(3) Link between Child's Grade and Child Abuse

Results displayed in Table 3.9 show positive association between grade and child abuse. Specifically, grade was found positively correlated with psychological abuse, physical neglect, emotional neglect, educational neglect and abuse as a whole. This result suggests that with increasing grade, the incidence of abuses also increased.

(4) Relationship between Child's Caste and Child Abuse

Correlation results displayed in Table 3.9 further denote positive association between caste (General/OBC/SC) and child abuse. Specifically, caste was found positively correlated with sexual abuse, physical neglect, emotional neglect, and abuse as a whole. This result suggests that abuses were found higher in SC students than OBC and General Category students.

3. Stepwise Multiple Regression Analysis (SMRA)

Based on the perusal of correlation results, it was considered adequate to go for Stepwise Multiple Regression Analysis (SMRA) to explore the relative contribution of school setting and school environment (Predictors) to child abuse and neglect (Criterion). The results of these analyses are in order:

Results displayed in Table 3.10 evinced that the Child Physical Abuse was predicted by four factors, i.e. rejection, permissiveness, setting and control. Specifically, rejection (E) has contributed positively (β = .275) whereas, permissiveness (C) contributed negatively (β = –.129) followed by setting (–.126) and control (F) (β = –.103). Though independently, rejection predicted 3.1 per cent variance, permissiveness predicted 2.6 per cent variance, setting predicted 1.5 per cent variance and control predicted 0.6 per cent variance. But the composite contribution of all four factors were found 7.8 per cent variance in criterion variable i.e. physical abuse.

Further, results show that psychological abuse was predicted by three dimensions of school environment (rejection, permissiveness and creative stimulation) and school setting. Specifically, setting has contributed negatively (β = –.205) whereas, rejection (E) has contributed positively (β = .260). Moreover permissiveness (β = –.096) and creative stimulation (β = –.098) both contributed negatively. Though independently setting predicted 3.8 per cent variance, rejection predicted 2.9 per cent variance, permissiveness predicted 2 per cent variance, and creative

Table 3.10: Step-wise Multiple Regression Analysis for Child Abuse on the Dimensions of School Environment and Setting

	R	R^2	R^2 *Change*	*Beta β*	*F Value*
			(Criterion Variable) Physical Abuse		
Rejection (E)	.176	.031	.031	.275	31.96**
Permissiveness (C)	.238	.057	.026	-.129	30.05**
Setting	.269	.072	.015	-.126	25.89**
Control (F)	.279	.078	.006	-.103	21.03**
		Psychological Abuse			
Setting	.194	.038	.038	-.205	39.07**
Rejection (E)	.275	.066	.029	.260	35.47**
Permissiveness (C)	.294	.087	.020	-.096	31.55**
Creative Stimulation (A)	.301	.090	.004	-.098	24.77**
		Sexual Abuse			
Rejection (E)	.115	.013	.029	.222	13.37**
Creative Stimulation (A)	.204	.042	.013	-.204	21.76**
Setting	.216	.047	.005	-.071	16.29**
		Physical Neglect			
Rejection (E)	.155	.024	.024	.225	24.74**
Creative Stimulation (A)	.192	.037	.013	-.133	19.11**
		Emotional Neglect			
Rejection (E)	.171	.029	.029	.285	30.14**
Creative Stimulation (A)	.242	.059	.029	-.140	31.19**
Setting	.270	.073	.014	-.123	26.20**
Permissiveness (C)	.278	.078	.005	-.100	20.96**
		Educational Neglect			
Rejection (E)	.140	.020	.020	.231	20.16**
Permissiveness (C)	.237	.056	.036	-.221	29.78**
Setting	.269	.072	.016	-.128	26.03**
		Abuse as a whole			
Rejection (E)	.193	.037	.037	.315	38.67**
Creative Stimulation (A)	.265	.070	.033	-.146	37.75**
Setting	.311	.097	.027	-.167	35.73**
Permissiveness (C)	.320	.103	.006	-.112	28.53**

**P<0.01.

stimulation predicted 0.4 per cent variance. But the composite contributions of all factors were found 9.1 per cent variance in criterion variable.

Regression results further show that Sexual Abuse was predicted by three factors i.e. rejection, creative stimulation, and school setting. Specifically, rejection (E) has contributed positively (β = .222) whereas, creative stimulation contributed negatively (β = –.204). Further, school setting also contributed negatively (β = –.071). Though independently, rejection predicted 2.9 per cent variance, creative stimulation predicted 1.3 per cent variance and setting predicted 0.5 per cent variance. But the composite contributions of all three factors were found 4.7 per cent variance to sexual abuse.

Regression results again display that Physical Neglect was predicted by two dimensions of school environment i.e. rejection, and creative stimulation. Specifically, rejection (E) has contributed positively (β = .225) whereas, creative stimulation contributed negatively (β = –.133). Though independently, rejection predicted 2.4 per cent variance, and creative stimulation predicted 1.3 per cent variance. But the composite contributions of both factors were found 3.7 per cent variance in criterion variable.

Further, results show that Emotional Neglect was predicted by three dimensions of school environment (rejection, permissiveness and creative stimulation) and school setting. Specifically, Rejection (E) has contributed positively (β = .285) whereas creative stimulation (β = –.140), school setting (β = –.123) and permissiveness (β = –.100) have contributed negatively. Though independently rejection predicted 2.9 per cent variance, creative stimulation predicted 2.9 per cent variance, school setting predicted 1.4 per cent variance and permissiveness predicted 0.5 per cent variance. But the composite contributions of all four factors were found 7.7 per cent variance in criterion variable.

Similarly, Educational Neglect was predicted by three factors i.e. rejection, permissiveness and setting. More specifically, Rejection (E) has contributed positively (β = .231) whereas permissiveness (β = –.221) contributed negatively followed by school setting (β = –.128). Though independently rejection predicted 2 per cent variance, permissiveness predicted 3.6 per cent variance, and setting contributed 1.6 per cent variance. But the composite contributions of all three factors were found 7.2 per cent variance in criterion variable.

Further, abuse as a whole was predicted by four factors (rejection, creative stimulation, setting and permissiveness).

Specifically, rejection (E) has contributed positively (β = .315) whereas, negative contributions were made by creative stimulation (β = –.146), school setting (β = –.167) and permissiveness (β = –.112). Though independently, rejection predicted 3.7 per cent variance, creative stimulation contributed 3.3 per cent variance, and setting contributed 2.7 per cent variance and permissiveness contributed 0.6 per cent variance. But the composite contributions of all four factors were found 10.3 per cent variance in criterion variable (abuse as a whole).

Results found on objective-I, proved the significant roles of environmental and sociodemographic factors in occurrence of child abuse in school setting.

SECTION-2

In this section results obtained on objective II are displayed and reported. The second objective of the study is to assess psychological characteristics of school personnel (teachers). Teacher's demographic characteristics were assessed with the help of personal data sheet. Apart from this childhood abusive experiences of teachers were measured with the help of Childhood Abuse Questionnaire (CAQ). Further teacher's personality was determined by using NEO PI-R. Responses on measures were scored according to defined rules. Scores were treated statistically in terms of Bivariate and Multivariate analyses, apart from this qualitative analysis (Frequencies and Percentage) were also applied to get the clear picture of incidents and forms of abuses in schools as reported by school personnel. In the first part, results of quantitative analysis are reported whereas; in second part findings of qualitative analysis are presented.

A. Teachers' Personality in Relation to Demographic Factors

Teacher's demographic characteristics were determined with the help of personal data sheet. Further, personality pattern of teachers/ school personnel was assessed with NEO PI-R. Data obtained from school personnel were scored and analyzed in terms of correlational analysis and step-wise multiple regression analysis. Results are displayed in Tables 3.11 and 3.12 and figures and interpreted in following section:

Correlation Results

I. Relationship between Five Dimensions of Personality and Demographic Factors

Correlation results (Table 3.11) denote relationships between demographic factors and dimensions of personality of teachers.

Table 3.11: Inter-correlations between Demographic Factors and Dimensions of Personality

Variables	*1*	*2*	*3*	*4*	*5*	*6*	*7*	*8*	*9*	*10*	*11*
1. School Type	—										
2. Gender	.463**	—									
3. Caste	–.90	–.113	—								
4. Age	–.542**	–.371**	.032	—							
5. Marital Status	.526	.256	.027	–.729**	—						
6. Family Type	–.063	–.210	–095	.338*	–.157	—					
7. Neuroticism	–.204	–.059	–112	–.110	.104	+.415**	—				
8. Extroversion	–049	.014	–.251	–.184	.219	–.139	.397**	—			
9. Openness	–.067	.218	–.178	–.180	.352*	–.120	.373**	.526**	—		
10. Agreeableness	.088	.129	–.281*	–.118	.234	–.132	.389**	.658**	.428**	—	
11. Consciousness	.100	.140	–.185	–.122	271	–.055	.251	.726**	.506**	.809**	—

As Table 3.11 shows, school type (Government *vs.* Private) was found positively correlated with gender (r = .463** P<.01) and marital status (r = .526** P<.01). However, school type was found to be negatively correlated with age (r = –.542**, P<.01). Similarly, gender was found negatively correlated with age (r = –.371**, P<.01). However, caste was found strongly linked with agreeableness dimensions of personality (r = –.281*, P<.05). Similarly, age was also found to be negatively correlated with marital status (r = –.729**, P<.01) and positively related with family type (r = .338*, P<.05). Similarly, marital status was positively related with openness (r = .352*, P<.05). Family type was found negatively related with neuroticism (r = +.415**, P<.01). A close positive link of neuroticism with extroversion, openness, and agreeableness was identified (r = .397**, .373**, and .389** P<.01). The Extroversion was found to be positively correlated with openness, agreeableness and consciousness (r = .526**, .658** and .726** P<.01). Similarly, openness was found to be positively correlated with agreeableness and consciousness (r = .428** and .506** P<.01). The agreeableness was also found to be positively correlated with consciousness (r = .809**, P<.01). Results thus, evinced strong association between five dimensions of personality and demographic factors of school personnel.

Multivariate Analysis

Based on the perusal of correlation results, it was considered appropriate to go for the stepwise multiple regression analysis (SMRA) to examine the relative contributions of antecedent factors i.e., demographic factors (Family Type, Marital Status, School Type, Gender, Caste and District) to the five dimensions of Personality. The findings of this analysis are depicted below in order.

(I) Prediction of Five Dimensions of Personality from Demographic Factors: It is clear from regression results (Table 3.12) that dimensions of personality were predicted by some demographic factors.

Table 3.12: Step-wise Multiple Regression Analysis for Teachers Personality on Demographic Factors

Predictor Variables	*Criterion Variables*				
	R	*R^2*	*R^2 Change*	*β*	*F*
		Neuroticism			
Family Type	.415	.172	.172	–.415	9.999**
		Openness			
Marital Status	.352	.124	.124	.352	6.774**
School Type	.460	.211	.088	–.348	6.296**
Gender	.535	.286	.075	.309	6.148**
		Agreeableness			
Caste	.281	.079	.079	–.281	4.124**
		Consciousness			
District	.302	.091	.091	.302	4.821**
Marital Status	.444	.197	.106	.330	5.762**

*P<0.05, **P<0.01.

The neuroticism was predicted by family type which explained negatively (β^2 = –.415, R^2 = .172), and contributed 17.2 per cent variance in criterion variable. Marital status contributed maximum positively (β^2 = .352, R^2 = .124.), which contributed 12.4 per cent variance. Further, school type predicted negatively to openness (β^2 = –.348, R^2 = .211), and it contributed 8.8 per cent variance. Again gender predicted maximum positively (β^2 = .309, R^2 = .286) and it contributed 7.5 per cent variance on criterion variable and its contribution along with marital status and school type and gender were identified 28.7 per cent variance to openness. Agreeableness was predicted by caste and (β^2 = –.281, R^2 = .079), its contributions was 7.9 per cent variance in criterion variable. District contributed maximum positively to consciousness (β^2 = .302, R^2 = .091), which contributed 9.1 per cent variance on criterion variable. Marital Status has also predicted maximum positively to consciousness (β^2 = –.330, R^2 = .197), and it contributed 10.6 per cent variance to consciousness, but along with district overall contribution to consciousness was identified 19.7 per cent variance.

B. Specific Forms of Child Abuse in School Setting (Reported by Teachers)

Respondents' percentages for their reporting of the main form of child abuse were determined with the help of child abuse Interview Schedule. Responses were content analyzed. The main forms of child abuse reported by teachers of both setting (total sample) are indicated in Table 3.13.

As is apparent from the table and wheel graph, that physical punishment and torture (physical abuse) is the main form of child abuse in schools as 77.5 per cent school personnel reported this factor as a primary form of child abuse and neglect. Other forms of abuse in preferential order are: psychological abuse (67.5%), mental/emotional neglect (name calling, discrimination, sarcastic comments etc.) (55%), aggressive behaviour towards children (attacking, kicking) (52.5%), bullying behaviour (47.5%), discrimination and partiality (32.5%), ignorance of children (neglecting behaviour) (25%), Verbal Abuse and Insulting in the classroom (17.5%), Doing unwanted behaviours with Girls Students (15%), Doing Racist Comments on a Particular Student or targeting a particular student during teaching in classroom (12.5%), Demoralizing (12.5%), Teasing (7.5%), Exposing Pornographic Pictures or Literature (7.5%), Trying to Establish Unethical Relationship with Students (5.5%) and Child Labour (5.0%) were type of abuses often found in schools.

Table 3.13: Specific Forms of Child Abuse in School Setting as Reported by Teachers

Sl. No.	*Specific Type of Child Abuse in Schools*	*Frequencies*	*Percentage (%)*
1.	Physical Punishment and Physical Torture	31	77.5
2.	Psychological Abuse	23	67.5
3.	Mental/Emotional Neglect	22	55
4.	Aggressive Behaviour towards Children	21	52.5
5.	Bullying Behaviour	19	47.5
6.	Discrimination and Partiality	13	32.5
7.	Educational Neglect	10	25
8.	Verbal Abuse and Insulting in the Classroom	7	17.5
9.	Sexual Abuse (Doing unwanted behaviour with Girl Students)	6	15
10.	Doing Racist Comments/Targeting a Particular Student	5	12.5
11.	Demoralizing	5	12.5
12.	Teasing	3	7.5
13.	Exposing Pornographic Acts or Literature	3	7.5
14.	Trying to Establish Unethical Relationship with Students	1	5.5
15.	Child Labour	2	5

On the basis of percentage scores for each items wheel graph was prepared to present vivid picture of forms of abuses as reported by teachers (*see* Fig. 3.14).

SECTION-3

Third objective of the study is to explore the extent and specific forms of abuse in school settings as reported/witnessed by school teachers. In order to determine the pattern and forms of abuse in schools situated in rural and urban settings, School personnel/ teachers were interviewed on an unstructured interview schedule. They were requested to respond on three open-ended questions—

I. What do you understand by child abuse and neglect?
II. Which types of abuses are often found in school setting?
III. Which type of abuses have you witnessed in your school or around the school setting?

Responses given by school personnel on each question were recorded and frequencies were transformed into percentage (%)

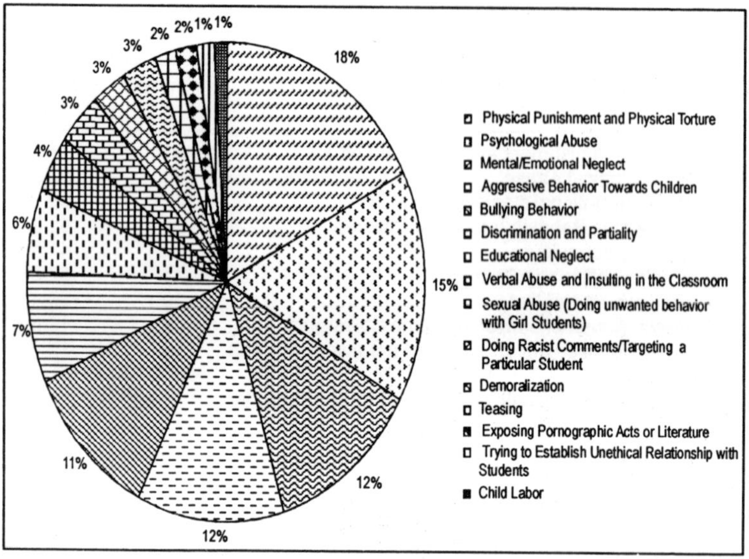

Fig. 3.14: Specific Forms of Child Abuse in School Setting as Reported by Teachers.

to identify the actual percentage of abuse and its forms in schools. In the subsequent section, results based on each question are displayed in tables and figures and interpreted below.

1. *What do you understand by child abuse and neglect?*

Responses obtained on question-1 were recorded. Table 3.14 shows the different forms of abuses as reported by teachers.

Table 3.14: Forms of Abuses Reported by Teachers of Government and Private Schools

S. No.	*Forms of abuses*	*Abuses (%) in schools as reported by Teachers*	
		Government School	*Private School*
1	Physical abuse	25	28
2	Mental torture	24	22
3	Making discrimination between children	12	15
4	Neglect	21	19
5	Demoralization	9	16
6	As a crime	9	–

On the basis of above scores mentioned in Table 3.14, wheel graphs were prepared (Fig. 3.15 and Fig. 3.16).

It is clear from results (Table 3.14 and Fig. 3.15 and Fig. 3.16), that majority of teachers working in government and private schools consider that child abuse is vulnerable in schools in many forms. According to government school teachers, child abuse includes—Physical Punishment (25%), Mental Torture (24%), Discrimination among children (12%), Neglect (21%) and Demoralization (9%) and Child Abuse as a Crime (9%). For private school teachers child abuse refers to Physical punishment (28%), Mental torture (22%), Neglect (19%), Discrimination among students (15%), and Demoralization (16%).

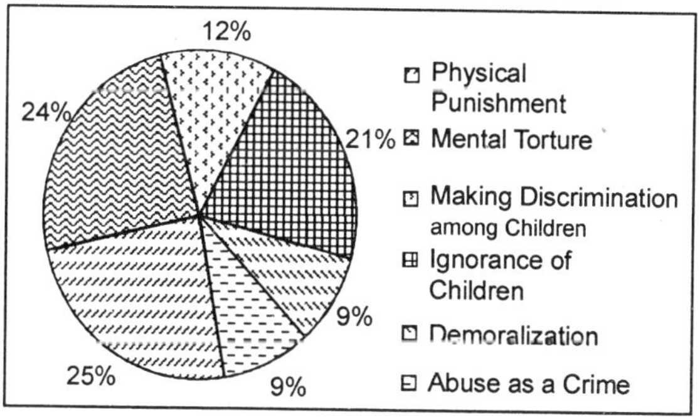

Fig. 3.15: Forms of Abuses as Reported by Government School Teachers.

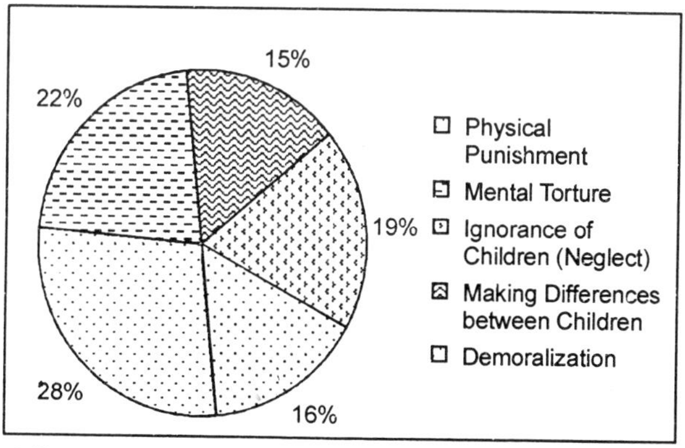

Fig. 3.16: Forms of Abuses as reported by Private School Teachers.

2. *Which types of abuses are often found in school setting?*

Furthermore, responses obtained on question-2 were also recorded and percentage of frequency was determined. Table 3.15 shows the different forms of abuses generally found in schools as reported by government and private school teachers.

Table 3.15: Forms of Abuses Generally Found in Schools (Reported by Government and Private School Teachers)

S. No.	*Forms of abuses in schools*	*Frequencies (%)*	
		Government School	*Private School*
1	Mental torture	37	41
2	Physical abuse	27	27
3	Neglect	12	23
4	Sexual harassment	12	9
5	Bullying	12	–

On the basis of percentage scores mentioned in Table 3.15, wheel graphs were prepared (Fig. 3.17 and Fig. 3.18).

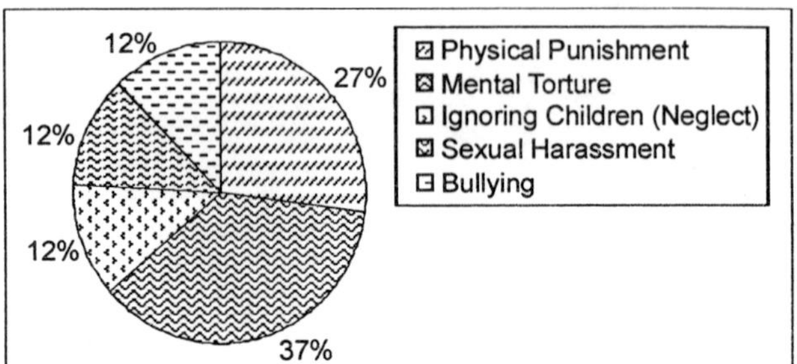

Fig. 3.17: Kind of Abuses witnessed in School Reported by Government School Teachers.

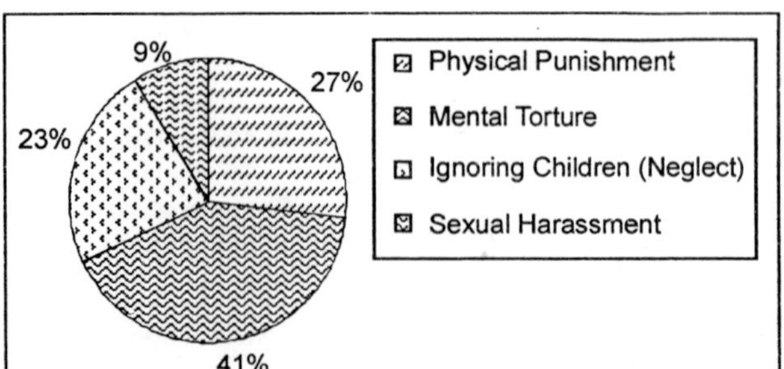

Fig. 3.18: Kind of Abuses Occurs in School as Reported by Private School Teachers.

It is clear from Fig. 3.17 and Fig. 3.18, that majority of teachers working in government and private schools consider that child abuse is witnessed in many forms in schools. Forms of abuses identified in Government schools are—Mental Torture (37%), Physical Punishment (27%), Neglect (12%), Sexual harassment (12%) and Bullying (12%). Whereas, in Private schools, types of abuses includes—Mental torture (41%), Physical punishment (27%), Neglect (23%) and Sexual harassment (9%).

3. *Which types of abuse are witnessed in your school?*

Furthermore, responses obtained on question-3 were also recorded and percentages based on frequencies were calculated. Table 3.16 shows the different forms of abuses witnessed by teachers in schools where they are working.

Table 3.16: Forms of Abuses Witnessed by Teachers in Their Schools

S. No.	*Forms of abuses*	*Percentages (%)*	
		Government School	*Private School*
1.	Bullying	50	15
2.	Sexual exploitation	30	20
3.	Verbal abuse	10	35
4.	Physical punishment	10	30

On the basis of above scores mentioned in Table 3.16, wheel graphs (Fig. 3.19 and Fig. 3.20) were prepared for government and private schools separately.

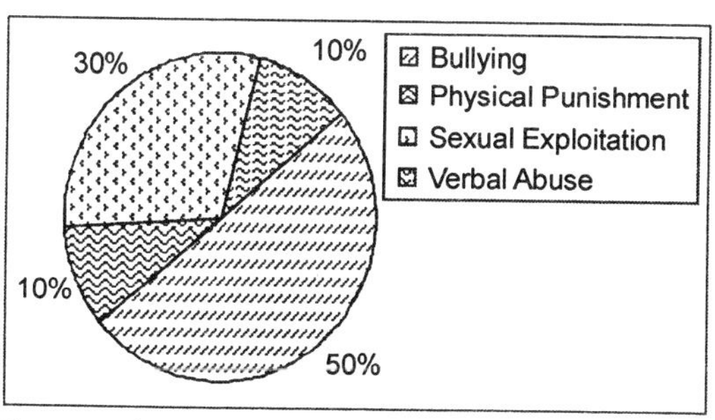

Fig. 3.19: Types of Abuses Witnessed in Schools (Reported by Government School Teachers).

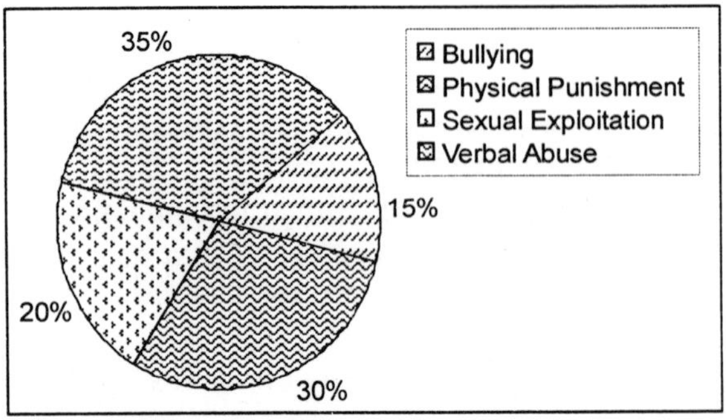

Fig. 3.20: Types of Abuses Witnessed in Schools (Reported by Private School Teachers).

It is apparent from Fig. 3.19 and Fig. 3.20, that majority of teachers working in government and private schools reported that child abuse is present in many forms in their schools also. Forms of abuses identified in government schools in preferential order are—Bullying (50%), Sexual exploitation (30%), Physical punishment (10%) and Verbal abuse (10%). Whereas, in Private Schools types of abuses identified include—Verbal abuse (35%), Physical punishment (30%), Sexual exploitation (20%) and Bullying (15%).

On the basis of data reported earlier, it is evident that child abuses in schools are present at high level in many forms. Further, in 4th section of the result, the consequences of child abuse on children (students) are reported and interpreted.

The Psychological Consequence of Child Abuse on Students

The psychological consequences of child abuse in schools on students were assessed under objectives four and five. Results are displayed and reported in following section.

SECTION-4

The fourth objective of the research is to measure the impact of child abuse on cognitive, affective, motivational and behavioural functioning of students. Data obtained on various measures were scored and treated statistically in terms of Univariate/Multivariate, Bivariate and Step-wise Multiple Regression Analysis (SMRA) by using SPSS 21st Version. Obtained results are displayed and reported in five sub-sections in accordance with various types of psychological outcomes of child abuse in schools. First multiple analysis of variance (MANOVA)/analysis of variance (ANOVA) results are reported followed by correlation and regression results.

Comparative Analysis

1. Impact on Cognitive Processes

The magnitude and forms of cognitive functioning (verbal ability and working memory) were studied as function of child abuse, type of school, gender and grade of students. Data obtained on various Cognitive Measures, viz. Verbal Ability, Memory Span and Working Memory were scored according to the defined rules as given in manuals. Several statistical analyses were done and results are displayed in tables and figures respectively.

(a): Verbal Ability in relation to type of school, gender, grade and child abuse in schools: Scores obtained on verbal ability test were treated statistically in terms of Mean, SD and multiple analysis of variance (MANOVA). Results are displayed in Table 3.17 (A and B) and figures. Table 3.17 (A) displays Mean and SD scores of verbal ability as a whole and its dimensions by type of school, gender, and grade and child abuse.

It is clear from Table 3.17 (A) that the level of verbal ability (as a whole) and its domains varied in accordance with type of school, gender, grade and child abuse level. Further, to determine the significant impact of independent variables; (type of school, gender, grade and child abuse) on verbal ability multiple analysis of variance (MANOVA) was computed. Results are displayed in Table 3.17 (B). Besides this, graphs have been prepared for main effects and interaction effects.

Verbal Ability (as a whole): MANOVA results [Table 3.17(B)] denote the significant impact of type of school, grade and level of abuse on verbal ability. It is clear from Fig. 3.21, that private school students performed far superior on verbal ability (M = 27.52) than their government school counterparts (M = 23.57).

The significant main effect of grade (Fig. 3.22) suggests that High school (9-10th grade) students (M = 24.24) performed very poor on verbal ability (as a whole) than Junior High school (6-8th grade), (M = 26.32) and intermediate level (11-12th grade) students (M = 26.07) .

Table 3.17 (A): Mean and S.D. of Verbal Ability and its Dimensions by Type of School, Gender, Grade and Child Abuse in Schools

Verbal Ability and Its Dimensions?			*Government Schools*				*Private Schools*			
			Boys		*Girls*		*Boys*		*Girls*	
			High Abused	*Low Abused*	*High Abused*	*Low Abused*	*High Abused*	*Low Abused*	*High Abused*	*Low Abused*
6-8th Grade	Verbal Ability (as a whole)	Mean	25.19	23.09	25.19	23.00	28.3	31.02	25.74	29.1
		(SD)	(5.64)	(7.86)	(5.64)	(7.86)	(4.88)	(5.02)	(6.15)	(4.63)
	Word Analogy	Mean	4.07	4.18	4.07	4.18	4.48	5.21	4.24	4.55
		(SD)	(1.23)	(1.78)	(1.23)	(1.78)	(1.56)	(1.71)	(1.61)	(1.47)
	Opposite Word	Mean	2.37	2.21	2.37	2.21	2.25	3.06	1.94	2.53
		(SD)	(1.22)	(1.10)	(1.22)	(1.10)	(1.09)	(1.20)	(1.30)	(1.47)
	Word Similarity	Mean	6.69	5.82	6.69	5.82	8.18	8.42	7.50	8.48
		(SD)	(2.72)	(3.03)	(2.72)	(3.03)	(1.57)	(1.9)	(2.35)	(1.51)
	Word Classification	Mean	5.24	4.86	5.24	4.86	5.83	5.71	5.44	6.00
		(SD)	(1.61)	(2.01)	(1.61)	(2.01)	(1.42)	(1.2)	(2.0)	(1.1)
	Sentence Completion	Mean	6.91	5.89	6.91	5.87	7.53	7.98	6.91	7.6
		(SD)	(1.55)	(2.23)	(1.55)	(2.23)	(1.15)	1.04	1.48	1.18

(Contd.)

9-10th Grade	Verbal Ability (as a whole)	Mean	19.59	25.57	14.2	24.48	26.72	27.35	28.8	27.16
		(SD)	(9.44)	(8.72)	(9.68)	(7.86)	(5.48)	(5.38)	(5.41)	(5.57)
	Word Analogy	Mean	2.85	4.29	1.80	3.67	4.11	4.10	4.77	4.31
		(SD)	(1.93)	(1.72)	(1.48)	(1.61)	(1.43)	(1.70)	(1.27)	(1.43)
	Opposite Word	Mean	1.78	1.43	1.00	1.79	2.22	2.85	2.85	2.58
		(SD)	(1.31)	(1.08)	(.70)	(1.11)	(1.28)	(1.23)	(1.17)	(1.22)
	Word Similarity	Mean	5.93	7.57	3.60	7.48	7.50	7.63	8.07	7.84
		(SD)	(3.28)	(2.79)	(2.88)	(2.23)	(2.29)	(1.89)	(1.99)	(2.13)
	Word Classification	Mean	4.19	5.64	3.2	4.83	5.81	5.85	5.7	5.72
		(SD)	(2.61)	(2.09)	(2.58)	(2.05)	(1.27)	(1.54)	(1.56)	(1.36)
	Sentence Completion	Mean	5.04	6.64	4.6	6.77	7.19	7.28	7.61	7.22
		(SD)	(2.57)	(2.09)	(2.88)	(2.11)	(1.38)	(1.35)	(1.10)	(1.57)
11-12th Grade	Verbal Ability (as a whole)	Mean	24	25.65	26.82	26.11	20.00	33.40	26.03	26.52
		(SD)	(4.63)	(5.57)	(5 72)	(6.26)	(8.26)	(1.51)	(5.96)	(4.86)
	Word Analogy	Mean	3.72	3.98	4.04	4.71	2.88	5.40	3.77	3.80
		(SD)	(1.37)	(1.51)	(1.61)	(1.48)	(1.35)	(0.89)	(1.55)	(1.50)
	Opposite Word	Mean	2.04	2.61	2.70	2.56	1.50	4.40	2.54	2.32
		(SD)	(1.25)	(1.61)	(1.15)	(1.23)	(1.30)	(0.54)	(1.48)	(1.28)
	Word Similarity	Mean	6.9	6.78	6.88	7.16	6.63	9.40	7.57	8.32
		(SD)	(2.66)	(2.48)	(2.93)	(2.43)	(2.5)	(0.89)	(2.04)	(1.97)
	Word Classification	Mean	5.17	5.48	5.8	5.4	4.00	5.6	5.29	5.72
		(SD)	(1.67)	(1.98)	(1.29)	(1.33)	(2.39)	(0.54)	(2.08)	(1.42)
	Sentence Completion	Mean	6.17	6.8	7.52	6.8	5.75	8.00	7.03	6.64
		(SD)	(1.75)	(1.36)	(1.28)	(1.82)	(3.01)	(1.41)	(1.67)	(1.38)

Table 3.17 (B): Summary of 2×2×3×2 MANOVA of Verbal Ability and its Dimensions as a Function of Type of School, Gender, Grade and Child Abuse

Source	*Dimensions of Verbal Ability*					
	Word Analogy	*Opposite Word*	*Word Similarity*	*Word Classification*	*Sentence Completion*	*Verbal Ability (as a whole)*
Type of school (A)	15.22***	21.26***	56.46***	16.56***	43.28***	61.35***
Gender B)	0.761	1.171	0.701	0.012	0.038	1.217
Grade (C)	10.036***	6.832***	1.676	1.597	3.598*	7.055***
Child abuse (D)	23.708***	15.420***	12.545***	8.155***	7.037**	27.682***
A×B	0.007	1.895	0.75	1.92	1.134	0.002
A×C	7.093***	8.467***	1.574	9.29***	8.943***	8.831***
A×D	0.722	9.441***	0.081	0.027	0.393	1.037
B×C	0.562	0.3	0.36	3.489*	1.609	1.18
B×D	2.636	8.595***	0.17	0.386	5.009*	4.342*
C×D	2.043	2.394	6.174***	4.324*	6.913***	6.422***
A×B×C	5.798***	2.207	2.389	0.94	1.237	4.371*
A×B×D	7.332**	12.987***	3.078	0	1.635	7.435**
A×C×D	9.734***	2.312	12.630***	7.422***	17.837***	21.881***
B×C×D	1.258	7.862***	1.333	1.924	5.810***	6.580***
A×B×C×D	2.122	3.151	2.372	0.493	0.975	3.221

*P>0.05, **P>0.01.

The significant main effect of child abuse on verbal ability (Table 3.17 and Fig. 3.23) denotes that verbal ability was found inferior in high abused group of students (M = 24.21) as compared to their low abused counterparts (M = 26.88).

Further, type of school × grade interaction graph (Fig. 3.24) denotes that although private school students performed superior on verbal ability, however little decline with increasing grade was found in this group. Contrary to this, in case of government school children, a sharp decline is observed from junior class students to high school but better performance is observed in intermediate level students.

Similarly, the significant interaction effect of gender x child abuse (Fig. 3.25) clearly showed that high abused group of girls performed slightly better than abused group of boys but in case of low abused group, boys performed far better than girl students on overall verbal ability.

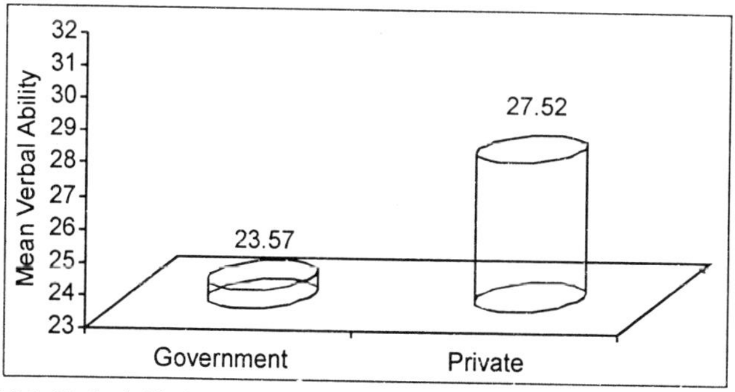

Fig. 3.21: Verbal Ability as a Function of Type of School.

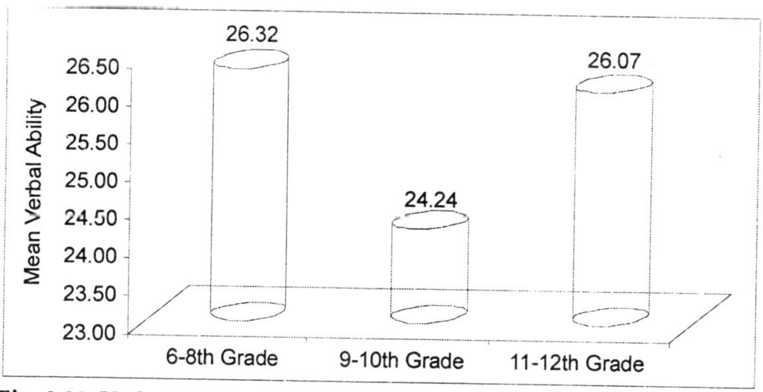

Fig. 3.22: Verbal Ability (as a whole) as a Function of Grade.

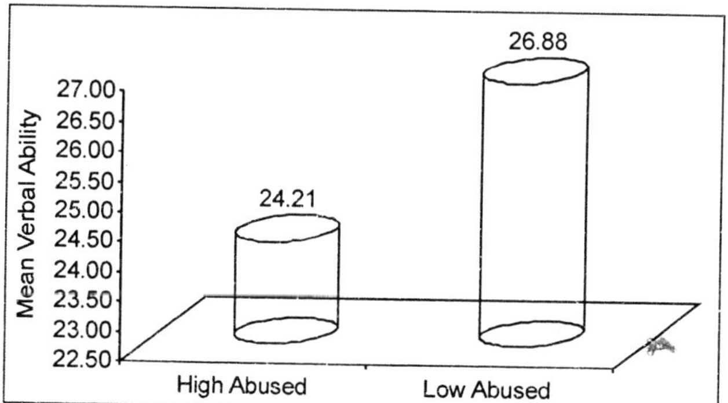

Fig. 3.23: Verbal Ability (as a whole) as a Function of Child Abuse

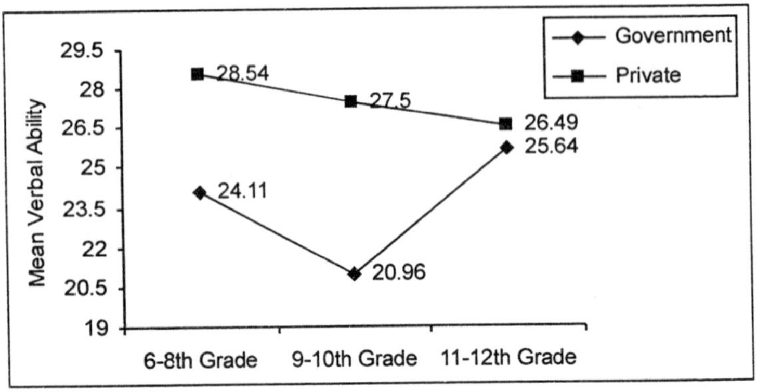

Fig. 3.24: Verbal Ability (as a whole) as a Function of Interaction of Type of School and Grade.

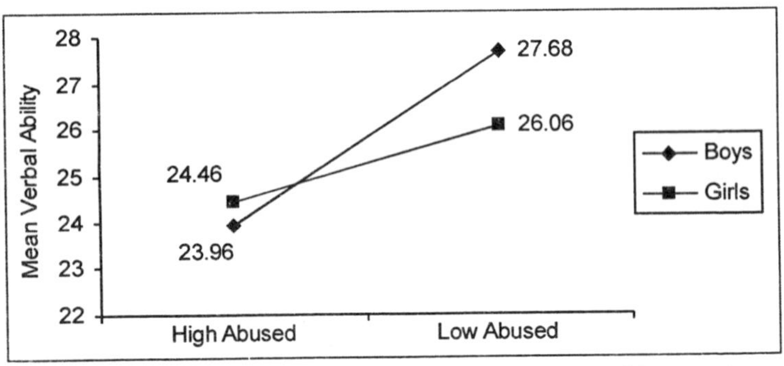

Fig. 3.25: Verbal Ability (as a whole) as a Function of Interaction of Gender and Child Abuse.

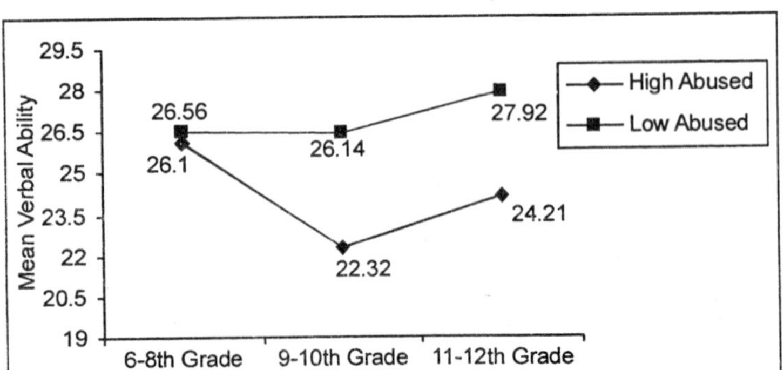

Fig. 3.26: Verbal Ability (as a whole) as a Function of Interaction of Grade and Child Abuse.

The significant Grade x Child Abuse interaction effect (Fig. 3.26) revealed that in case of low abused group intermediate level students performed far better than junior high school and high school students. However, in case of high abused group, high school students did very poor than junior high school students and Intermediate level students.

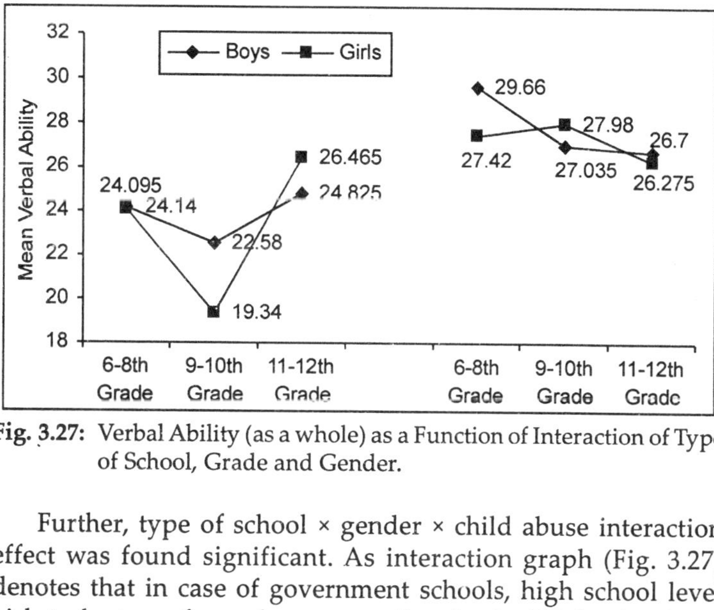

Fig. 3.27: Verbal Ability (as a whole) as a Function of Interaction of Type of School, Grade and Gender.

Further, type of school × gender × child abuse interaction effect was found significant. As interaction graph (Fig. 3.27) denotes that in case of government schools, high school level girl students performed very poor than Junior High school and Intermediate level counterparts. A similar pattern was found in case of boys also though little differences in all three grades were identified. Further, in case of private schools, girl students of High school did better than junior and intermediate level counterparts. However, boys of Junior High school level showed far superior verbal ability as compared to Intermediate level and high school level students.

Furthermore, interaction effect of type of school x gender x child abuse was also found significant. Interaction graph (Fig. 3.28) showed that in case of high abused group, girl students of government school performed very poor than their private school counterparts. Similar pattern was found in case of boys, though difference was lesser. Further, in case of low abused group boys of

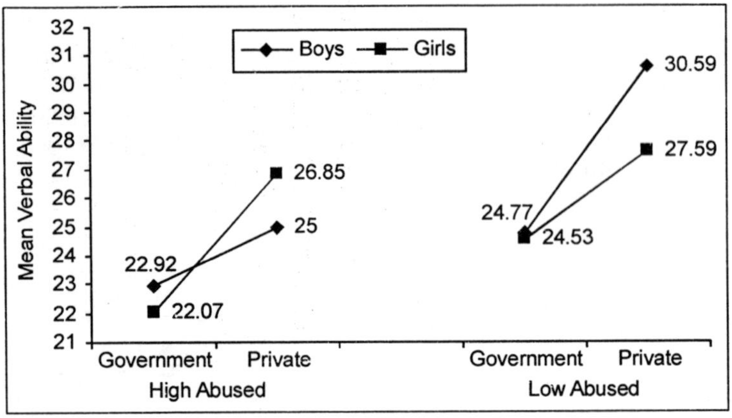

Fig. 3.28: Verbal Ability (as a whole) as a Function of Interaction of Type of School, Gender and Child Abuse.

private school performed far superior on verbal ability than those of government schools. Similar pattern was found in case of girls, though difference was lesser.

Again, type of school x grade x child abuse interaction effect was found significant. It is clear from interaction graph (Fig. 3.29) that in case of abused group, government school students of high school level performed very poor on verbal ability as compared to junior high school and intermediate level students. But reverse pattern was found in case of private school students in which

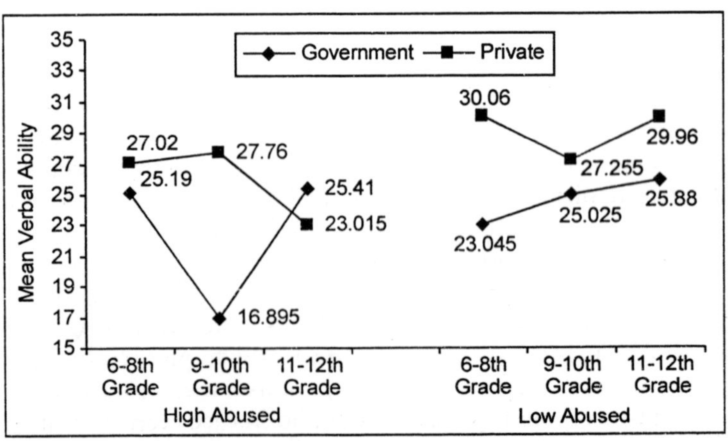

Fig. 3.29: Verbal Ability (as a whole) as a Function of Interaction of Type of School, Grade and Child Abuse.

intermediate level students performed inferior than junior and high school level students. Again, regarding low abused group, an increasing pattern on this ability was found with growing grades in government school students. However, in case of private schools, junior class and intermediate students have performed better than high school students.

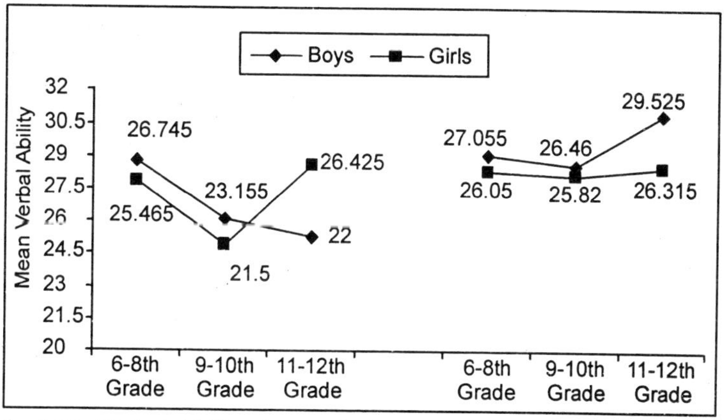

Fig. 3.30: Verbal Ability (as a whole) as a Function of Interaction of Gender, Grade and Child Abuse.

The significant interaction effect of gender x grade x child abuse on overall verbal ability (Fig. 3.30) suggests that in case of high abused group, a sharp decline from junior to high school and intermediate level is identified in male students. However, high school level girls have shown very poor verbal ability than junior high school and intermediate level counterparts. In case of low abused group, little variations across three grades of girl students were found, but intermediate level of male students have shown far superior verbal ability than those of junior high school and high school counterparts. (Table 3.17 B).

Impacts on Dimensions of Verbal Ability

Multiple analysis of variance (MANOVA) was calculated for dimensions of verbal ability to determine the impact of type of school, gender, grade and school abuse. Results are displayed in table and figures and reported for each domains of verbal ability separately (Table 3.17B).

(I) Word Analogy: As results indicate that word analogy ability in students varied as a function of type of school, class grade and level of school abuse. This ability was found higher in students of private schools (M = 4.30) as compared to government school counterparts (M = 3.70) (Fig. 3.31).

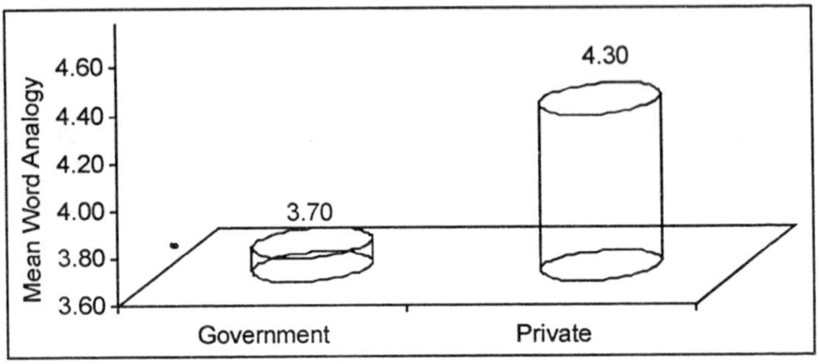

Fig. 3.31: Word Analogy as a Function of Grade.

Further, significant main effect of grade, suggests that high school (9-10th grade) students (M = 3.73) performed more poor on word analogy than junior high school (6-8th grade) (M = 4.37) and intermediate level (11-12th grade) students (M = 4.03) (Fig. 3.32).

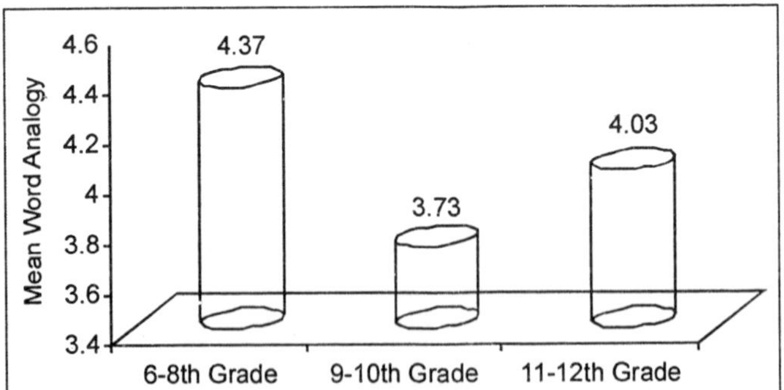

Fig. 3.32: Word Analogy as a Function of Grade.

The Word Analogy was also significantly influenced by child abuse (Fig. 3.33). As results reveal high abused group of children performed far poor on word analogy (M = 3.70) than low abused children (M = 4.30).

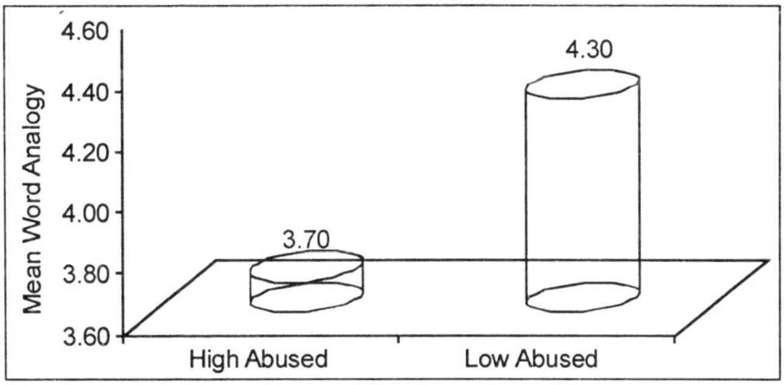

Fig. 3.33: Word Analogy as a Function of Child Abuse.

Apart from main effects, certain interaction effects were found significant. Results are reported and interpreted below.

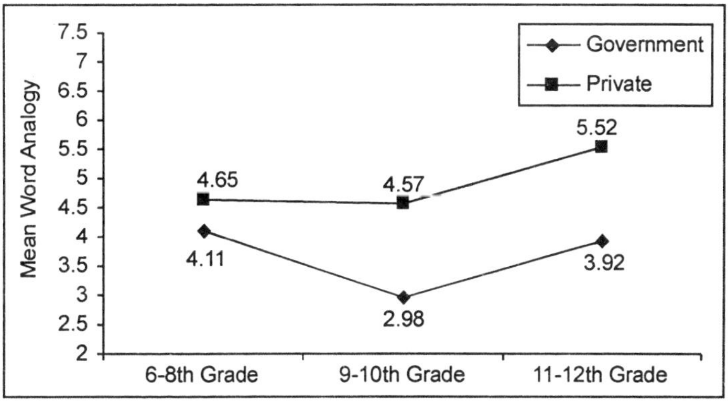

Fig. 3.34: Word Analogy as a Function of Interaction of Type of School and Grade.

The significant type of school x grade interaction effect (Fig. 3.34) indicates that in case of government schools, a sharp decline was found in high school students (9-10th grade) than junior high school and intermediate level students. However, in case of private schools, intermediate level students performed far better than junior high school and high school level students.

Further, interaction effect of type of school x gender x grade on word analogy (Fig. 3.35) indicates that in case of government schools, intermediate level (11-12th grade), girl students were found far superior than junior high school (6-8th grade) students

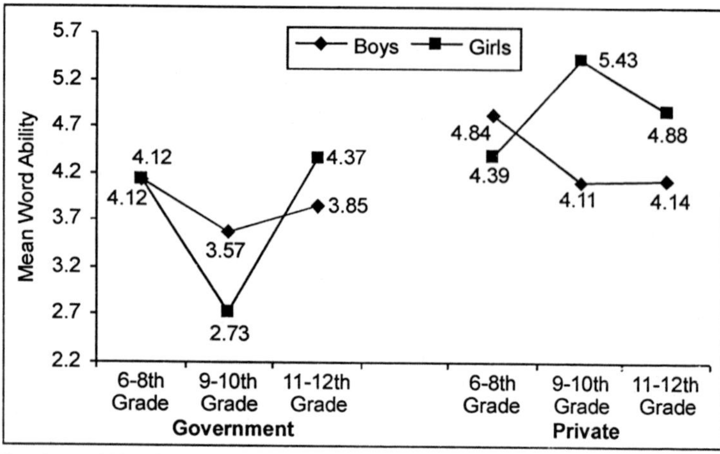

Fig. 3.35: Word Analogy as a Function of Interaction of Type of School, Gender and Grade.

but minimum word analogy was expressed by high school (9-10th grade) counterparts, however in case of boys little decline with increasing grade was found. Contrary to this, in case of private schools, high school level (9-10th grade) girl students were found far superior on this ability than intermediate level (11-12th) and junior high school (6-8th grade) girl students but boys showed decline with the increasing grade levels.

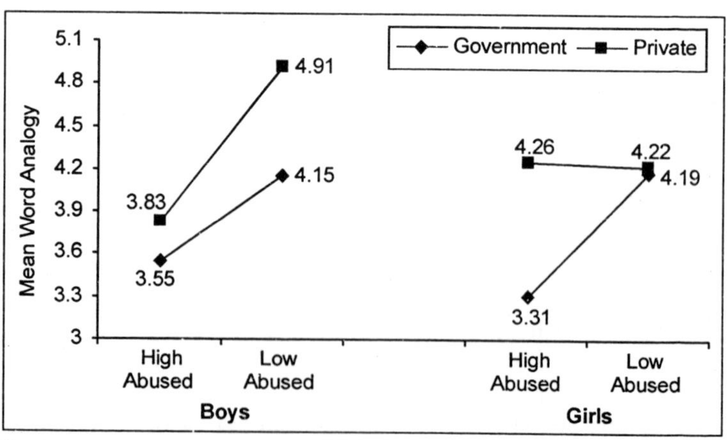

Fig. 3.36: Word Analogy as a function of Interaction of Type of School, Gender and Child Abuse.

Again, significant type of school x gender x child abuse interaction effect (Fig. 3.36) indicates that abused boys belonging to both, government and private schools performed inferior as compared to low abused boys but different pattern was identified in case of girls. In case of private schools, girls of high abused and low abused groups did not differ significantly but in case of Government schools, word analogy was found very poor in high abused group than low abused counterparts.

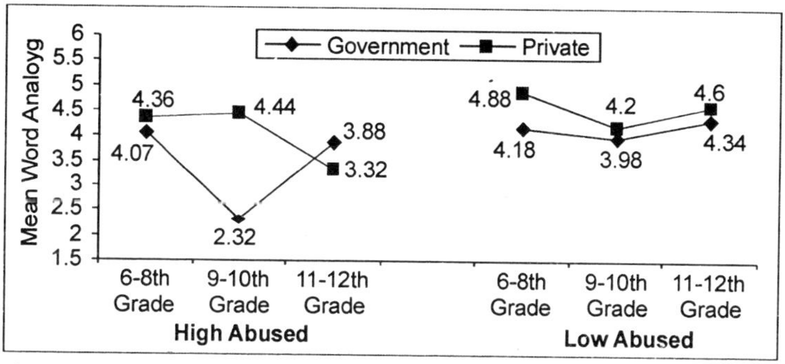

Fig. 3.37: Word Analogy as a Function of Interaction of Type of School, Grade and Child Abuse

Again, type of school x grade x child abuse interaction effect (Fig. 3.37) was found significant which denotes that in case of high abused students of government schools, minimum word analogy was found in high school (9-10th grade) as compared to junior high school (6-8th) and intermediate level (11-12th grade) students. Whereas, minimum analogy was reported by high school level (9-10th grade) students of private school than junior high school (6-8th grade) and intermediate (11-12th grade) students. Further, in case of low abused group minimum word analogy was shown by high school students of both government and private schools. However, intermediate level students of Government schools expressed better analogy than junior high school students but reverse pattern was found in private schools. Junior high school students showed better word analogy than intermediate level students.

(II) Opposite Word: MANOVA results (Table 3.17 and Figure 3.38) evince the influence of type of school, grade and child abuse on opposite word ability.

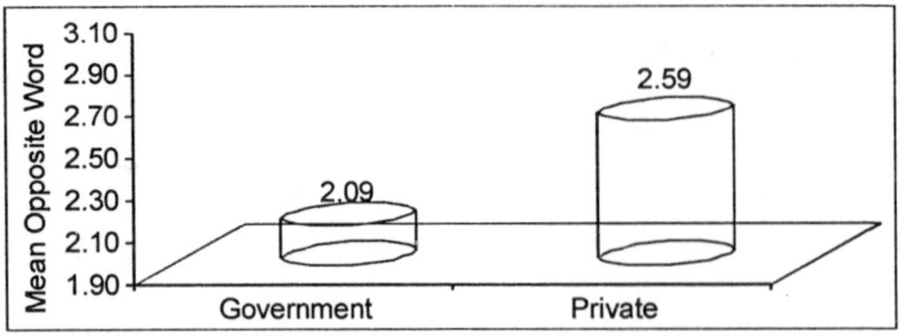

Fig. 3.38: Opposite Word as a Function of Type of School.

Significant main effect of type of school (Fig. 3.38) revealed that government school students performed very poor (M = 2.09) than private school students (M = 2.59) on this ability.

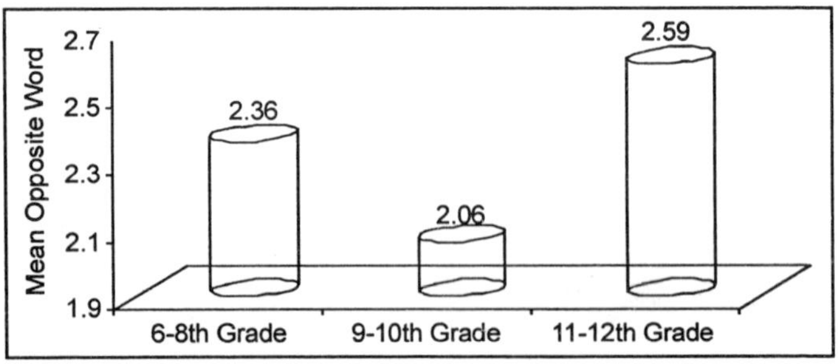

Fig. 3.39: Opposite Word as a Function of Grade.

Further, significant main effect of grade (Fig. 3.39), reveals that high school (9-10th grade) students scored lesser on opposite word (M = 2.06) than junior high school (6-8th grade) (M = 2.36) and intermediate level (11-12th grade) students (M = 2.59).

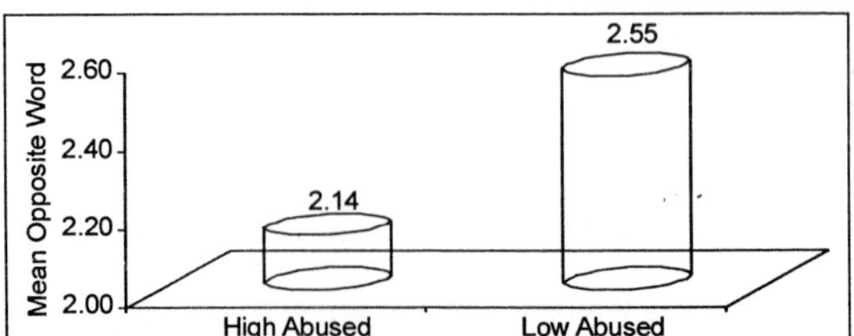

Fig. 3.40: Opposite Word as a Function of Child Abuse.

The main effect of child abuse was also found significant (Fig. 3.40), which revealed that high abused students performed more poor on opposite word (M = 2.14) than low abused students (M = 2.55). Certain interaction effects were also found significant.

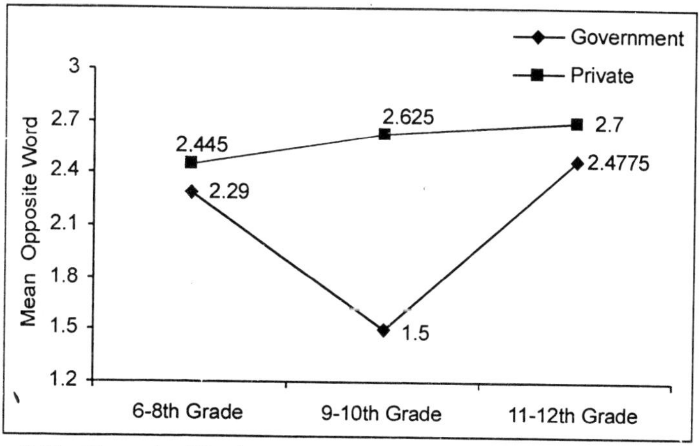

Fig. 3.41: Opposite Word as a Function of Interaction of Type of School and Grade.

The type of school x grade interaction effect (Fig. 3.41) was found significant which revealed that in case of private schools increasing patterns on this ability were found in students of all three grades (6-8th, 9-10th and 11-12th). Whereas, in case of government schools students' performance on opposite word task was far inferior in high school (9-10th grade) students than junior

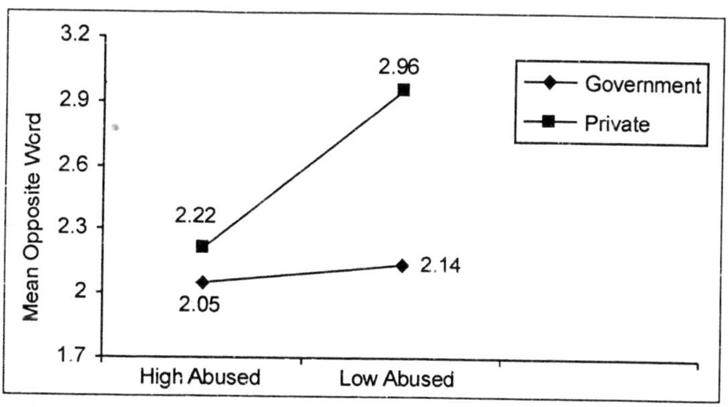

Fig. 3.42: Opposite Word as a Function of Interaction of Type of School and Child Abuse.

high school (6-8th grade) children and intermediate level (11-12th grades) students.

Furthermore, significant interaction effect of type of school x child abuse (Fig. 3.42) indicates that in case of abused group, government school students scored lesser on opposite word as compared to their private school counterparts but difference was found low. Contrary to this, low abused children of private schools scored far high on opposite word (M = 2.96) than government schools' children (M = 2.14).

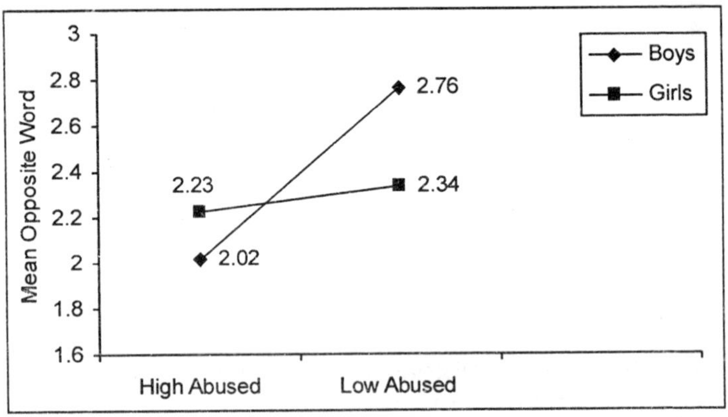

Fig. 3.43: Opposite Word as a Function of Interaction of Gender and Child Abuse.

Further, significant interaction effect of gender x child abuse (Fig. 3.43) indicates that high abused boys performed far inferior than low abused boys, contrary to this, girls of both groups did not differ significantly on this task.

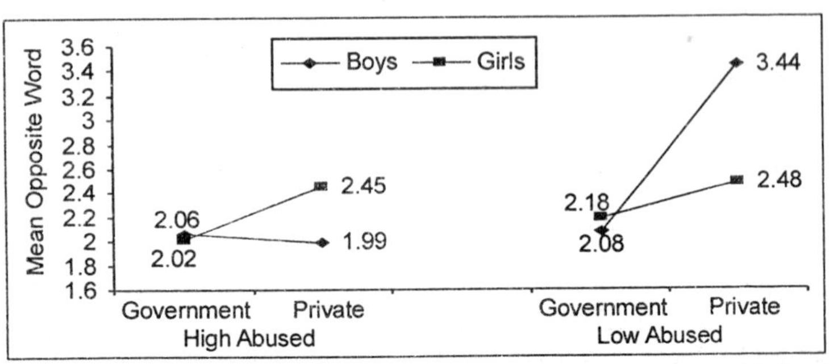

Fig. 3.44: Opposite Word as a Function of Interaction of Type of School, Gender and Child Abuse.

Furthermore, type of school x gender x child abuse interaction effect (Fig. 3.44) has indicated that abused boys belonging to both government and private schools performed equally very inferior. Whereas, low abused group of private schools did better than those of government school students. Contrary to this, boys and girls of low abused group differed across type of school. Both boys and girls of government school scored very poor and did not differ on verbal ability (opposite word). However, boys of private school did extremely well on verbal ability as compared to girls.

(III) Word Similarity: Word Similarity varied significantly in accordance with type of school and level of abuse.

As results indicate (Fig. 3.45), Government school children performed very poor (M = 6.44) on word similarity task as compared to private school students (M = 7.97).

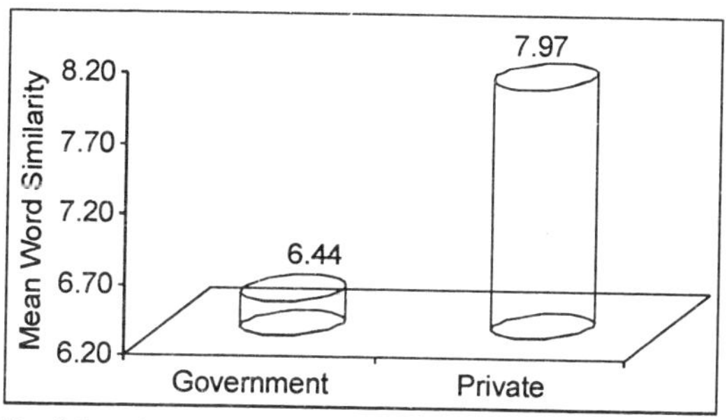

Fig. 3.45: Word Similarity as a Function of Type of School.

Furthermore, the significant main effect of child abuse denoted (Fig. 3.46) that high abused children scored less on word similarity (M = 6.84) than low abused children (M = 7.56).

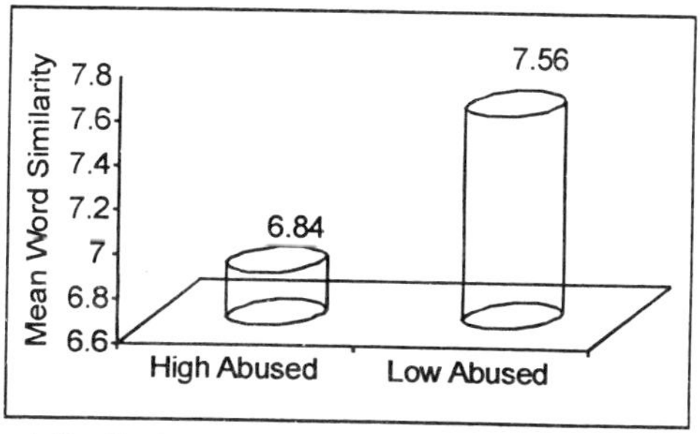

Fig. 3.46: Word Similarity as a Function of Child Abuse.

Apart from main effects, certain interaction effects were found significant.

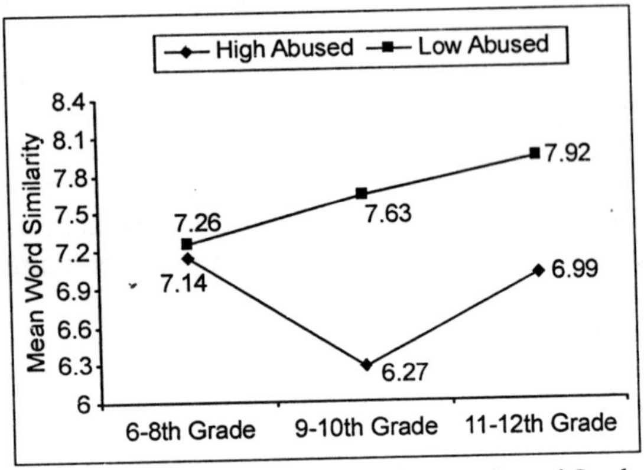

Fig. 3.47: Word Similarity as a Function of Interaction of Grade and Child Abuse.

The significant grade x child abuse interaction effect (Fig. 3.47) revealed that in case of low abused group developing pattern was found with increasing grades of students on word similarity. Contrary to this, in case of abused group, high school (9-10th grade) students performed very poor as compared to intermediate level and junior high school students.

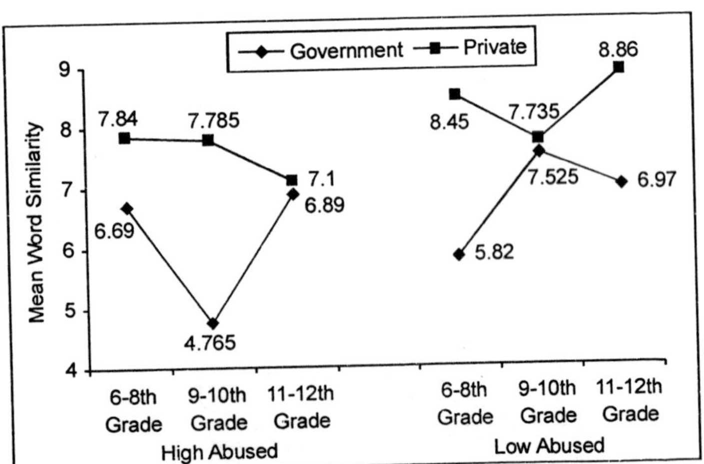

Fig. 3.48: Word Similarity as a Function of Interaction of Grade and School Type.

Further, Type of school x Grade x Child Abuse interaction effect was also found significant on word similarity task. As interaction graph (Fig. 3.48) denotes that in abused group of students, high school age children of government school scored very less on word similarity as compared to intermediate level and junior high school students. However, a little decline on word similarity was identified in intermediate level students as compared to high school and junior high school students. A different pattern was identified in case of low abused group of children. In this group, high school level children of both government and private schools have performed equally well. However, junior high school students of private school did better than government school counterparts. Similarly, intermediate level students of private school performed far better than government school counterparts on word similarity.

(IV) Word Classification: It is clear from results (Table 3.17 and Fig. 3.49) that main effect of type of school was found significant, which denotes that government school students performed poor on word classification (M = 4.99) than private school students (M = 5.55).

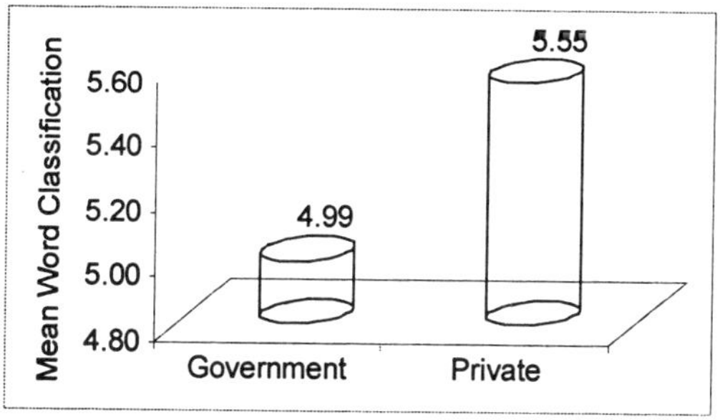

Fig. 3.49: Word Classification as a Function of Type of School.

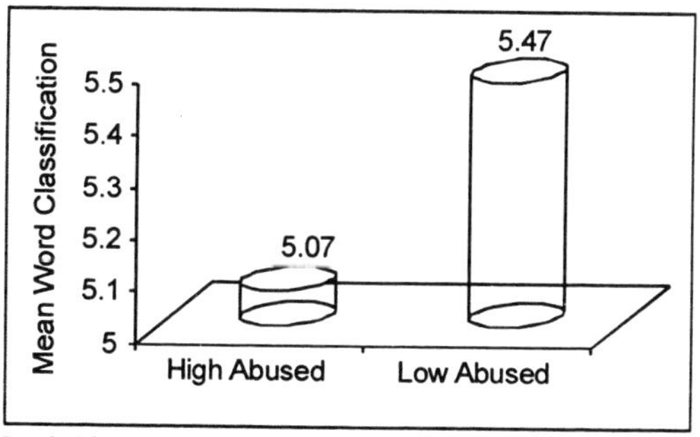

Fig. 3.50: Word Classification as a Function of Child Abuse.

Similarly, the main effect of child abuse was also found significant (Fig. 3.50), which showed that high abused students performed very poor on word classification task (M = 5.07) than low abused students (M = 5.47).

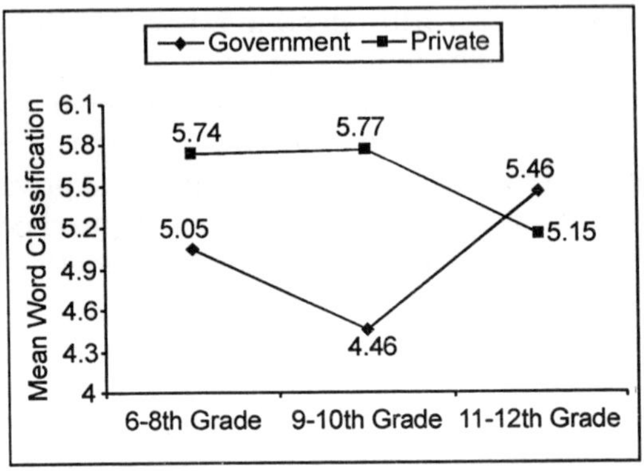

Fig. 3.51: Word Classification as a Function of Interaction of Type of School and Grade.

Further, significant interaction effect of type of school x grade (Fig. 3.51) revealed that in case of private school, very little differences on word classification were found among three grades. However, government school students of junior high school (6-8th class) and intermediate level (11-12th class) students scored high on word classification than high school (9-10th class) students.

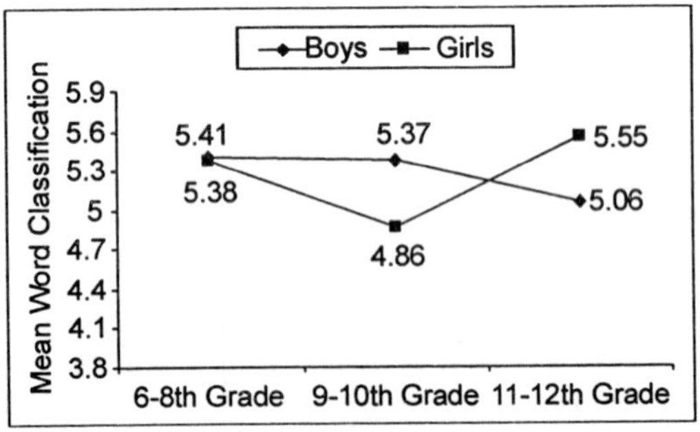

Fig. 3.52: Word Classification as a Function of Interaction of Gender and Grade.

The interaction effect of gender x grade (Fig. 3.52) denoted that girl students of junior high school (6-8th grade) compete with their boys counterparts with very little difference on word classification task. But, in the case of high school (9-10th grade) students, boys scored higher as compared to girls. Interestingly, girls belonging to intermediate level (11-12th grade) performed better than boys.

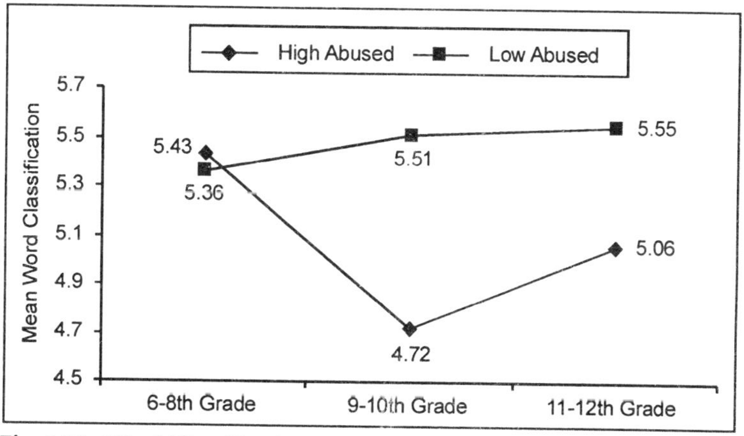

Fig. 3.53: Word Classification as a Function of Interaction of Grade and Child Abuse.

Similarly, significant interaction effect of grade x child abuse (Fig. 3.53) indicates that in case of high abused group, high school level students (9-10th) performed very poor on word classification as compared to intermediate level and junior high school students. However, an increasing pattern from junior high school to high school and intermediate level was identified in low abused group.

Type of school x grade x child abuse interaction effect was also found significant on word classification task (Fig. 3.54). In case of high abused group, high school level students of government school scored far poor than junior high school and intermediate level counterparts. However, reverse pattern was found in private school students. Intermediate level students did very poor than high school and junior high school students. Contrary to this, an increasing pattern was found with growing age (grades) in low abused children studying in government

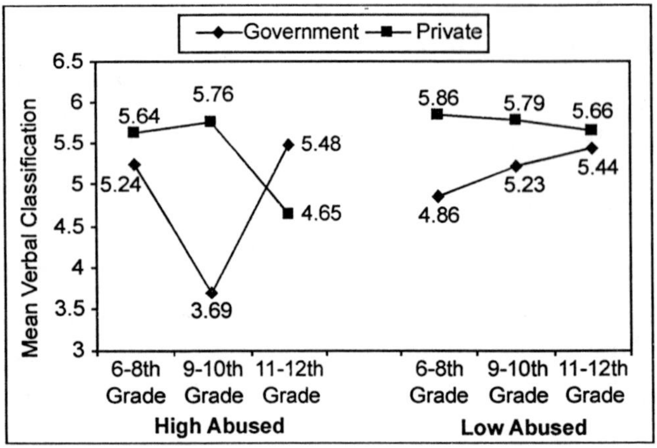

Fig. 3.54: Word Classification as a Function of Interaction of Type of School, Grade and Child Abuse.

schools. However, in case of private schools, junior class (6-8th grade) students performed little better than high school and intermediate level students.

(V) Sentence Completion: It is clear from MANOVA results (Table 3.17) that the influences of type of school, grade and child abuse on sentence completion were found significant. As Figure 3.55 displays government school students performed far inferior (M = 6.32) than private school students (M = 7.23) on sentence completion task.

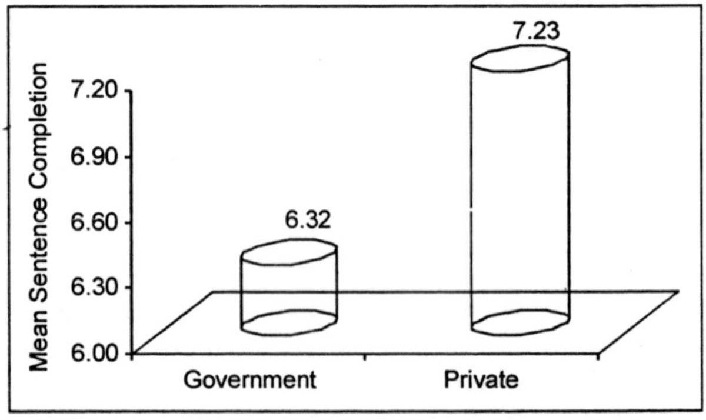

Fig. 3.55: Sentence Completion as a Function of Type of School.

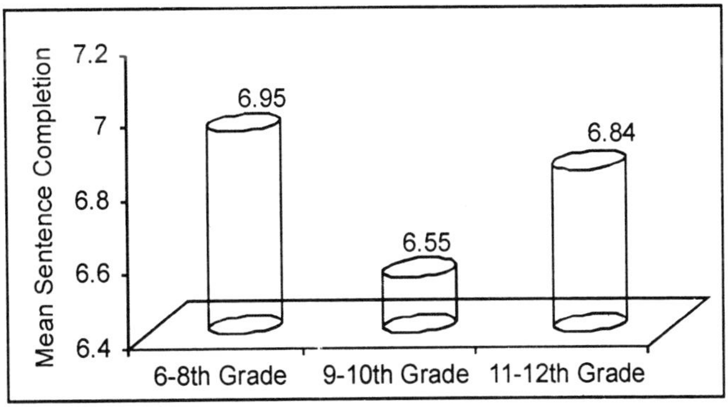

Fig. 3.56: Sentence Completion as a Function of Grade.

Again Figure 3.56 indicates varying pattern on sentence completion across different grades of students. Junior high school (6-8th) and intermediate level (11-12th grade) students (M = 6.95 and M = 6.84) scored higher on sentence completion as compared to high school (9-10th grade) students (M = 6.55).

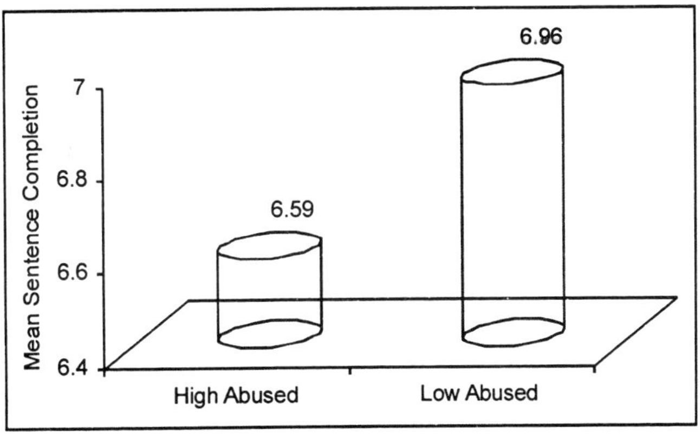

Fig. 3.57: Sentence Completion as a Function of Child Abuse.

Similarly, significant main effect of child abuse denoted that high abused students (M = 6.59) performed far inferior than low abused students (M = 6.96) on sentence completion task (Fig. 3.57).

Furthermore, significant type of school × grade interaction effect (Fig. 3.58) revealed that on sentence completion junior high school and high school students of private schools performed far better than government school counterparts, but no difference was found in case of intermediate level students of both types of schools.

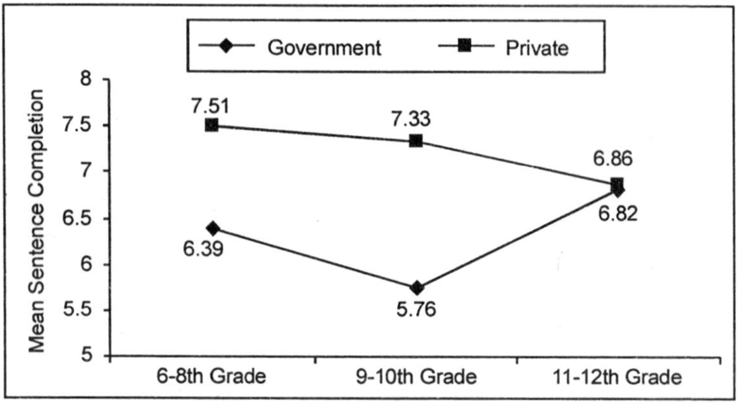

Fig. 3.58: Sentence Completion as a Function of Interaction of Type of School and Grade.

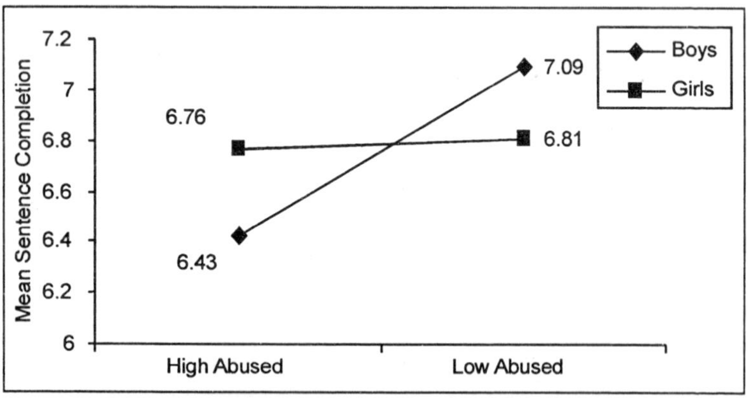

Fig. 3.59: Sentence Completion as a Function of Interaction of Gender and Child Abuse.

Likewise, gender × child abuse interaction effect was also found significant on sentence completion. As Figure 3.59 shows, highly abused boys performed more poor than low abused group, but very little difference between high and low abused girls was found on sentence completion task.

The significant Grade x Child Abuse interaction effect (Fig. 3.60) revealed that in case of low abused group, very little difference was found on sentence completion in all three grades of students. However, abused students of high-school scored far inferior than intermediate and junior high school students.

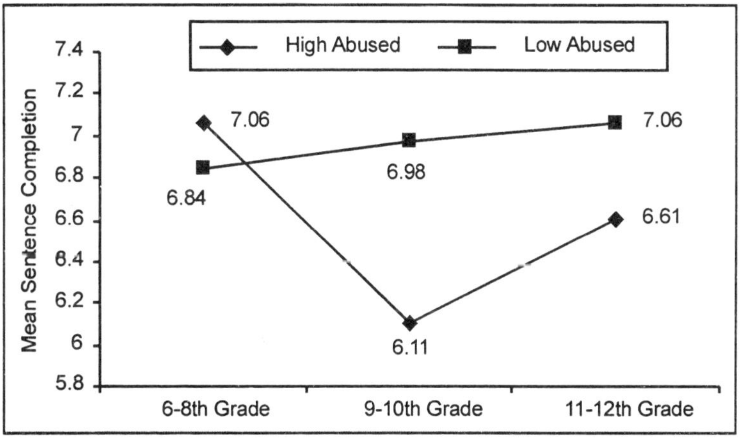

Fig. 3.60: Sentence Completion as a Function of Interaction of Grade and Child Abuse.

Furthermore, the interaction effect of type of school x grade x child abuse on sentence completion was found significant. An overview of interaction graph (Fig. 3.61), suggests that in case of abused group, high school students of government school performed very poor than their private school counterparts. In case of junior high school (6-8th grade) lesser difference was found between both types of schools. However, in case of intermediate level, government school students outperformed their private school counterparts. Again in case of low abused group, a growing pattern with increasing grade level was found in government school students. However, low abused junior high school students of private school scored better than high school and intermediate level counterparts.

Further, gender x grade x child abuse interaction effect on sentence completion was found significant. In case of high abused group, high school level both boys and girls have performed very poor than rest of the groups. Specifically, a sharp decline with

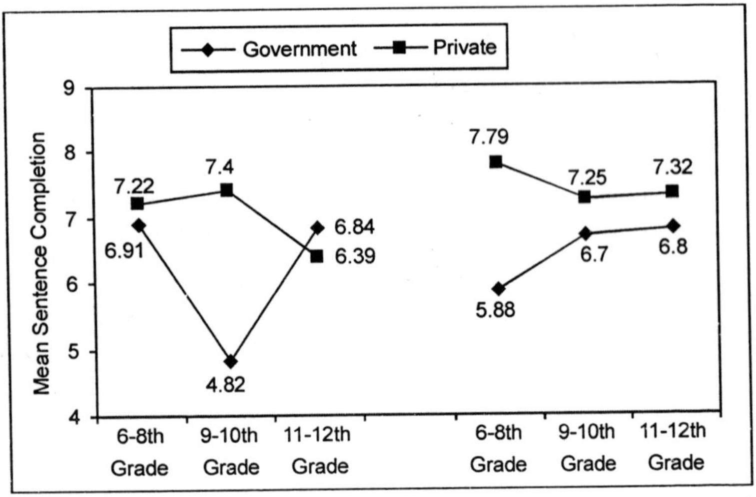

Fig. 3.61: Sentence Completion as a Function of Interaction of Type of School, Grade and Child Abuse.

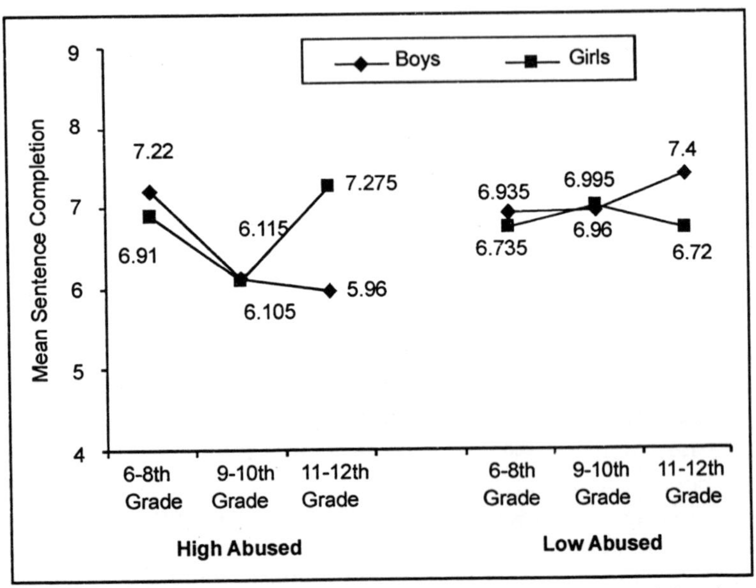

Fig. 3.62: Sentence Completion as a Function of Interaction of Gender, Grade and Child Abuse.

increasing grade is observed in case of boys whereas, junior high school and intermediate level girl students did far better than their high school counterparts. Again, interaction graph denotes that in case of low abused group, an increasing pattern with growing grade level was identified in case of boys. However high school level girl students did better on sentence completion than junior high school students and intermediate level students.

To sum up, abusive experiences in schools and government school system have played inhibitory role in the development of verbal ability in students.

Further, Memory process (memory span and working memory) was selected as another cognitive variable and the role of child abuse, type of school, gender and grade in memory level of students was investigated.

2. *Impact on Memory Process*

(I) Memory Span: Scores obtained on memory span task were analyzed in terms of Univariate analysis and results are displayed in Tables 3.18 and 3.19. As results indicate that mean scores of memory span differed across type of school, gender, grades and child abuse.

Table 3.18: Mean and SD of Memory Span by Type of School, Gender, Grade and Child Abuse

Variables		*Government*				*Private*			
		Boys		*Girls*		*Boys*		*Girls*	
		High Abused	*Low Abused*	*High Abused*	*Low Abused*	*High Abused*	*Low Abused*	*High Abused*	*Low Abused*
6-8th Grade	Mean	4.24	3.89	4.24	3.89	4.31	3.59	3.92	3.52
	(SD)	1.268	1.133	1.268	1.133	1.267	1.321	1.287	1.338
9-10th Grade	Mean	2.96	3.71	2.20	3.17	4.24	3.89	3.95	3.55
	(SD)	1.091	.726	1.789	1.209	1.264	1.123	1.327	1.241
11-12th Grade	Mean	3.20	3.21	4.47	3.84	2.84	3.29	4.48	4.68
	(SD)	1.103	1.160	1.138	1.445	1.221	1.136	1.127	1.670

ANOVA results (Table 3.19) show that type of school and grade have influenced memory span significantly.

Table 3.19: Summary of 2 × 2 × 3 × 2 ANOVA (Two Levels of Type of School, Gender, Grade and Child Abuse) of Memory Span

Source	*Sum of Squares*	*df*	*Mean Square*	*F*
Type of School (A)	81.645	1	81.645	54.08**
Gender (B)	1.367	1	1.367	.905
Grade (C)	43.872	2	21.936	14.53**
Child Abuse (D)	.983	1	.983	.651
A×B	1.968E-005	1	1.968E-005	.000
A×C	19.526	2	9.763	6.46**
A×D	.034	1	.034	.023
B×C	9.238	2	4.619	3.05*
B×D	4.007	1	4.007	2.654
C×D	3.673	2	1.837	1.217
A×B×C	21.318	2	10.659	7.06**
A×B×D	1.357	1	1.357	.899
A×C×D	23.810	2	11.905	7.88**
B×C×D	11.430	2	5.715	3.78*
A×B×C×D	2.116	2	1.058	.701

*P<0.05, *P<0.01.

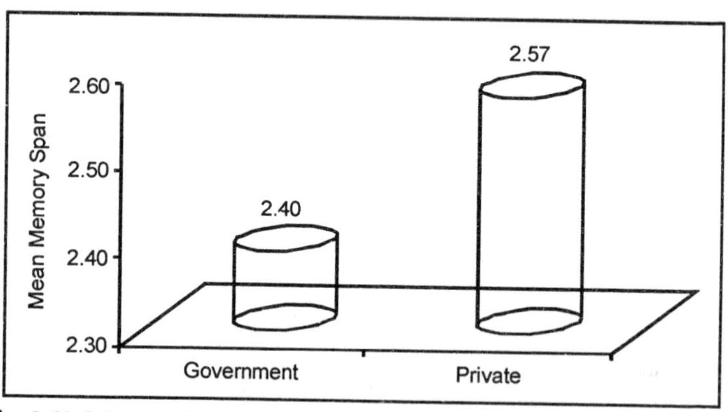

Fig. 3.63: Memory Span as a Function of Type of School.

Significant main effect of type of school revealed (Fig. 3.63) that memory span was found better in students of private schools (M = 2.57) than government school students (M = 2.40).

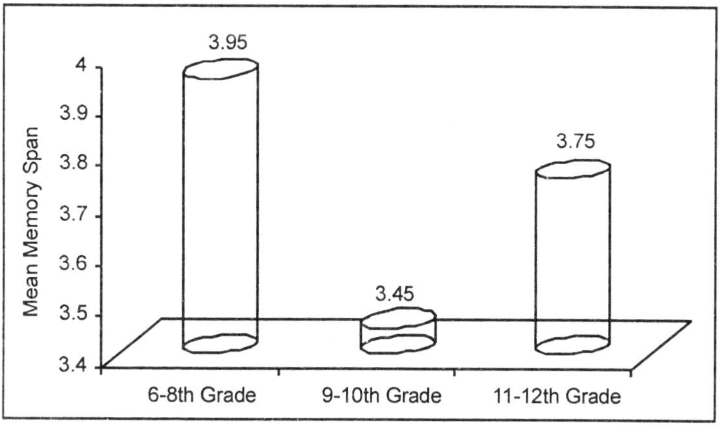

Fig. 3.64: Memory Span as a Function of Grade.

Further, significant main effect of grade (Fig. 3.64), suggests that junior high school students showed superior memory span than intermediate level students and very poor level of memory span was found in high school students.

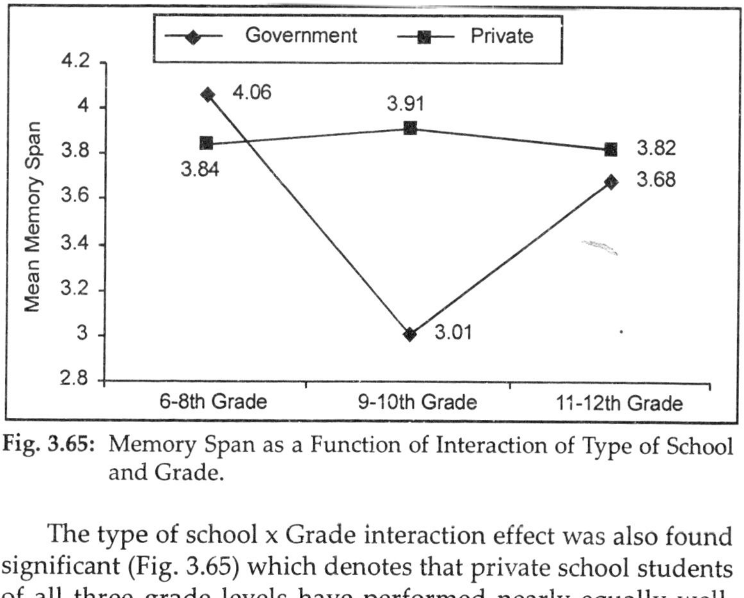

Fig. 3.65: Memory Span as a Function of Interaction of Type of School and Grade.

The type of school x Grade interaction effect was also found significant (Fig. 3.65) which denotes that private school students of all three grade levels have performed nearly equally well. However, government school students of high school level have performed very poor. Interestingly junior high school students showed (M = 4.06) far superior memory span than intermediate level students.

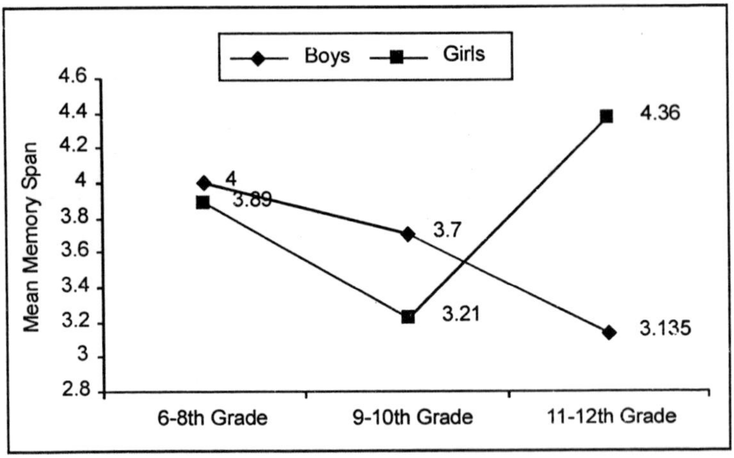

Fig. 3.66: Memory Span as a Function of Interaction of Gender and Grade.

Again, significant gender x grade interaction effect (Fig. 3.66) revealed that in case of boys, decline in memory span was found with growing grade level. However, in case of girls, high school level students showed inferior memory span than junior high school students. But memory span of intermediate level girl students was found far superior.

Further, type of school x gender x grade interaction effect (Fig. 3.67) was also found significant. Interaction graph (Fig. 3.67) indicates that regarding government school students, a sharp decline in memory span was found with increasing grade of male students. However, girl students of high school showed very poor memory span than junior and intermediate level students. A different pattern was found in case of private school students. With increasing grade level girl students showed superior memory span however, reverse pattern was found in case of boys of private schools.

Further, type of school x grade x child abuse interaction effect was found significant. As Figure 3.68 indicates that in case of high abused group, high school students of government schools showed very poor level of memory span than intermediate level and junior

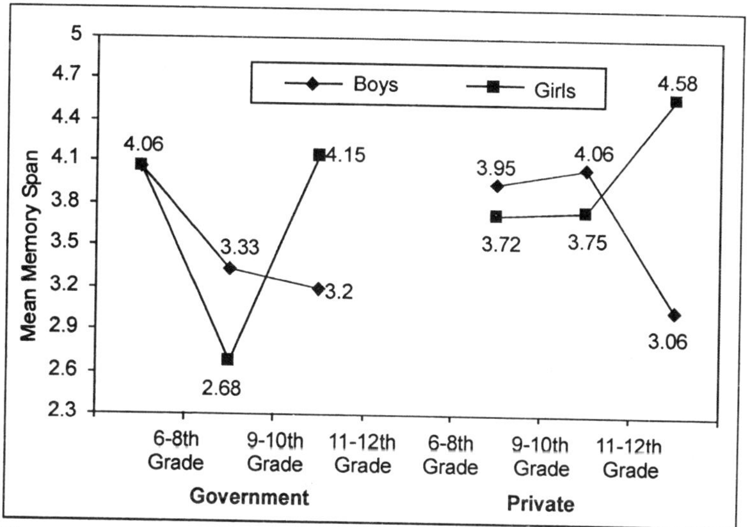

Fig. 3.67: Memory Span as a Function of Interaction of Gender, Grade and Type of School.

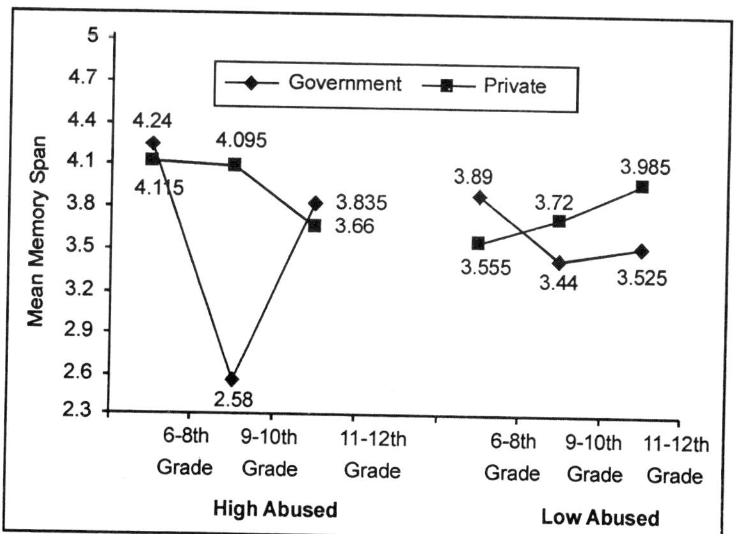

Fig. 3.68: Memory Span as a Function of Interaction of Type of School, Grade and Child Abuse.

high school counterparts. But in case of private schools, little decline was found with increasing grade. Again in case of low abused group decline in memory span was found with increasing grades in government schools however reverse pattern was found in case of private school students of low abused group in which intermediate level students expressed superior memory span than high school and junior high school students.

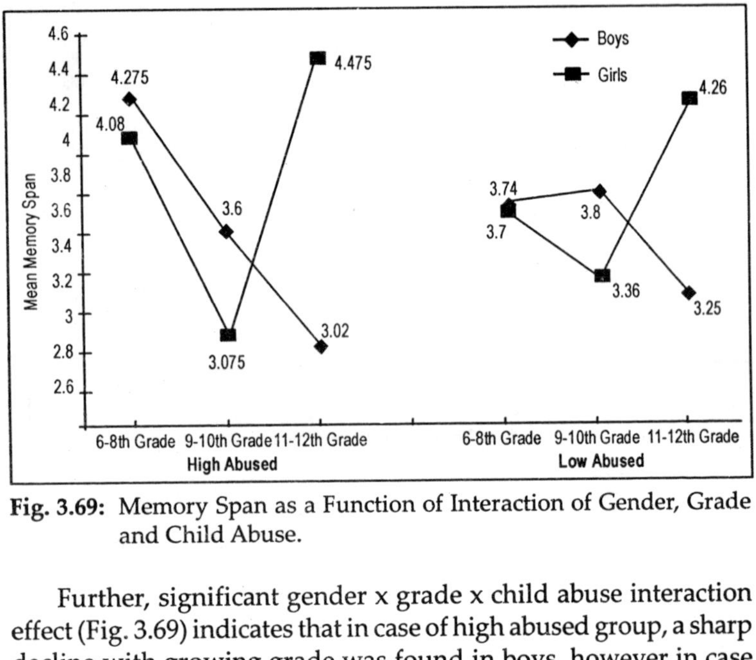

Fig. 3.69: Memory Span as a Function of Interaction of Gender, Grade and Child Abuse.

Further, significant gender x grade x child abuse interaction effect (Fig. 3.69) indicates that in case of high abused group, a sharp decline with growing grade was found in boys, however in case of high school level girl students memory span was far inferior than junior and intermediate level girl students. Contrary to this, in low abused group, intermediate level girls have shown far superior memory than junior high school and high school level students. Whereas, boys of high school level have shown better memory span than junior high school and intermediate level students. Results thus, indicate that memory span increased with growing grade however abusive experiences disrupted the proper development of memory span.

(II) Impact on Working Memory of Students

Scores obtained on working memory task, i.e. reading span task (RSPAN), visual pattern recall (VSPAN) and operation span task (OSPAN) were treated statistically.

To understand the effect of grade, gender and child abuse on development of working memory, 2×2×2 factorial analysis of variance was computed for various domains of working memory and working memory (WM) as a whole. Results are displayed in Table 3.20 and figures and reported in the following section.

Table 3.20: Mean, S.D. and Significant F-Values for Different Components of Working Memory (WM) by Grade, Gender and Child Abuse in Schools

Variables	*Grade*		*Gender*		*Abuse*		*F = Value A = Grade B = Gender C = Child-abuse*
	Junior students (6-8th Grade)	*Senior students (9-12th Grade)*	*Boys*	*Girls*	*High Abuse*	*Low Abuse*	
Phonological WM	M = 12.33 S.D.(3.54)	M = 14.86 S.D.(3.55)	M = 13.8 S.D.(3.55)	M = 13.31 S.D.(3.87)	M = 12.39 S.D.(2.92)	M = 14.76 S.D.(3.94)	FA = 21.46** FC = 16.59** FAxB = 3.98*
Visuo-Spatial WM	M = 14.89 S.D.(3.71)	M = 16.83 S.D.(4.10)	M = 16.08 S.D.(4.10)	M = 15.62 S.D.(3.94)	M = 15.25 S.D.(4.00)	M = 16.48 S.D.(3.98)	FA = 21.46**
Central Executive WM	M = 12.42 S.D.(3.10)	M = 14.14 S.D.(3.11)	M = 12.86 S.D.(3.15)	M = 13.70 S.D.(3.18)	M = 12.29 S.D.(2.84)	M = 14.28 S.D.(3.24)	FA = 10.27** FC = 14.24** FAxC = 2.90*
Working Memory (overall)	M = 39.55 S.D.(7.26)	M = 45.89 S.D.(7.33)	M = 42.86 S.D.(8.20)	M = 42.77 S.D.(7.60)	M = 40.06 S.D.(6.55)	M = 45.19 S.D.(8.30)	FA = 21.46** FC = 16.59**

**P<.01, *P<.05.

1. Phonological Working Memory

Table 3.20 indicates that phonological working memory was significantly influenced by grade and child abuse. Significant main effect of grade [F(1,112) = 21.46, P<.01] denotes that senior students performed far better on phonological component of working memory as compared to junior class students. Further, significant main effect of abuse [F(1,112) = 16.59, P<.01] revealed that phonological working memory of high abused children was far inferior than low abused children. Further, grade x gender interaction effect [F (1,112) = 3.98, P<.05] was found significant.

As interaction graph shows that in case of junior students, girls were found inferior than boys on phonological WM whereas, among senior students, little difference was found in boys and girls.

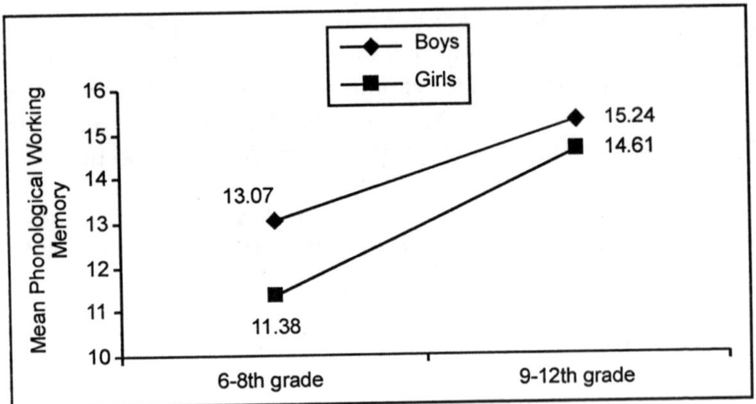

Fig. 3.70: Phonological Working Memory as a Function of Grade and Gender.

2. Visuo-Spatial Sketch Pad

ANOVA results (Table 3.20) denote that main effect of grade was found significant which reveals that senior students scored higher on visuo-spatial sketch pad working memory as compared to junior students. Thus, a developmental pattern with increasing grade was further identified in visuo-spatial working memory. Child abuse and gender effects were found non-significant.

3. Central Executive

As is apparent from Table 3.20, central executive working memory was significantly influenced by grade and level of abuse. Significant main effect of grade denotes that senior students performed superior on central executive as compared to junior students. Contrary to this, significant main effect of abuse revealed that high abused children scored low on central executive working memory task than low abused counterparts.

Significant grade x abuse interaction effect as displayed in interaction graph (Fig. 3.71) shows that in case of high abused group, little improvement in central executive working memory was found with increasing grade. Whereas, in case of low abused group, senior students were found far superior on central executive working memory than junior students.

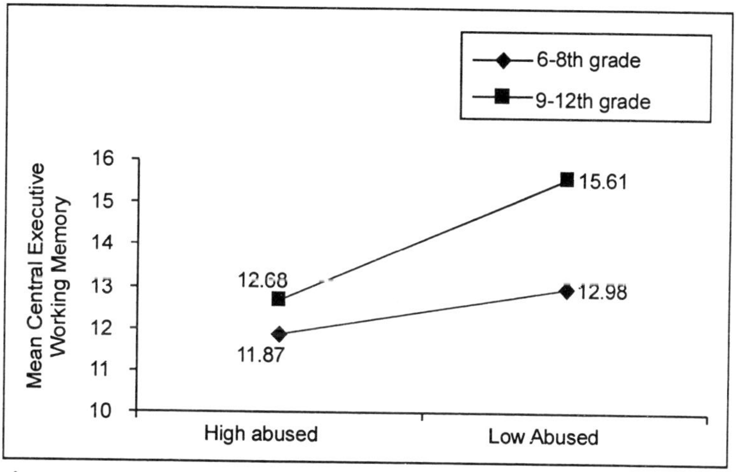

Fig. 3.71: Central Executive Working Memory as a Function of Grade and Child Abuse.

4. Working Memory (As a Whole)

It is also clear from results (Table 3.20, Fig. 3.72), working memory (overall) was found significantly influenced by grade and abuse level. Significant main effect of grade evinced a developmental trend from junior (6-8th grade) to senior (9-12th grade) group. More specifically, senior students scored far superior on working memory than junior students. Whereas, significant main effect of abuse denoted that high abused children were found very inferior on working memory as compared to low abused children. Moreover, abuse x grade interaction effect was also found to be significant.

As Figure 3.72 shows that in case of low abused group, senior students performed superior on working memory (overall) as compared to junior students. Whereas, in case of high abused group, improvement on working memory was found very slow and steady from junior to senior group.

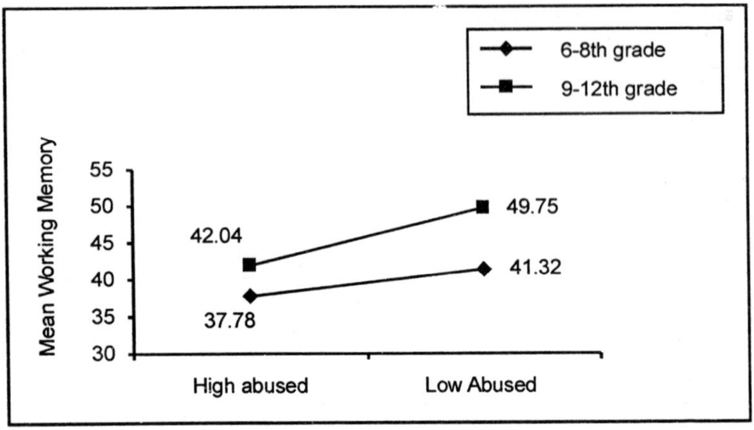

Fig. 3.72: Working Memory (overall) as a Function of Grade and Child Abuse.

Present results suggest that working memory improves with growing grade, however abusive experiences of children interrupt the proper development of working memory. More specifically, high abused children performed very poor on various components of working memory whereas, gradual improvement in working memory was found in case of low abused group of children. Gender effect was found non-significant.

2. *Impact of Child Abuse (in Schools) on Motivational Process*

The Motivational processes (Academic achievement and Aspiration) in relation to Type of School, Grade, Gender and Child Abuse were examined on different group of students. Scores obtained on achievement motivation test and aspiration scale were treated statistically in terms of descriptive and comparative analysis. Results are displayed in tables and figures and reported in following section.

(I) Academic Achievement Motivation in Students: Results displayed in Table 3.21 suggest that students differed significantly on academic achievement motivation level as a function of type of school, gender, grade and child abuse.

Table 3.21: Mean and SD of Academic Achievement Motivation by Type of School, Gender, Grade and Child Abuse in School Setting

		Government School				*Private School*			
		Boys		*Girls*		*Boys*		*Girls*	
		High Abused	*Low Abused*	*High Abused*	*Low Abused*	*High Abused*	*Low Abused*	*High Abused*	*Low Abused*
6-8th	Mean	28.04	26.89	28.04	26.89	29.10	27.98	27.32	28.25
Grade	SD	3.092	3.247	3.092	3.247	4.375	5.341	5.139	5.801
9-10th	Mean	25.41	27.43	23.40	26.88	29.78	31.30	29.05	29.27
Grade	SD	6.778	5.155	4.393	6.603	4.697	6.140	3.741	4.037
11-12th	Mean	28.20	28.32	28.31	29.09	26.00	4.440	28.00	28.68
Grade	SD	3.571	3.544	4.278	5.035	27.80	3.493	2.941	4.028

In order to determine the impact of type of school, grade, gender and child abuse on academic achievement motive of students, ANOVA analysis was done. Results are displayed in Table 3.22.

Table 3.22: Summary of 2x2x3x2 ANOVA of Academic Achievement Motivation as a Function of Type of School, Gender, Grade and Child Abuse

Source	*Sum of Squares*	*df*	*Mean Square*	*F*
Type of School (A)	224.982	1	224.982	10.92**
Gender (B)	8.705	1	8.705	.423
Grade (C)	5.692	2	2.846	.138
Child Abuse (D)	60.810	1	60.810	2.953
A×B	.077	1	.077	.004
A×C	485.468	2	242.734	11.78**
A×D	.003	1	.003	.000
B×C	92.026	2	46.013	2.234
B×D	2.784	1	2.784	.135
C×D	173.831	2	86.915	4.22**
A×B×C	18.291	2	9.146	.444
A×B×D	5.696	1	5.696	.277
A×C×D	61.148	2	30.574	1.484
B×C×D	11.995	2	5.998	.291
A×B×C×D	47.798	2	23.899	1.160

**P<0.01.

It is clear from results (Table 3.22 and Fig. 3.73) that type of school exerted significant effect on academic achievement of students.

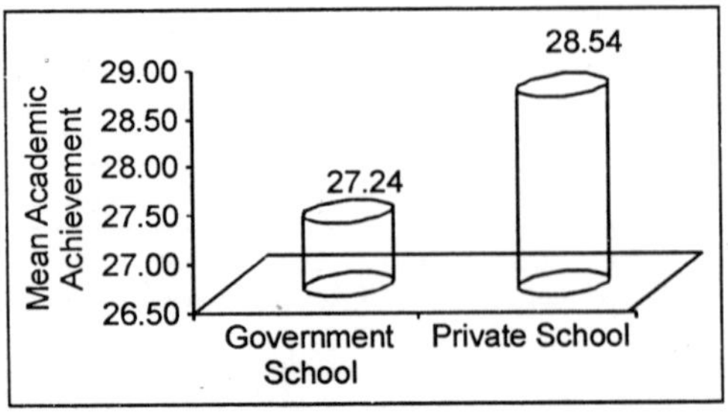

Fig. 3.73: Academic Achievement as a Function of Type of School.

As Figure 3.73 indicates, government school students showed low academic achievement motive (M = 27.24) than private school students (M = 28.54). The effects of gender, grade and child abuse level were found non-significant. However certain interaction effects were found significant.

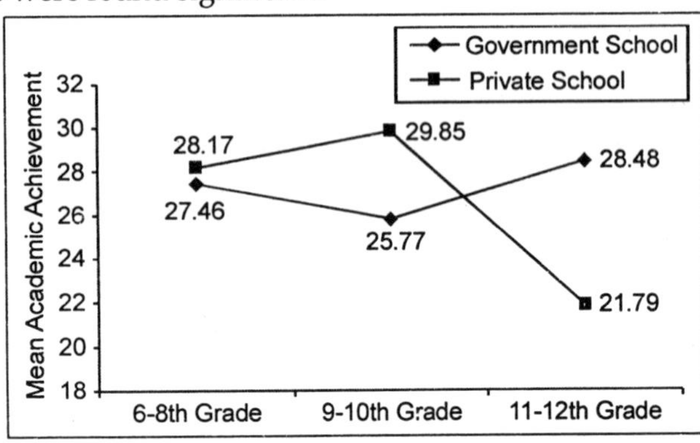

Fig. 3.74: Academic Achievement Motive as a Function of Interaction of Type of School and Grade.

Significant type of school × grade interaction effect (Fig. 3.74) denotes that in case of private school, academic achievement was found higher in high school students as compared to junior high school students, but intermediate level students have displayed very low level of achievement motive. Reverse pattern was found in case of government school students. Greater level of academic achievement is identified in intermediate level students than junior high school and high school level students.

Significant grade x child abuse interaction effect (Fig. 3.75) revealed that in case of high abused group, high school students

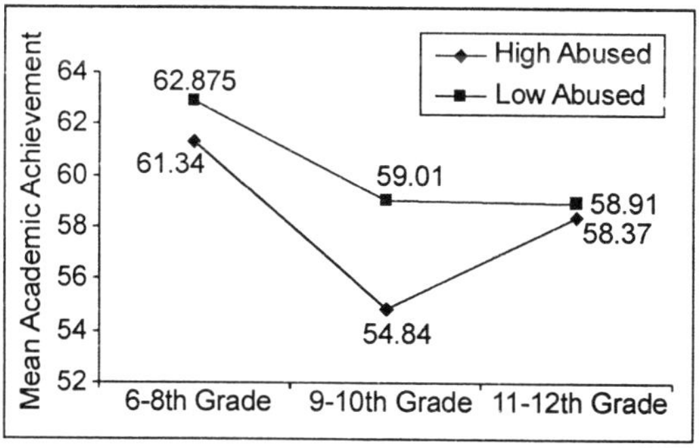

Fig. 3.75: Academic Achievement as a Function of Interaction of Grade and Child Abuse.

were found far inferior in academic achievement than intermediate level and junior high school level students. In case of low abused group, a decreasing pattern in academic achievement is identified with increasing grade level. In other words, junior high school students of both groups (high abused and low abused) have scored better than rest of the group.

Level of Aspiration: As results displayed in Table 3.23 show that students varied on aspiration level across groups.

Table 3.23: Mean and SD of Aspiration Level by Type of School, Gender, Grade and Child Abuse

		Government				*Private*			
		Boys		*Girls*		*Boys*		*Girls*	
		High Abused	*Low Abused*	*High Abused*	*Low Abused*	*High Abused*	*Low Abused*	*High Abused*	*Low Abused*
6-8th Grade	Mean	63.51	62.50	63.51	62.50	57.23	61.75	61.12	64.75
	SD	5.60	8.89	5.60	8.80	10.23	10.34	12.65	5.72
9-10th Grade	Mean	45.67	55.14	51.20	57.56	60.41	60.88	62.11	62.44
	SD	21.60	17.67	3.63	10.48	6.93	8.34	7.04	6.69
11-12th Grade	Mean	61.46	59.96	60.22	61.89	51.25	56.60	60.57	57.16
	SD	7.86	5.80	7.95	6.25	16.47	9.18	9.66	11.16

Further, the effects of type of school, gender, grade and child abuse on aspiration was determined by 2 × 2 × 3 × 2 ANOVA analysis. ANOVA results (Table 3.24) report that main effect of gender was found significant. It is clear from Fig. 3.76 that girls (M = 60.42) showed higher level of aspiration as compared to boys (M = 58.03).

Table 3.24: Summary of 2x2x3x2 ANOVA of Aspiration Level as a Function of Type of School, Gender, and Grade and Child Abuse

Source	*Sum of Squares*	*DF*	*Mean Square*	*F*
Type of School (A)	114.953	1	114.953	1.42
Gender (B)	758.822	1	758.822	9.42**
Grade (C)	3268.813	2	1634.406	20.30**
Child Abuse (D)	571.292	1	571.292	7.09**
A×B	119.882	1	119.882	1.489
A×C	4161.935	2	2080.967	25.85**
A×D	8.965	1	8.965	.111
B×C	40.676	2	20.338	.253
B×D	87.313	1	87.313	1.085
C×D	273.330	2	136.665	1.698
A×B×C	283.916	2	141.958	1.764
A×B×D	89.382	1	89.382	1.110
A×C×D	1079.632	2	539.816	6.707**
B×C×D	34.776	2	17.388	.216
A×B×C×D	266.951	2	133.475	1.658

**P<0.01

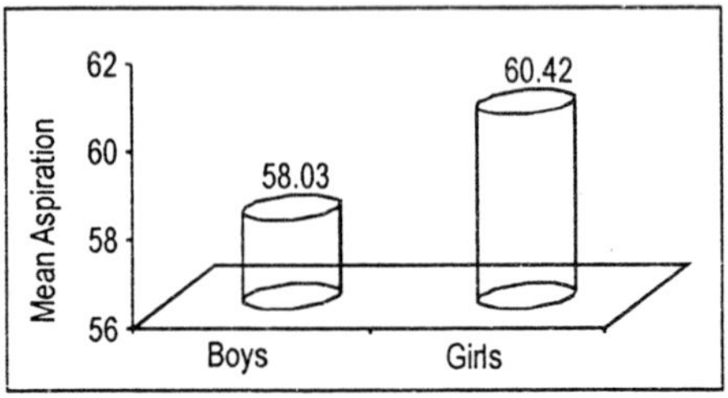

Fig. 3.76: Aspiration as a Function of Gender.

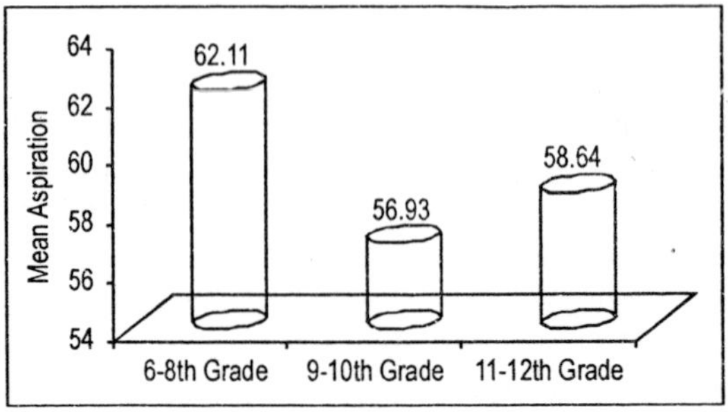

Fig. 3.77: Aspiration as a Function of Grade.

Similarly, the main effect of grade was also found significant (Fig. 3.77) which suggests that junior high school students showed higher aspiration level than intermediate level and minimum level was found in high school students.

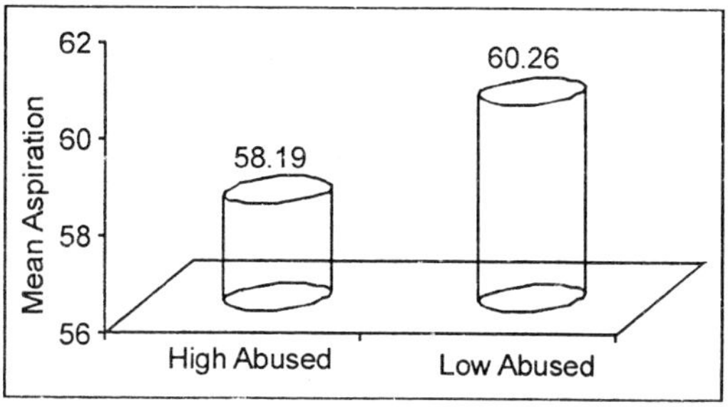

Fig. 3.78: Aspiration as a Function of Child Abuse.

The level of aspiration varied significantly between high abused and low abused group of students (Fig. 3.78). High abused students expressed far inferior level of aspiration (M = 58.19) than low abused counterparts.

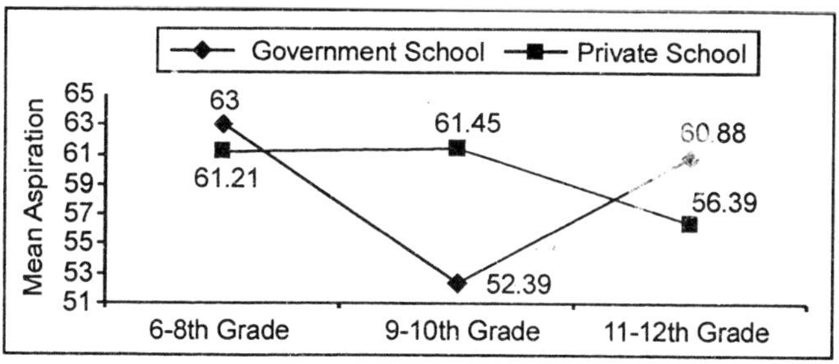

Fig. 3.79: Aspiration as a Function of Interaction of Type of School and grade.

Type of school x grade interaction effect was also found significant. As interaction graph (Fig. 3.79) indicates that in case of government school, high school level students expressed minimum aspiration level as compared to intermediate level and junior high school level students. But reverse pattern was found in case of private school students.

Furthermore, the significant effect of type of school x grade x child abuse on level of aspiration (Fig. 3.80) evinced that in high abused group the level of aspiration was found very poor in high

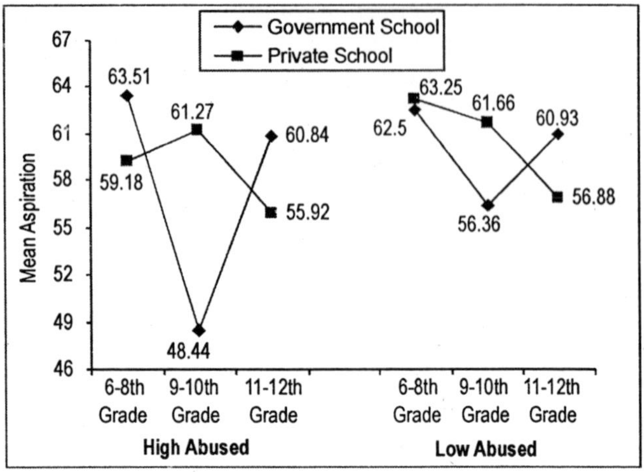

Fig. 3.80: Aspiration as a Function of Interaction of Type of School, Grade and Child Abuse.

school level students as compared to junior and intermediate level students in government schools but reverse pattern was found in case of private school students. Again, similar pattern was found in low abused group. Minimum level of aspiration was shown by government school students of high school level than junior high school students and intermediate level, but gradual decline with increasing grade was found in private school students of low abused students.

C. Impact on Affective Process

Affective processes (depression and anxiety) as a function of type of school, gender, and grade and child abuse were also investigated. Scores obtained on depression and anxiety tests were treated statistically. Results are displayed in Table 3.25 and 3.26 and figures and reported below.

(1) Depression—Results displayed in Table 3.25, suggest that different group of students differed significantly on depression level.

ANOVA results (Table 3.26 and Fig. 3.81) suggest that government school children were found more depressed (M = 47.39) than Private school children (M = 42.66). Rest of the main effects were found non-significant. However, some of the interaction effects were found significant.

Table 3.25: Mean and SD of Depression Scores by Type of School, Gender, Grade and Child Abuse

Variables		Government				Private			
		Boys		Girls		Boys		Girls	
		High Abused	Low Abused	High Abused	Low Abused	High Abused	Low Abused	High Abused	Low Abused
6-8th	Mean	48.54	48.46	48.54	48.46	42.77	40.04	38.38	39.88
Grade	SD	12.38	11.41	12.38	11.41	12.67	10.68	14.68	14.77
9-10th	Mean	54.33	36.71	50.2	42.27	46.52	46.88	50.86	45.9
Grade	SD	10.38	5.32	11.81	9.3	9.74	9.33	9.76	11.28
11-12th	Mean	45.33	53.27	48.45	44.13	31	47.2	44.09	38.4
Grade	SD	10.39	7.25	10.75	14.63	19.22	8.37	16.53	16.8

Table 3.26: Summary of 2×2×3×2 ANOVA of Depression Scores as a function of Type of School, Gender, Grade and Child Abuse

Source	Sum of Squares	df	Mean Square	F
Type of school (A)	2649.925	1	2649.925	18.25**
Gender (B)	1.811	1	1.811	.012
Grade (C)	695.722	2	347.861	2.396
Child abuse (D)	248.429	1	248.429	1.711
A×B	48.846	1	48.846	.336
A×C	2791.672	2	1395.836	9.61**
A×D	588.102	1	588.102	4.05*
B×C	148.067	2	74.034	.510
B×D	536.171	1	536.171	3.69*
C×D	2204.887	2	1102.443	7.59**
A×B×C	288.831	2	144.416	.995
A×B×D	342.275	1	342.275	2.357
A×C×D	825.003	2	412.501	2.84*
B×C×D	1953.587	2	976.793	6.72**
A×B×C×D	709.338	2	354.669	2.443

*P < .05, **P < 0.01.

The significant type of school x grade interaction effect (Fig. 3.82) denoted that government school students of junior high school (class 6-8th) and intermediate level (11-12th) expressed lower level of depression but high school (9-10th grade) students showed high level of depression. Contrary to this, in case of private school, high school (9-10th class) students showed lower level of depression as compared to junior high school (6-8th class) and intermediate level students (11-12th class).

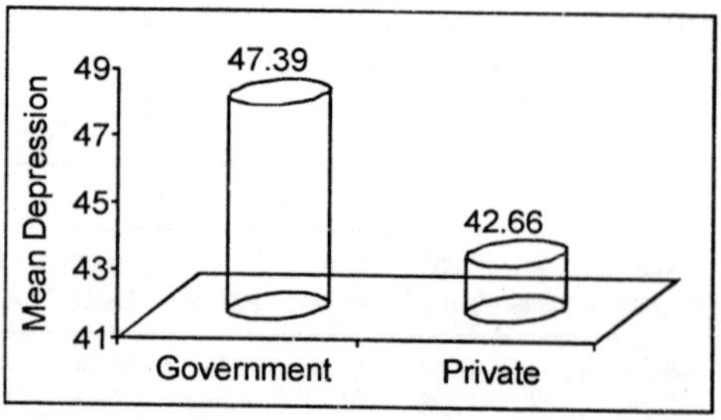

Fig. 3.81: Depression as a Function of Type of School.

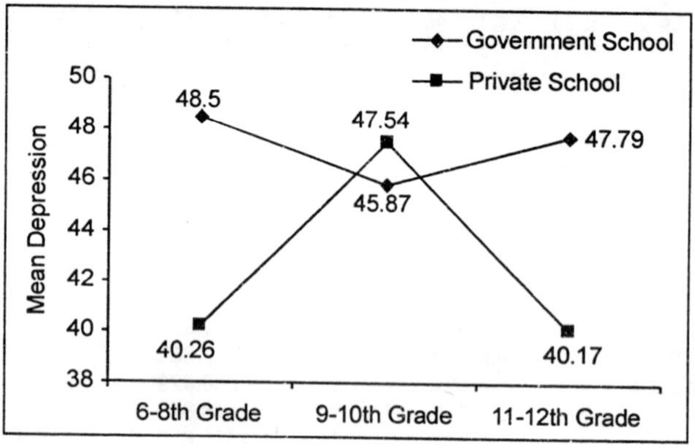

Fig. 3.82: Depression as a Function of Interaction of Type of School and Grade.

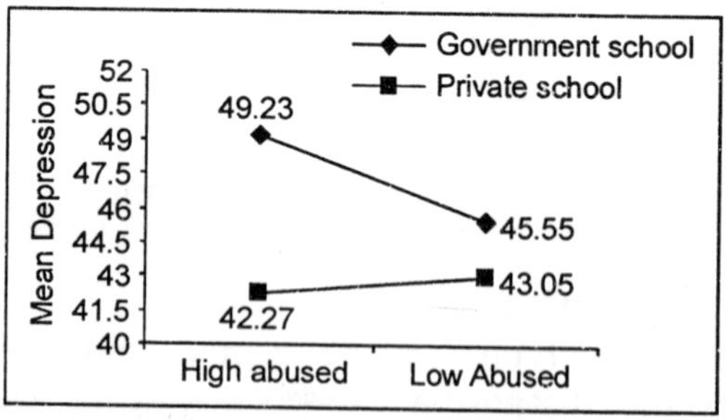

Fig. 3.83: Depression as a Function of Interaction of Type of School and Child Abuse.

Similarly, significant interaction effect of type of school x child abuse (Fig. 3.83) revealed that higher level of depression was found in high abused students of government school than their low abused counterparts. But in case of private school students depression level was very low and very little difference was found between high abused and low abused group.

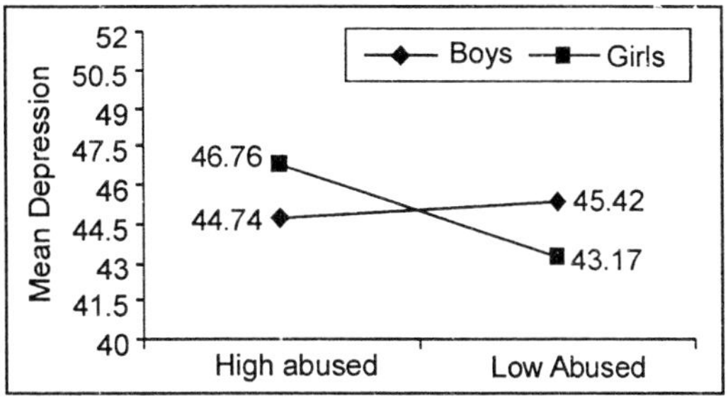

Fig. 3.84: Depression as a Function of Interaction of Gender and Child Abuse.

The significant interaction effect of gender x child abuse (Fig. 3.84) showed that girls belonging to high abused group expressed very high level of depression than their low abused counterparts. But, in case of boys, very little difference was found between high abused boys and low abused on depression level.

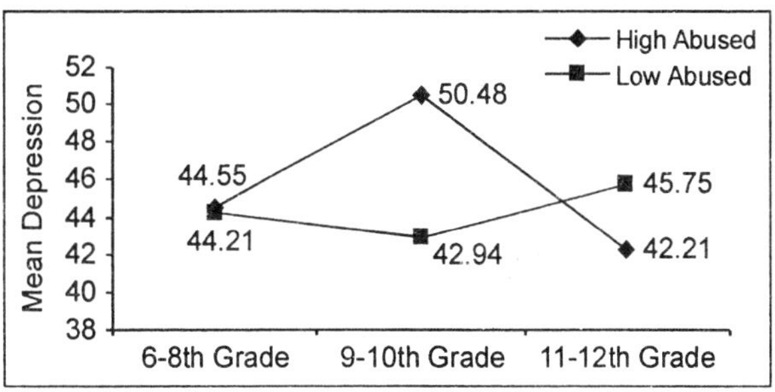

Fig. 3.85: Depression as a Function of Interaction of Grade and Child Abuse.

The significant interaction effect of grade x child abuse (Fig. 3.85) revealed that in case of high abused group, high school level students expressed higher level of depression as compared to junior high school and intermediate level students. Contrary to this, in case of low abused group, depression level was found little higher in intermediate level students than junior high school and high school students.

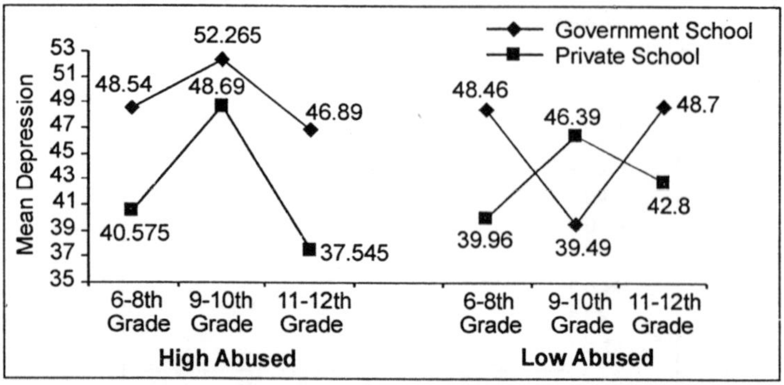

Fig. 3.86: Depression as a Function of Interaction of Type of School, Grade and Child Abuse.

Type of school x grade x child abuse interaction effect was also found significant on level of depression. Results (Fig. 3.86) indicate that in abused group depression level was found very high in high school level students. Junior high school students also showed more depression than intermediate level students of government school. Similar pattern was found in case of private school students of abused group. However, in case of low abused group, government school students of junior high school (6-8th) and intermediate level (11-12th grade) expressed higher level of depression as compared to high school students. But in case of private school students, depression level was found greater in high school students than their intermediate and junior high school counterparts.

Again, the significant interaction effect of gender x grade x child abuse, displayed in Figure 3.87, suggests that in case of high abused group, the level of depression was found equally very high in boys and girl students of high school level. The minimum level of depression was found in boys of intermediate level among rest of the group of students. In case of low abused group, decline in level of depression was found with increasing grade in case of girls. But intermediate level boys expressed maximum depression among all group of students.

(ii) Impact on Anxiety: Statistical analysis was also done for anxiety score. Results displayed in Table 3.27, indicate that level of anxiety differed in accordance with type of school, gender, class grade of students and level of child abuse.

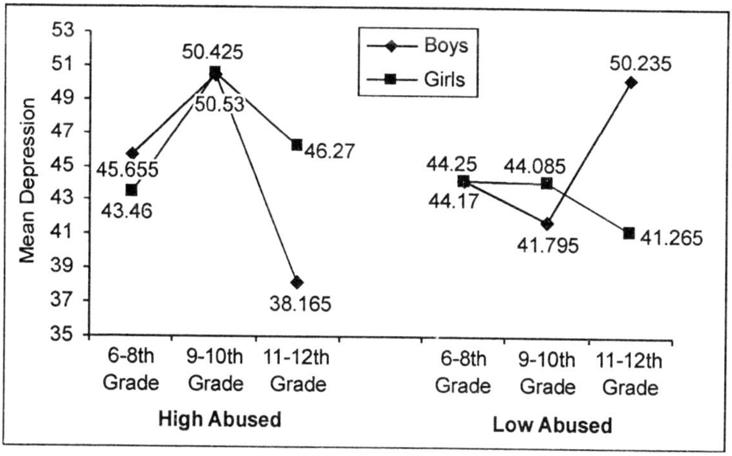

Fig. 3.87: Depression as a Function of Interaction of Gender, Grade and Child Abuse.

Table 3.27: Mean and SD of Anxiety by Type of School, Gender, Grade and Child Abuse

Variables		Government				Private			
		Boys		Girls		Boys		Girls	
		High Abused	Low Abused	High Abused	Low Abused	High Abused	Low Abused	High Abused	Low Abused
6-8th	Mean	41.96	38.43	41.96	38.43	40.13	35.27	35.26	39.03
Grade	SD	8.11	7.95	8.11	7.95	8.15	9.87	12.59	12.68
9-10th	Mean	42.3	40.64	42.2	37.04	43.63	39.15	44.2	41
Grade	SD	9.59	9.52	10.66	7.14	9.22	8.71	9.97	9.31
11-12th	Mean	40	44.38	41	40.13	34.5	40.8	44.03	35.24
Grade	SD	9.36	11.8	7.99	11.65	15.81	7.32	8.63	13.13

Further ANOVA analysis was done and results are presented in Table 3.28 and figures respectively. Results (Table 3.28 and Fig. 3.88) indicate that level of anxiety in students varied across grade and child abuse. High school level (9-10th class) students showed higher level of anxiety (M = 41.27) as compared to intermediate (11-12th class) students (M = 40.01) and Junior high school (6-8th class) students (M = 38.81). The significant impacts of grade and child abuse on anxiety level of students were found. As Figure (3.88) denotes, higher level of anxiety was found in high school (9th-10th grade) students than intermediate level and minimum anxiety was expressed by junior high school students.

Table 3.28: Summary of 2×2×3×2 ANOVA of Anxiety as a Function of Type of School, Gender, Grade and Child Abuse

Source	Sum of Square	df	Mean Square	F
Type of school (A)	209.765	1	209.765	2.311
Gender (B)	2.180	1	2.180	.024
Grade (C)	673.712	2	336.856	3.71**
Child abuse (D)	373.639	1	373.639	4.11**
A×B	119.457	1	119.457	1.316
A×C	517.201	2	258.601	2.84*
A×D	.662	1	.662	.007
B×C	4.549	2	2.275	.025
B×D	155.039	1	155.039	1.708
C×D	226.233	2	113.116	1.246
A×B×C	135.065	2	67.532	.744
A×B×D	10.152	1	10.152	.112
A×C×D	201.208	2	100.604	1.109
B×C×D	1027.320	2	513.660	5.66**
A×B×C×D	402.928	2	201.464	2.220

*P<0.05, **P<0.01

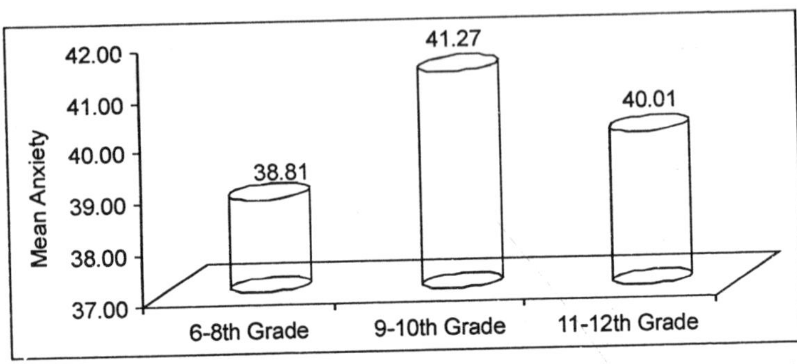

Fig. 3.88: Anxiety as a Function of Grade Level.

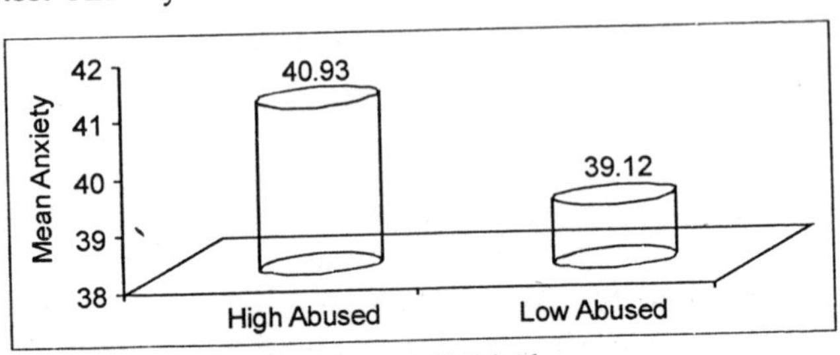

Fig. 3.89: Anxiety as a Function of Child Abuse.

Further, significant main effect of child abuse (Fig. 3.89) reveals that high abused children showed higher level of anxiety (M = 40.93) as compared to low abused children (M = 39.12).

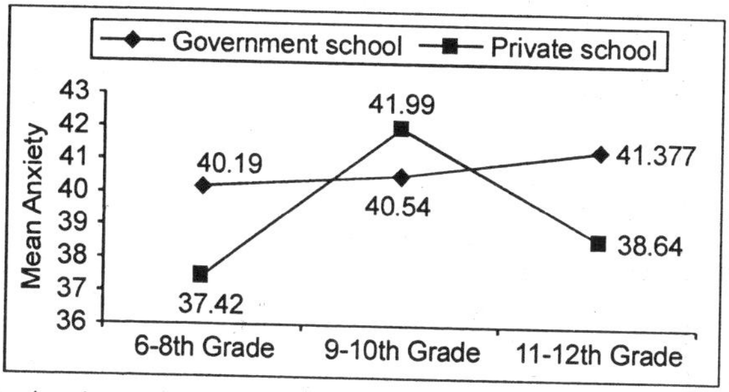

Fig. 3.90: Anxiety as a Function of Interaction of Type of School and Grade.

In addition, significant interaction effect of type of school x grade (Fig. 3.90) denotes that in case of private school, higher level of anxiety was found in high school students as compared to intermediate level and minimum was found in junior high school students. However, in government school students, anxiety level was found little more in intermediate level students than their high school and junior high school counterparts.

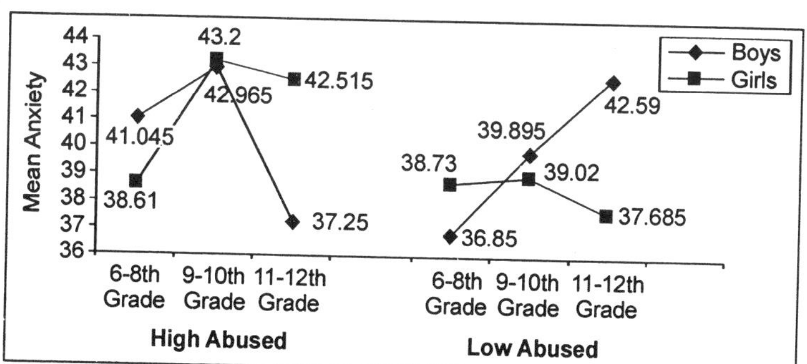

Fig. 3.91: Anxiety as a Function of Interaction of Gender, Grade and Child Abuse.

Again, significant interaction effect of gender x grade x child abuse (Table 3.28, Fig. 3.91) revealed that in case of abused group, anxiety level was found maximum in high school level students of both gender. Minimum anxiety was found in boys of intermediate level than junior high school students. In case of girls, intermediate level students showed greater anxiety than junior high school students.

D. Behavioural Consequences of Child Abuse in School

In order to ascertain the influence of child abuse on behavioural functioning (both positive and negative behaviours) of students, responses were obtained on Child Behaviour Checklist. Data were scored and treated statistically in terms of MANOVA, Bivariate and SMRA analyses. MANOVA results are reported in following section.

I. Positive Behaviours: The effects of type of school, gender, grade and child abuse in schools on positive behaviours i.e., social interaction, helping behaviour, disciplinary behaviour and study behaviour, Mean, S.D., Multiple analysis of variance (MANOVA) were calculated. Results are displayed in tables and figures and reported below.

(i) Social Interaction: Results displayed in Table 3.30 and Figure 3.92 and 3.93 indicate the significant effects of gender and grade on social interaction.

As displayed in Figure 3.92, girls showed superior social interaction (M = 21.15) as compared to boys (M = 20.08).

Again, main effect of grade was also found significant (Fig. 3.93), which revealed that poor interaction was displayed by high school (9-10th grade) students (M = 19.74) as compared to intermediate (11-12th grade) (M = 20.82) and junior high school (6-8th) students (M = 21.28). Interaction effects were also found significant.

Significant type of school x grade interaction effect (Fig. 3.94), suggested that in case of government school, high school (9-10th grade) students expressed lesser social interaction as compared to junior high school (6-8th grade) and intermediate level (11-12th grade) students. But reverse pattern was found in case of private school students. High school (9-10th grade) students showed little more social interaction behaviour than their intermediate level (11-12th grade) and junior high school level (6-8th grade) counterparts.

(ii) Helping Behaviour: Helping behaviour differed significantly across type of school, grade and child abuse (Table 3.30). Significant interaction effect of type of school x grade

Table 3.29: Mean and S.D. of Child Positive Behaviours by Type of School, Gender, Grade and Child Abuse in Schools

Dimension of Child Positive Behaviour			Government Schools				Private Schools			
			Boys		Girls		Boys		Girls	
			High Abused	Low Abused	High Abused	Low Abused	High Abused	Low Abused	High Abused	Low Abused
6-8th Grade	Social Interaction	Mean	22.53	21.05	22.82	22.14	20.58	19.67	19.94	21.47
		(SD)	(3.97)	(4.80)	(3.11)	(4.503)	(4.75)	(6.19)	(4.70)	(4.93)
	Helping Behaviour	Mean	28.47	31.21	30.10	31.96	26.70	27.63	26.88	28.88
		(SD)	(7.41)	(7.52)	(5.97)	(6.53)	(6.45)	(7.98)	(6.84)	(7.13)
	Discipline	Mean	27.88	27.53	29.22	28.21	27.47	26.17	25.56	29.25
		(SD)	(6.41)	(7.23)	(5.22)	(6.34)	(5.02)	(7.54)	(5.86)	(5.80)
	Study Behaviour	Mean	19.88	18.68	18.61	19.00	18.43	16.27	19.53	19.12
		(SD)	(4.15)	(6.29)	(4.22)	(5.44)	(4.29)	(4.43)	(5.63)	(4.25)
9-10th Grade	Social Interaction	Mean	18.19	18.93	17.60	19.00	20.15	21.40	22.02	20.70
		(SD)	(8.74)	(6.83)	(3.29)	(6.98)	(4.74)	(4.25)	(4.10)	(5.17)
	Helping Behaviour	Mean	22.89	31.50	24.80	26.85	28.83	29.58	31 48	27.77
		(SD)	(11.39)	(10.44)	(5.54)	(9.01)	(5.13)	(5.72)	(4.55)	(6.69)
	Discipline	Mean	23.30	29.00	25.60	26.60	28.13	28.68	28.45	27.84
		(SD)	(11.17)	(9.600	(9.29)	(8.15)	(5.44)	(5.90)	(5.44)	(7.16)
	Study Behaviour	Mean	15.26	17.29	18.20	16.58	17.85	18.43	17.64	16.71
		(SD)	(7.84)	(6.62)	(6.38)	(5.05)	(4.74)	(4.75)	(5.17)	(4.78)
11-12th Grade	Social Interaction	Mean	19.84	20.09	22.41	22.18	21.13	17.40	22.57	20.92
		(SD)	(6.87)	(4.21)	(3.98)	(3.92)	(3.48)	(4.16)	(3.97)	(4.16)
	Helping Behaviour	Mean	29.00	26.17	31.43	30.67	32.38	23.60	30.77	28.60
		(SD)	(7.38)	(7.49)	(5.16)	(5.23)	(3.81)	(5.17)	(5.19)	(4.99)
	Discipline	Mean	27.00	25.39	29.65	29.80	31.13	22.40	30.06	27.00
		(SD)	(7.34)	(6.67)	(5.07)	(4.59)	(4.58)	(5.03)	(5.01)	(4.27)
	Study Bchaviour	Mean	18.90	19.78	18.39	17.82	22.63	16.60	20.77	18.40
		(SD)	(6.61)	(5.63)	(4.44)	(4.62)	(7.03)	(3.20)	(5.65)	(2.65)

Table 3.30: Summary of 2×2×3×2 MANOVA of Positive Behaviours as a Function of Type of School, Gender, Grade and Child Abuse

Source of Variance	*Social Interaction*	*Helping Behaviour*	*Discipline*	*Study Behaviour*
Type of school (A)	.050	.078	.191	.568
Gender (B)	5.95*	2.987	3.83*	.021
Grade (C)	4.9**	1.423	.384	6.3**
Child abuse (D)	.846	.009	.684	4.7**
A×B	.113	.016	.506	.358
A×C	10.06**	9.80**	3.41*	1.780
A×D	.850	10.22**	3.92*	4.56*
B×C	2.010	1.843	1.748	.897
B×D	.308	.092	.770	.006
C×D	1.243	8.50**	5.68**	1.483
A×B×C	.120	.668	.157	2.704
A×B×D	.034	1.473	3.77*	1.981
A×C×D	2.115	2.618	4.29*	1.711
B×C×D	.873	4.92**	2.92*	2.458
A×B×C×D	.994	.112	.108	.696

*P<0.05, **P<0.01.

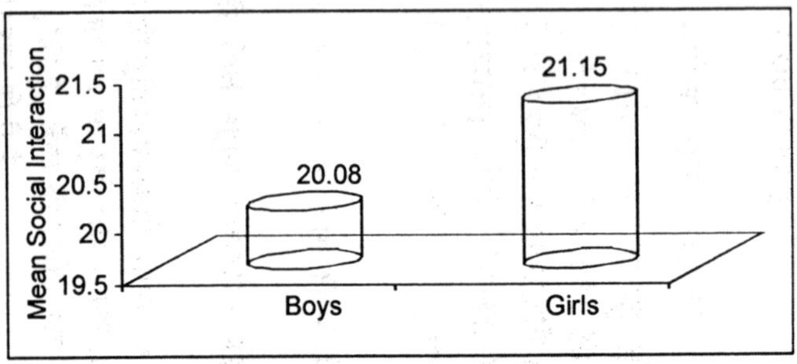

Fig. 3.92: Social Interaction as a Function of Gender.

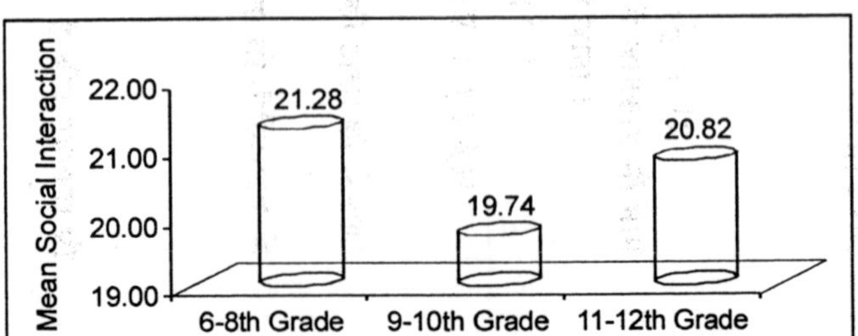

Fig. 3.93: Social Interaction as a Function of Grade.

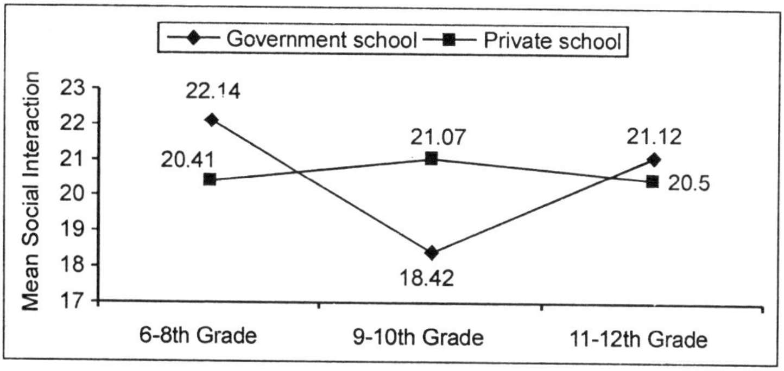

Fig. 3.94: Social Interaction as a Function of Interaction of Type of School and Grade.

(Fig. 3.95) revealed that junior high school (6-8th grade) students of government school expressed more helping behaviour than intermediate level (11-12th grade) students. Whereas, High school level (9-10th grade) students showed poor helping behaviour.

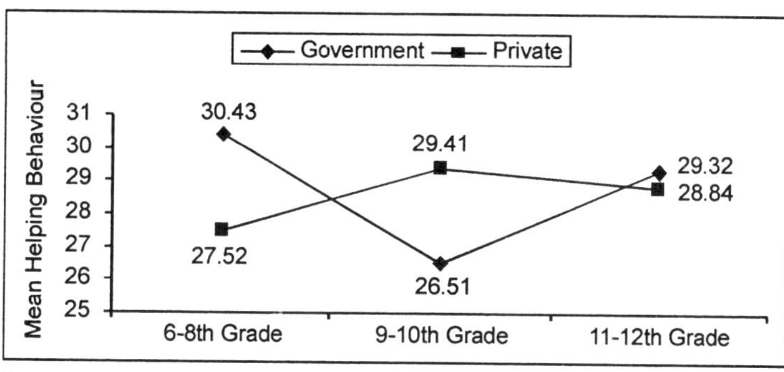

Fig. 3.95: Helping Behaviour as a Function of Interaction of Type of School and Grade.

But reverse pattern was found in private school students. High school level (9-10th grade) students expressed more helping behaviour than intermediate level students (11-12th grade) and junior high school level students (6-8th grade).

Further, significant interaction effect of type of school x child abuse (Fig. 3.96) revealed that high abused students of government school displayed lesser helping behaviour than their low abused counterparts. But in case of private schools, reverse pattern was

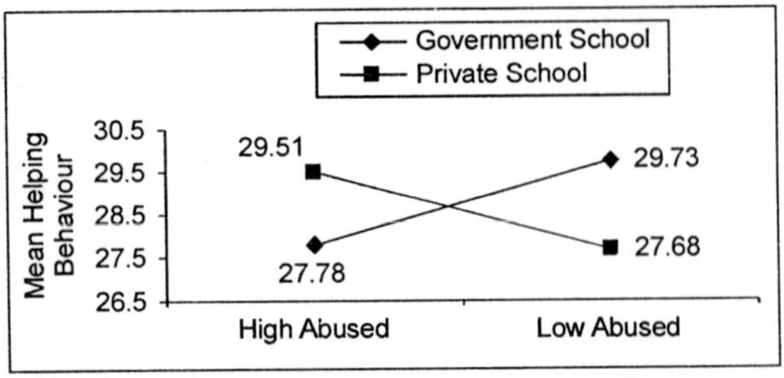

Fig. 3.96: Helping Behaviour as a Function of Interaction of Type of School and Child Abuse.

found. High abused group expressed more helping behaviour as compared to low abused group of students.

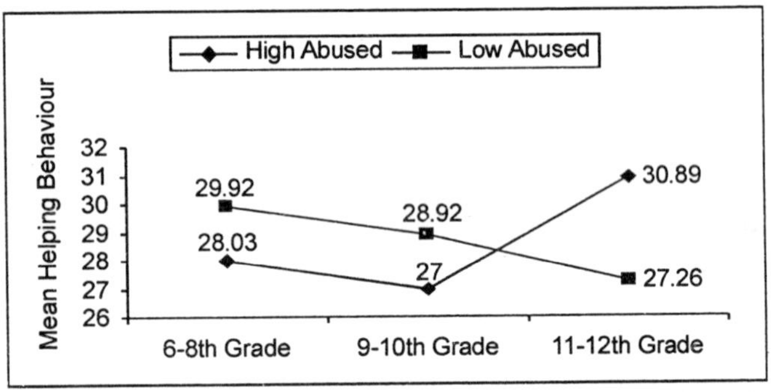

Fig. 3.97: Helping Behaviour as a Function of Interaction of Grade and Child Abuse.

Significant interaction effect of grade x child abuse (Fig. 3.97) denoted that in case of high abused group, helping behaviour was found lesser in high school level (9-10th grade) students as compared to junior high school students but it was found maximum in intermediate level students. However, in case of low abused group a decreasing pattern in helping was found with increasing grade level.

The interaction effect of gender x grade x child abuse was also found significant. Results (Fig. 3.98) suggest that in case of high abused group, boys and girls belonging to intermediate level (11-12th grade) expressed higher level of helping behaviour than their

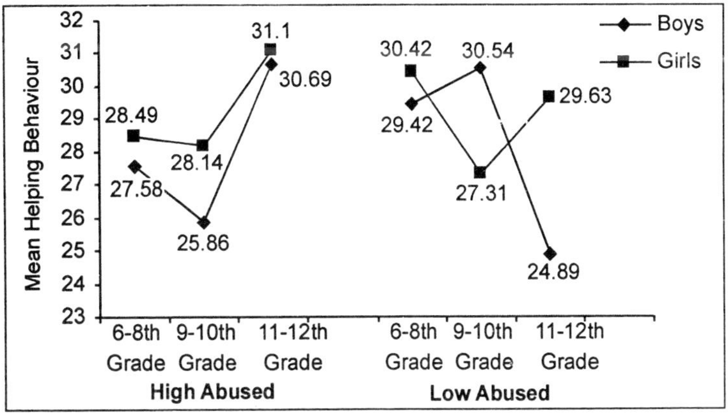

Fig. 3.98: Helping Behaviour as a Function of Interaction of Gender, Grade and Child Abuse.

junior high school (6-8th) and high school (9-10th grade) counterparts. A sharp decline was found in case of high school (9-10th grade) boys. Contrary to this, a different pattern was found in boys and girls of all three grades belonging to low abused group. High school level (9 10th grade) girl students expressed low level of helping behaviour as compared to junior high school level students (6-8th grade) and intermediate level students (11-12th grade). But, in case of high school level students (9-10th grade) boys expressed more helping behaviour as compared to junior high school level (6-8th grade) and minimum helping behaviour in intermediate level (11-12th grade) male students was identified.

(iii) Disciplinary Behaviour: The MANOVA results as reported in Table 3.30 and Figure 3.99 evinced the influence of gender on disciplinary behaviour in children.

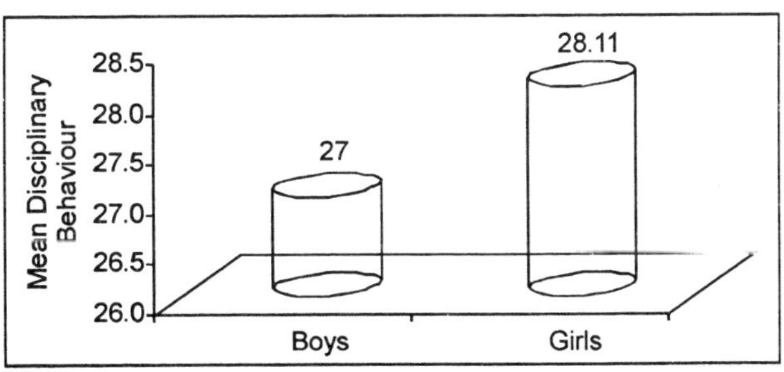

Fig. 3.99: Disciplinary Behaviour as a Function of Gender.

As Figure 3.99 displays, girls (M = 28.11) showed more disciplinary behaviour as compared to boys (M = 27.00).

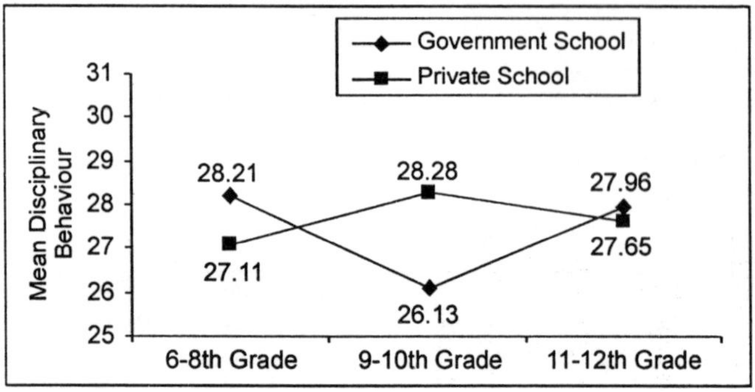

Fig. 3.100: Disciplinary Behaviour as a Function of Interaction of Type of School and Grade

Further, the significant interaction effect of type of school x grade (Fig. 3.100) revealed that in case of government school, junior high school and intermediate level students were found superior in disciplinary behaviour. But a sharp decline was found in case of high school level students (9-10th grade) of government schools. In case of private schools, reverse pattern was found. High school level students of private schools showed more disciplinary behaviour than intermediate level and junior high school students.

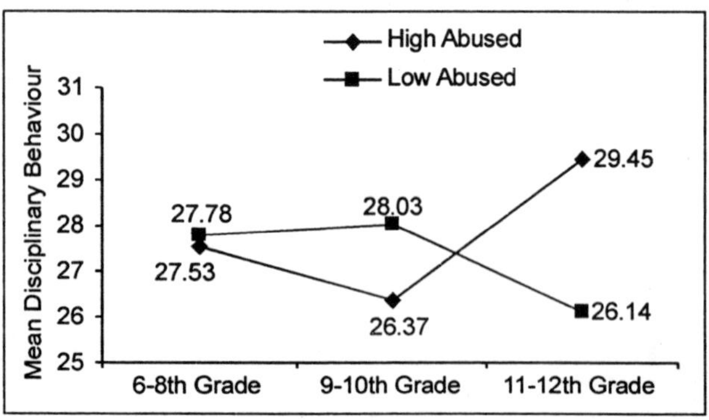

Fig. 3.101: Disciplinary Behaviour as a Function of Interaction of Grade and Child Abuse.

Significant interaction effect of grade x child abuse (Fig. 3.101)

revealed that in case of high abused group disciplinary behaviour was found minimum in high school students. Intermediate level students showed more discipline than junior high school students. Contrary to this, in case of low abused group, high school level students (9-10th grade) showed greater disciplinary behaviour than intermediate level students (11-12th grade) and junior high school level (6-8th grade) students.

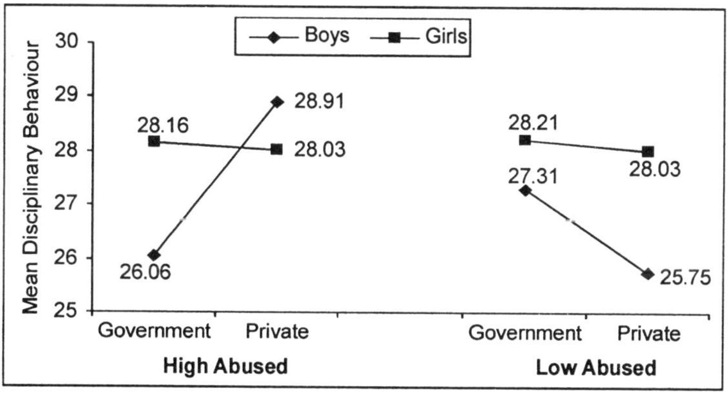

Fig. 3.102: Disciplinary Behaviour as a Function of Interaction of Type of School, Gender and Child Abuse.

Further, type of school x gender x child abuse interaction effect was also found significant (Fig. 3.102) which revealed that in case of high abused group, private school boys showed more disciplinary behaviour than government school boys. A very little difference was found between girls belonging to government and private schools. Contrary to this, in case of low abused group, boys of government schools showed more discipline than those of private schools. But little difference in disciplinary behaviour was found among girl students of government and private schools.

Similarly, the interaction effect of type of school x grade x child abuse was also found significant (Fig. 3.103), which suggests that in case of high abused group, high school level students (9-10th grade) of government schools were found worse on disciplinary behaviour. But junior high school students and intermediate level students showed superior level of disciplinary behaviour. Private school students of all three grades expressed almost equal level of discipline. Contrary to this, in low abused group, government school students showed disciplinary behaviour in increasing order

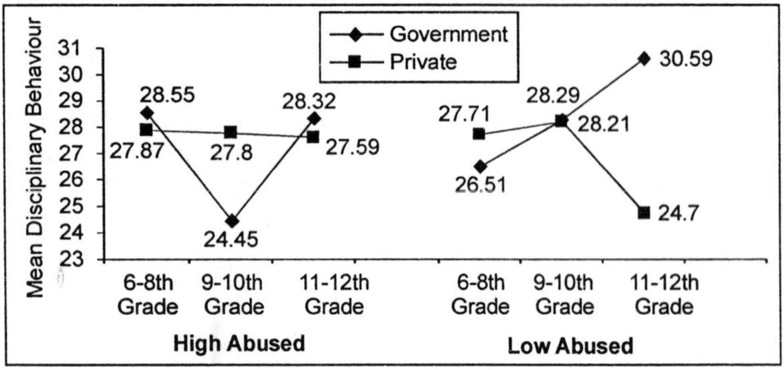

Fig. 3.103: Disciplinary Behaviour as a Function of Interaction of Type of School, Grade and Child Abuse.

across all three grades. However, a sharp decline was found in intermediate level (11-12th grade) students of private schools.

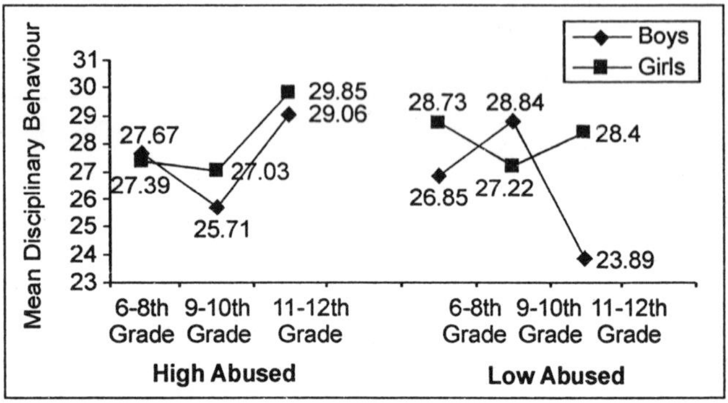

Fig. 3.104: Disciplinary Behaviour as a Function of Interaction of Gender, Grade and Child Abuse.

A significant interaction effect of gender x grade x child abuse (Fig. 3.104) denoted that in case of high abused group intermediate level students (both boys and girls) showed higher level of discipline. But a sharp decline was found in high school level (9-10th grade) boys than girls. Junior high school level students (both boys and girls) showed average level of discipline. Contrary to this, different pattern was identified in low abused group. High school level girls showed poor discipline than junior high school and intermediate level counterparts. But in case of boys, minimum discipline was found in intermediate level students than junior and high school level children.

(IV) Study Behaviour: The MANOVA results as reported in Table 3.31 evinced the significant influence of grade and child abuse on study behaviour (Figs. 3.105 and 3.106).

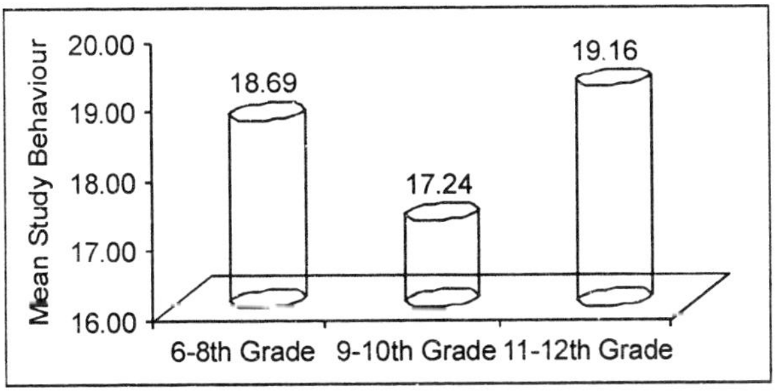

Fig. 3.105: Study Behaviour as a Function of Grade.

It is clear from Figure 3.105, intermediate level students showed superior study behaviour than junior high school students however, study behaviour was found very inferior in high school level students.

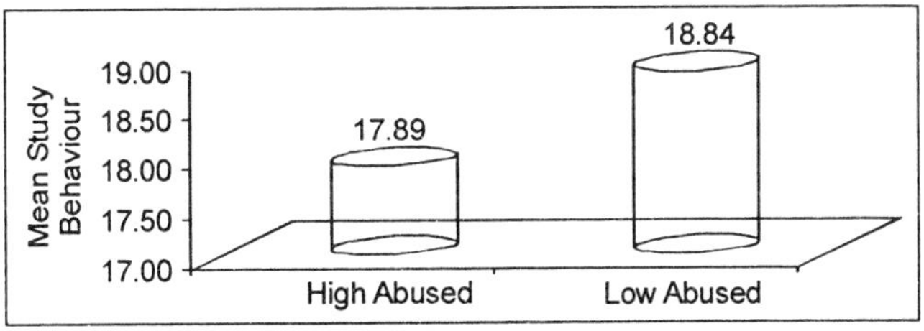

Fig. 3.106: Study Behaviour as a Function of Child Abuse.

The study behaviour also varied significantly by child abuse (Fig. 3.106). Results revealed that low abused group of students expressed better study behaviour (M = 18.84) than high abused students (M = 17.89).

Furthermore, significant interaction effect of type of school x child abuse (Fig. 3.107) revealed that government school students from both high and low abused group showed equal level of study behaviour. Besides this, in case of private school students high

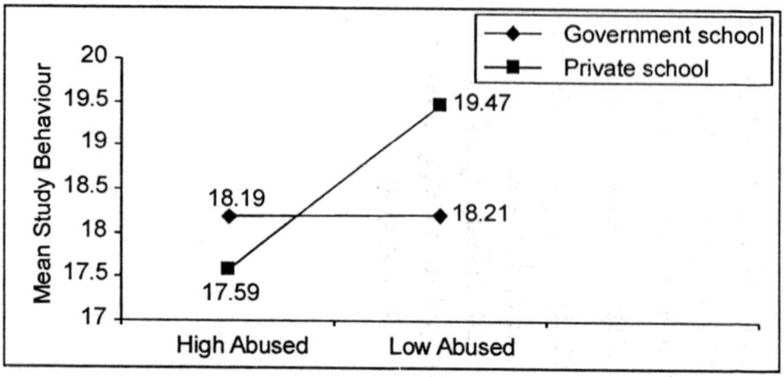

Fig. 3.107: Study Behaviour as a Function of Interaction of Type of School and Child Abuse.

abused group expressed very poor study behaviour than low abused group.

II. Negative Behaviours

The effects of type of school, gender, grade and child abuse in schools on negative behaviours i.e., aggressive behaviour, school bullying behaviour and non-compliance behaviour, Mean, S.D and, Multiple analysis of variance (MANOVA) were calculated and graphic representation of data were also done. Results are displayed in Tables 3.31 and 3.32 and figures and reported below.

(v) Aggressive Behaviour: Results displayed in Table 3.32 and Fig. 3.108 indicated that aggressive behaviour was significantly influenced by level of school abuse.

The significant main effect of child abuse in school setting (Fig. 3.108) displays that high abused children expressed greater level of aggressive behaviour (M = 8.36) as compared to low abused group (M = 6.80) of students.

In addition, type of school x grade interaction effect on aggressive behaviour was also found significant (Fig. 3.109), which denoted that in case of government schools, junior high school (6-8th grade) students expressed more aggressive behaviour than high school (9-10th) and intermediate level (11-12th grade) students. Contrary to this, intermediate level (11-12th grade) students of private schools showed more aggressive behaviour than junior high school (6-8th grade) and high school (9-10th grade) counterparts.

Table 3.31: Mean and S.D. of Child Negative Behaviours by Type of School, Gender, Grade and Child Abuse in Schools

Dimension of Child Negative Behaviour			*Government Schools*				*Private Schools*			
			Boys		*Girls*		*Boys*		*Girls*	
			High Abused	*Low Abused*	*High Abused*	*Low Abused*	*High Abused*	*Low Abused*	*High Abused*	*Low Abused*
6-8th Grade	Aggressive Behaviour	Mean	9.41	9.47	7.43	9.04	6.38	5.13	8.88	6.52
		(SD)	(5.36)	(7.01)	(5.35)	(6.37)	(4.56)	(3.64)	(5.96)	(5.51)
	Bullying	Mean	11.47	8.32	8.30	8.00	6.73	4.85	13.03	7.92
		(SD)	(7.18)	(5.57)	(6.71)	(5.09)	(5.73)	(4.05)	(7.95)	(8.23)
	Non-Compliance	Mean	11.18	9.95	8.64	9.04	8.88	7.23	11.41	9.05
		(SD)	(6.10)	(6.54)	(5.68)	(6.05)	(5.01)	(4.43)	(5.64)	(7.06)
9-10th Grade	Aggressive Behaviour	Mean	8.93	5.00	9.60	5.98	7.54	5.80	7.66	5.34
		(SD)	(8.64)	(3.91)	(5.32)	(4.48)	(4.06)	(4.63)	(4.43)	(4.31)
	Bullying Behaviour	Mean	9.96	4.36	14.40	6.54	8.93	6.73	9.02	5.90
		(SD)	(7.51)	(3.72)	(5.89)	(6.0)	(6.61)	(6.01)	(6.75)	(5.85)
	Non-Compliance	Mean	9.00	7.50	16.20	8.71	10.04	9.05	10.80	8.19
		(SD)	(6.19)	(4.04)	(3.56)	(5.42)	(3.88)	(3.55)	(4.75)	(5.01)
11-12th Grade	Aggressive Behaviour	Mean	7.65	9.13	5.92	6.29	11.13	8.00	9.74	5.92
		(SD)	(3.73)	(5.14)	(4.54)	(4.29)	(6.28)	(4.06)	(5.50)	(3.29)
	Bullying	Mean	8.00	8.04	6.05	6.62	15.25	8.40	12.86	7.40
		(SD)	(6.21)	(6.71)	(5.13)	(5.58)	(8.84)	(6.02)	(7.74)	(4.87)
	Non-Compliance	Mean	12.52	10.83	7.90	8.47	17.75	9.60	13.23	9.68
		(SD)	(6.39)	(5.17)	(5.03)	(4.93)	(4.46)	(4.27)	(5.41)	(4.18)

Table 3.32: Summary of 2×2×3×2 MANOVA as a Function of Type of School, Gender, Grade and Child Abuse for Negative Behaviours

Source of Variance	*Aggressive Behaviour*	*Bullying*	*Non-Compliance*
Type of school (A)	1.238	1.090	.795
Gender (B)	1.003	.565	.155
Grade (C)	1.815	.647	5.32**
Child abuse (D)	12.74**	37.81**	29.29**
A×B	1.075	.676	.106
A×C	5.83**	7.23**	4.86**
A×D	4.10**	1.562	2.231
B×C	2.84*	3.14*	7.78**
B×D	.101	.060	.001
C×D	3.08*	1.476	2.508
A×B×C	2.452	9.02**	7.70**
A×B×D	.354	.342	.617
A×C×D	3.93*	6.35**	5.14**
B×C×D	.145	.371	4.32**
A×B×C×D	.296	1.501	1.455

**P<.01,*P<.05.

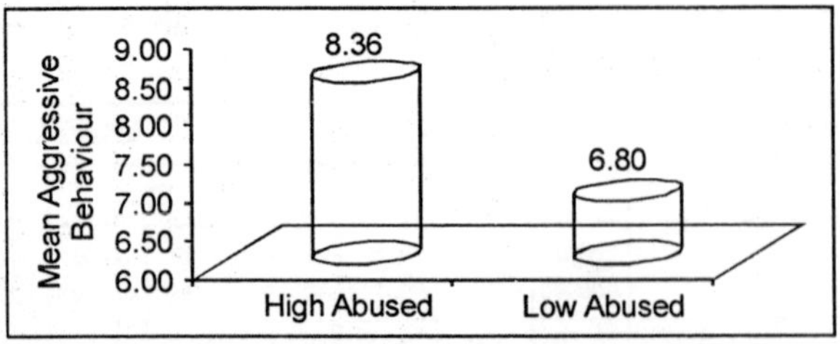

Fig. 3.108: Aggressive Behaviour as a Function of Child Abuse.

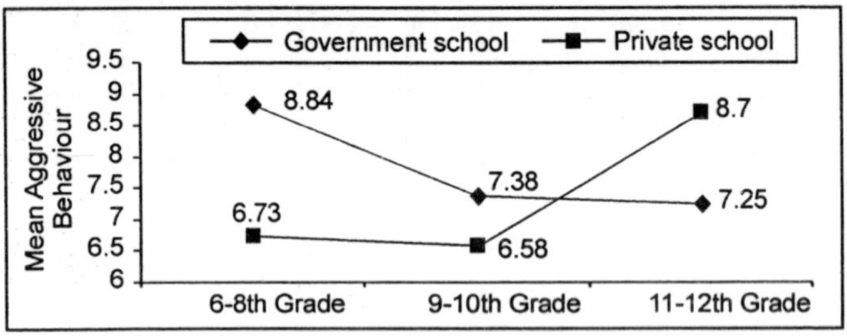

Fig. 3.109: Aggressive Behaviour as a Function of Interaction of Grade and Child Abuse.

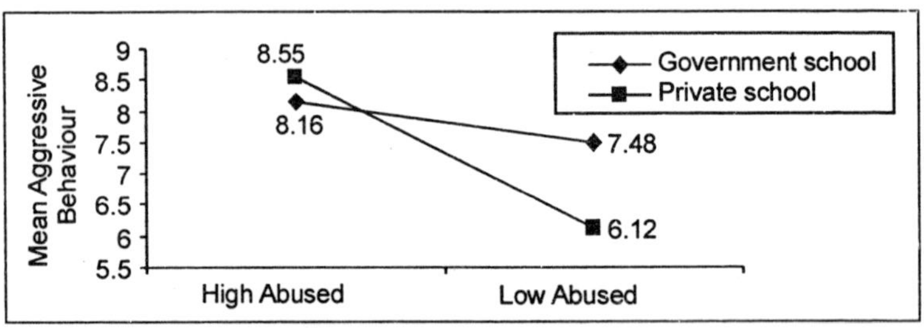

Fig. 3.110: Aggressive Behaviour as a Function of Interaction of Type of School and Child Abuse.

Furthermore, significant interaction effect of type of school x child abuse (Fig. 3.110) revealed that more aggressive behaviour was found in abused children of private schools than those of government school students. Contrary to this, minimum aggressive behaviour was shown by low/non-abused students of private schools and government schools counterparts.

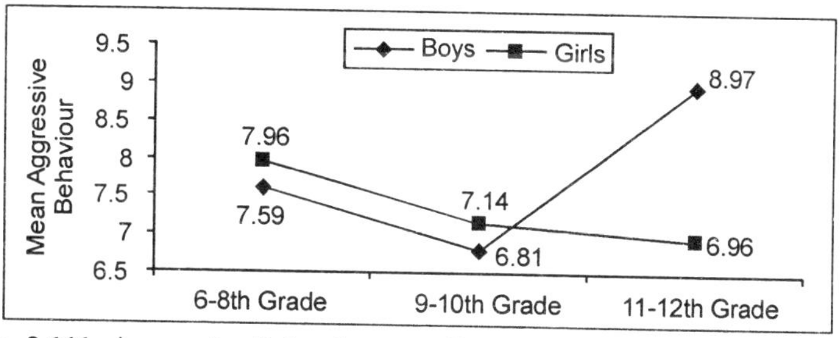

Fig. 3.111: Aggressive Behaviour as a Function of Interaction of Gender and Grade

Similarly, the significant interaction effect of gender x grade (Fig. 3.111) revealed that in case of girls decreasing pattern was found with increasing grade of students on aggressive behaviour. But in case of boys different pattern was identified, intermediate level students expressed higher aggressive behaviour than junior high school (6-8th grade) and high school level students.

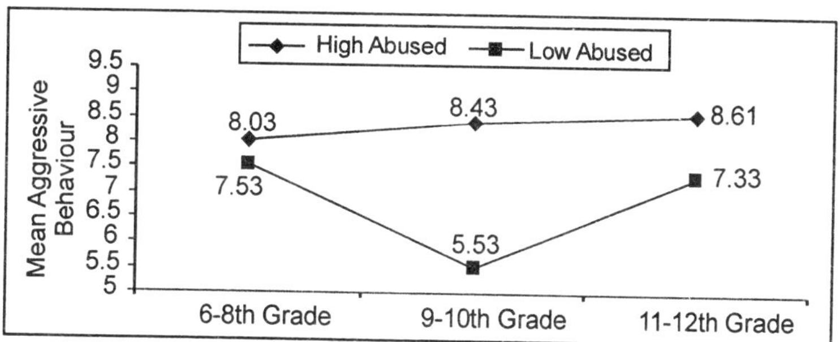

Fig. 3.112: Aggressive Behaviour as a Function of Interaction of Grade and Child Abuse.

Further, the significant interaction effect of grade x child abuse (Fig. 3.112) revealed that students belonging to high abused group expressed more aggressive behaviour with the increasing level of grades. But different pattern was found in case of low abused group. High school level students showed lesser aggressive behaviour than junior high school and intermediate level students.

Again, type of school x grade x child abuse interaction effect was found significant. Results (Fig. 3.113) indicate that in case of

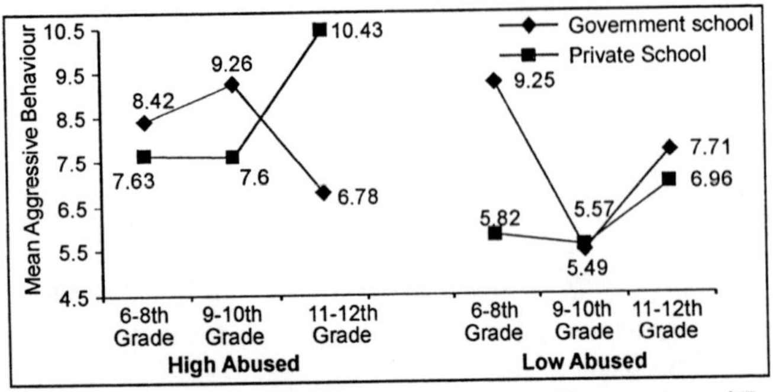

Fig. 3.113: Aggressive Behaviour as a Function of Interaction of Type of School, Grade and Child Abuse

abused group, maximum aggressive behaviour was found in intermediate level students, and lesser in junior high school students than high school counterparts of private schools, but in students of government schools reverse pattern was identified. In case of low abused group, aggressive behaviour was identified maximum in junior high school students than intermediate and high school level students of government schools but in case of private school students, aggressive behaviour was identified higher in intermediate level students than junior and high school level students.

(vi) Bullying Behaviour: Results indicated (Table 3.33) that bullying behaviour in children was significantly influenced by the level of abuse.

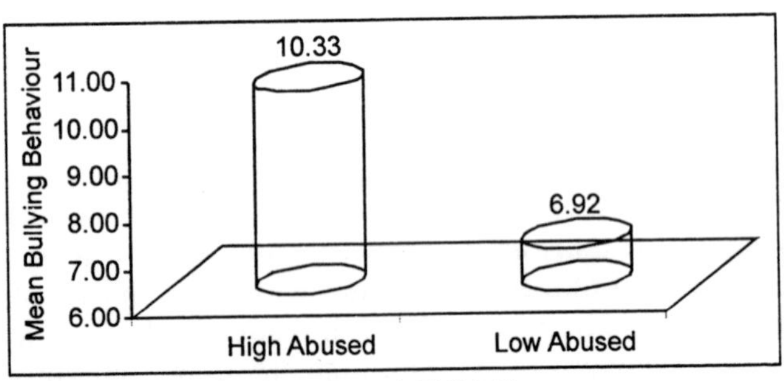

Fig. 3.114: Bullying as a Function of Child Abuse.

It is clear from (Fig. 3.114) results, that high abused group was found more involved in bullying behaviour (M = 10.33) as compared to low abused group of students (M = 6.92).

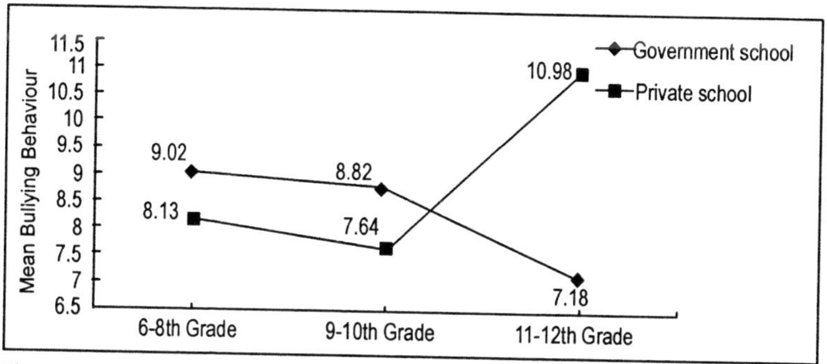

Fig. 3.115: Bullying as a Function of Interaction of Type of School and Grade.

The significant interaction effect of type of school x grade (Fig. 3.115) indicates that in case of government schools a decreasing pattern was found with the increasing level of grades in bullying behaviour. But reverse pattern was found in case of private schools. Maximum bullying behaviour was found in intermediate level students. But high school students showed lesser bullying behaviour than junior high school students.

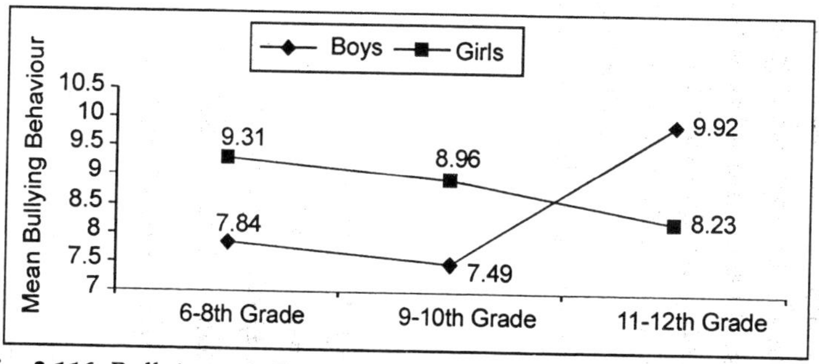

Fig. 3.116: Bullying as a Function of Interaction of Gender and Grade.

Similarly, the interaction effect of gender x grade on bullying behaviour was also found significant (Fig. 3.116) which denoted that male students of intermediate level showed far high bullying than junior high school (6-8th grade) and high school students (9-10th grade). Contrary to this, a decreasing pattern was found with the increasing level of grades in case of female students.

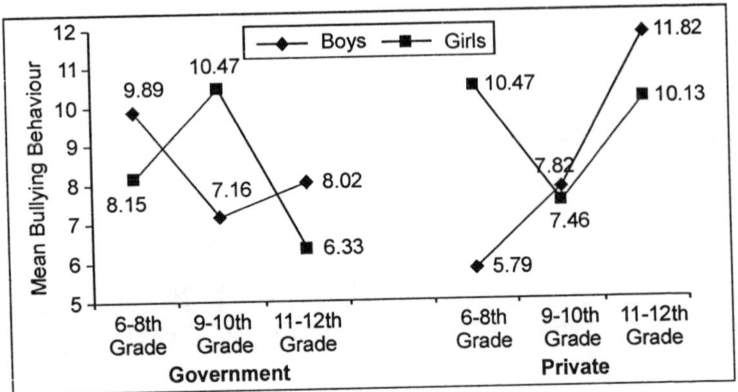

Fig. 3.117: Bullying as a Function of Interaction of Type of School, Gender and Grade.

Further, interaction effect of type of school x gender x grade on bullying behaviour was found significant. As Fig. 3.117 denotes, that in case of government schools, high school level (9-10th grade) girls expressed more bullying behaviour than junior high school (6-8th) and intermediate level (9-10th grade) girl students. But boys at junior high school (6-8th grade) showed more bullying behaviour than high school (9-10th grade) and intermediate level (11-12th grades) students. Contrary to this, in case of Private Schools, high school level (9-10th grade) girls showed lower level of bullying than junior high school (6-8th grade) and intermediate level (11-12th grades) girls. But in case of boys, maximum bullying behaviour was found in intermediate level students than their high school and junior high school counterparts.

Again type of school x grade x child abuse interaction effect was found significant. As Fig. 3.118 suggests, in case of high abused group, maximum bullying was found in intermediate level students of private school as compared to junior high school (6-8th grade) and high school level students, but reverse pattern was found in case of government school students of abused group. As high school students expressed more bullying behaviour than junior high school and minimum bullying was found in intermediate level students. Whereas, in case of low abused group, bullying was found lesser in all groups, more specifically, private school intermediate level students showed little higher bullying than junior high school and high school counterparts. But in case

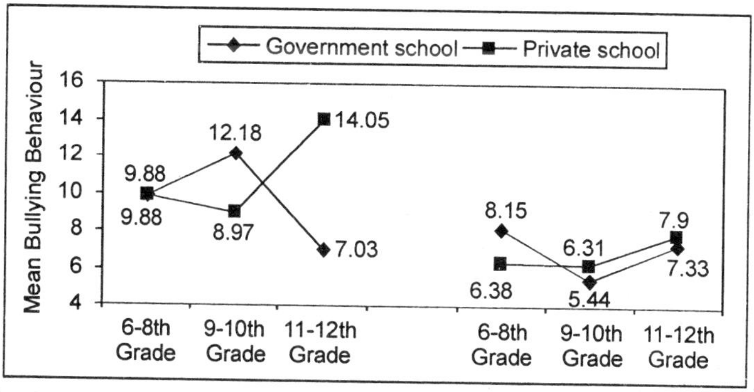

Fig. 3.118: Bullying as a Function of Interaction of Type of School, Grade and Child Abuse

of government schools junior high school students showed more bullying as compared to intermediate level and high school level students.

(vii) Non-Compliance: Results displayed in Table 3.34 indicate that Non-compliance behaviour was significantly influenced by grade of students and child abuse in schools.

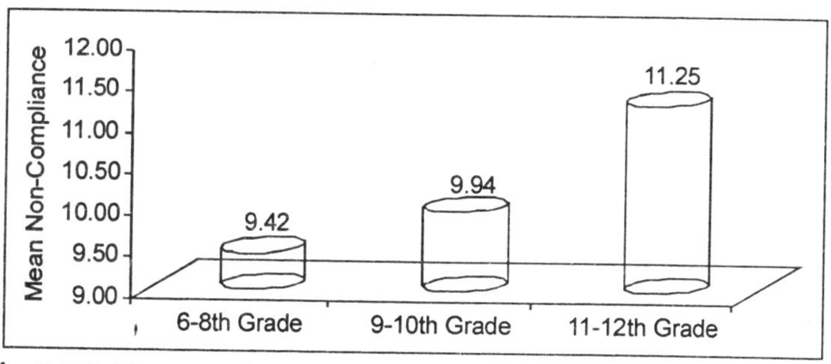

Fig. 3.119: Non-compliance as a Function of Grade.

The significant main effect of grade (Fig. 3.119) suggests that intermediate level (11-12th grade) students (M = 11.25) expressed higher level of non-compliance than high school (9-10th grade) students (M = 9.94) and junior high school (6-8th grade) students (M = 9.42).

The effect of child abuse was also found significant on non-compliance. As Fig. 3.120, indicates, high abused children displayed non-compliance more (M = 11.46) than those of low abused group (M = 8.94).

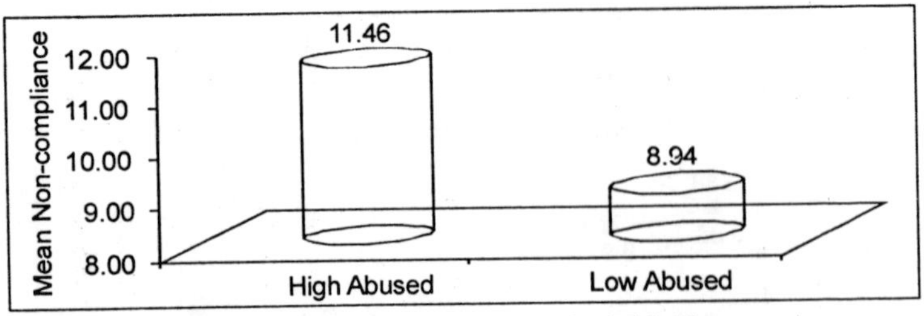

Fig. 3.120: Non-compliance as a Function of Child Abuse.

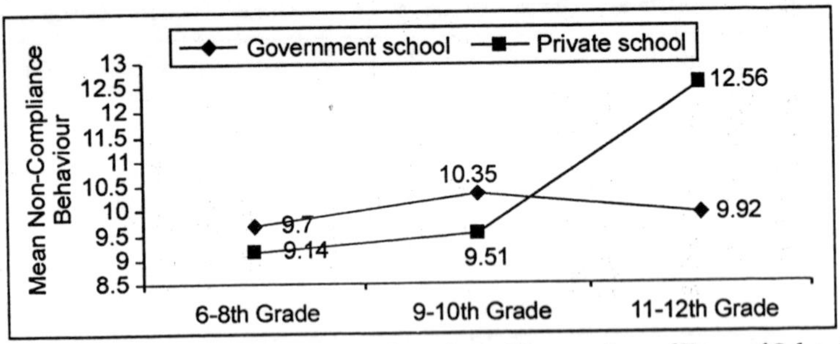

Fig. 3.121: Non-compliance as a Function of Interaction of Type of School and Grade.

Further, significant interaction of type of school x grade on non-compliance (Fig. 3.121) suggested that in case of government schools high school students expressed more non-compliance behaviour than intermediate level students and junior high school students. Contrary to this, in private schools, an increasing pattern was found with growing level of grades on non-compliance. Interestingly, intermediate level students showed more non-compliance than high school and junior high school students.

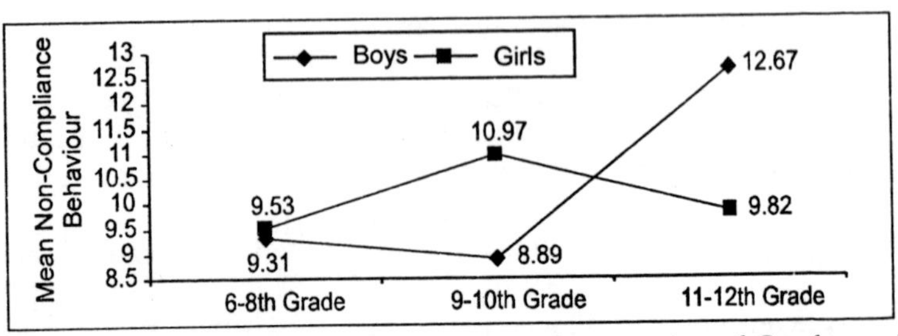

Fig. 3.122: Non-compliance as a Function of Interaction of Gender and Grade.

Similarly, the interaction effect of gender x grade on non-compliance behaviour was also found significant. Interaction graph (Fig. 3.122) denotes that intermediate level boys showed far more non-compliance behaviour than junior high school and high school level students. But in case of girls, non-compliance was found greater in high school students as compared to junior high school and intermediate level students.

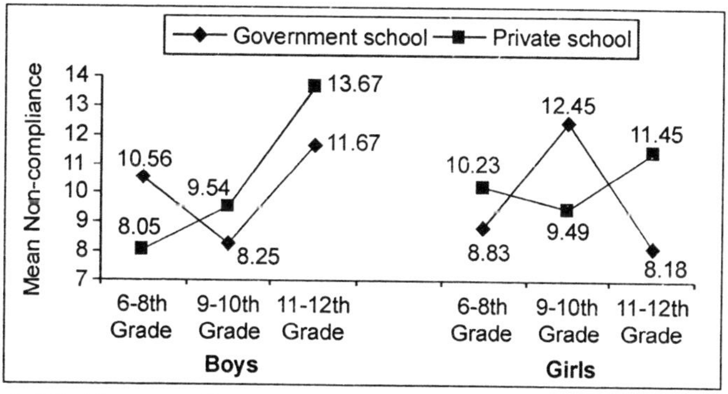

Fig. 3.123: Non-compliance as a Function of Interaction of Type of School, Gender and Grade.

The interaction effect of type of school x gender x grade on non-compliance was found significant. As Fig. 3.123 indicates that in case of boys, maximum non-compliance was shown by intermediate level students of private schools than high school and junior high school students, but in case of government school students, minimum non-compliance was shown by high school students than junior high school and intermediate level students. However, in case of girls, maximum non-compliance was shown by high school students of government school than junior high school and intermediate level students but reverse pattern was identified in case of private school girl students.

Furthermore, type of school x grade x level of abuse interaction effect was found significant. As Fig. 3.124 denotes, in case of high abused group, maximum non-compliance was expressed by intermediate level students and minimum by junior class students of government schools. But in case of private school students, high school students showed higher level of non-compliance than intermediate and junior high school level students. However, non-

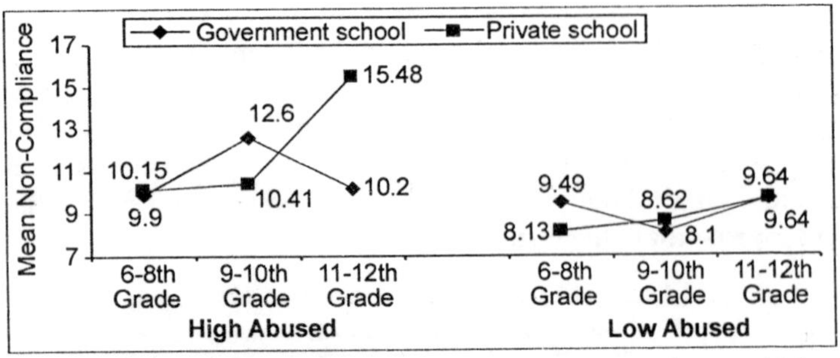

Fig. 3.124: Non-compliance as a Function of Interaction of Type of School, Grade and Child Abuse.

compliance was found at low level in low abused students. In this group, an increasing pattern of non-compliance was found with growing grades in case of private school students, but government school students of junior high school level showed more non-compliance than intermediate level and high school level students.

Results thus, proved that abusive experiences intensified the expression of negative behaviour in children and minimized the development of positive behaviour in different groups of students. However, it caused more damaging impact on high school (9-10th grade) students than junior high school and intermediate level students. The roles gender and type of school in behavioural functioning were partially supported.

Correlation Results

Correlations were computed to establish linkages between following factors:

1. Relationship between child abuse and cognitive variables;
2. Relationship between child abuse and motivational process;
3. Relationship between child abuse and affective process, and
4. Linkages between child abuse and children's behaviours.

1. Relationship between Child Abuse and Cognitive Processes

Correlations were computed between child abuse and forms of

cognitive processes (verbal ability, memory span and working memory). Results are depicted in Tables 3.33 and 3.34.

(a) Linkage between Child Abuse and Verbal Ability: Results shown in Table 3.33 indicate inverse relationship between child abuse and verbal ability.

Table 3.33: Correlation between Child Abuse and Verbal Ability

Dimensions of Child Abuse	*Word Analogy*	*Oppo-site Word*	*Word Simila-rity*	*Word Classi-fication*	*Sen-tence Com-pletion*	*Verbal Ability (as a whole)*
Physical Abuse	-.075*	-.134**	-.126**	-.048	-.085**	-.120**
Psychological Abuse	-.053	-.064*	-.080*	-.014	-.049	-.060
Sexual Abuse	-.159**	-.119**	-.129**	-.126**	-.153**	-.187**
Physical Neglect	-.089**	-.020	-.124**	-.094**	-.061*	-.121**
Emotional Neglect	-.086**	-.059	-.111**	-.037	-.013	-.095**
Educational Neglect	-.068*	-.017	-.077*	-.020	-.023	-.070*
Child Abuse (as a whole)	-.096**	-.082**	-.124**	-.056	-.070*	-.118**

*P< 0.05, **P<0.01.

Correlation results (Table 3.33) indicate that child abuse was found negatively correlated with verbal ability and its domains. Specifically, physical abuse was found negatively correlated with word analogy, opposite word, word similarity, sentence completion and verbal ability (as a whole). Psychological abuse was found negatively correlated with opposite words and word similarity. Sexual abuse was found negatively correlated with all domains of verbal ability and verbal ability as a whole. Similarly, physical neglect was found negatively correlated with world analogy, word similarity, word classification, sentence completion and verbal ability as a whole. Further, emotional neglect was found negatively correlated with word analogy, word similarity and verbal ability as a whole. Again, educational neglect was found negatively correlated with word analogy, word similarity and verbal ability as a whole. Similarly, child abuse (as a whole) was also found negatively correlated with word analogy, opposite word, word similarity, sentence completion and overall verbal ability.

These results suggest that child abuse has played negative role in the development of verbal ability in children.

Relationship between Child Abuse and Memory Process (Working Memory and Memory Span)

In order to determıne linkage between various types of child abuse and memory (working memory components and memory span) correlations were computed. Results are displayed in Table 3.34.

Table 3.34: Correlation between Child Abuse and Memory Processes (Working Memory and Memory Span)

Variables	*Working Memory and its components*				
Domains of Child Abuse	*Phonological Memory*	*Visuo-spatial working memory*	*Central Executive working memory*	*Overall working memory*	*Memory Span*
Physical abuse	–.211*	–.143	–.220*	–.259**	–.005
Psychological abuse	–.254**	–.226*	–.340**	–.369**	.061
Sexual abuse	–.016	–.092	–.120	–.088	–.043
Physical neglect	–.156	–.073	–.152	–.170	–.022
Emotional neglect	–.124	–.183*	–.180*	–.223*	–.036
Educational neglect	–.254**	–.176	–.212*	–.292**	–.022
Abuse as a whole	–.269	–.220*	–.305**	–.358**	–.019

*P< 0.05, **P<0.01.

Correlation results (Table 3.34) indicate that child abuse was found negatively correlated with working memory and its components. As Table 3.34 presents, physical abuse was found negatively related with phonological working memory, central executive, and overall working memory. Psychological abuse was also found inversely correlated with phonological working memory, visuo-spatial WM and overall WM. Likewise, emotional neglect was found inversely correlated with visuo-spatial WM, central executive WM and overall WM. Furthermore, educational neglect was also found inversely correlated with phonological WM, central executive WM and overall working memory. Abuse as a whole was found inversely correlated with phonological WM, visuo-spatial WM, central executive WM and overall working memory. Further, correlation results (Table 3.34) indicate negative but low correlation between forms of child abuse and memory span.

Relationship between Child Abuse and Motivational Process

In order to determine linkage between various types of child abuse and motivational process (Academic Achievement Motivation and Aspiration) correlations were computed. Results are shown in Table 3.35.

Table 3.35: Correlation between Child Abuse and Motivational Factors

Dimensions of Child abuse	*Academic Achievement Motivation*	*Aspiration*
Physical Abuse	-.034	-.122**
Psychological Abuse	-.024	-.112**
Sexual Abuse	-.128**	-.071*
Physical Neglect	-.080*	-.060
Emotional Neglect	-.072*	-.079*
Educational Neglect	-.021	-.108**
Child Abuse (as a whole)	-.060	-.120**

*P< 0.05, **P<0.01.

Correlation result (Table 3.35) indicate that child abuse was found negatively correlated with motivational processes (Academic Achievement and Aspiration). As Table 3.35 indicates physical abuse was negatively correlated with aspiration. Psychological abuse was also negatively associated with aspiration. Sexual abuse was found negatively correlated with academic achievement and aspiration. Similarly, physical neglect was negatively related with academic achievement. Emotional neglect was negatively linked with academic achievement and aspiration. Further, educational neglect was found negatively correlated with aspiration. Child abuse as a whole was found negatively associated with aspiration level.

Relationship between Child Abuse and Affective Process

In order to determine linkage between various types of child abuse and affective process (Depression and Anxiety) correlations were computed. Results are displayed in Table 3.36.

Correlation results (Table 3.36) indicate that child abuse was found negatively correlated with affective process and its domains. Specifically, psychological abuse showed positive association with

Table 3.36: Correlation between Child Abuse and Affective Process

Dimensions of Child abuse	*Depression*	*Anxiety*
Physical Abuse	.048	.025
Psychological Abuse	.102**	.093**
Sexual Abuse	.108**	.097**
Physical Neglect	.038	.071*
Emotional Neglect	.112**	.137**
Educational Neglect	.113**	.100**
Child Abuse (as a whole)	.111**	.107**

*P< 0.05, **P<0.01.

depression and anxiety. Similarly, sexual abuse was positively associated with depression and anxiety. Physical neglect was found positively associated with depression. Emotional neglect was found positively linked with depression and anxiety. Further, educational neglect was found positively correlated with depression and anxiety. Child abuse as a whole was also found positively linked with depression and anxiety.

Linkages between Child Abuse and Children's Behaviour

In order to determine linkage between various types of child abuse and children's behaviour correlations were computed. Results are depicted in Table 3.37.

Table 3.37: Correlation between Child Abuse and Students' Behaviour

Dimensions of Child abuse	*Positive Behaviours*				*Negative Behaviours*		
	Social Interaction	*Helping Behaviour*	*Discipline*	*Study Behaviour*	*Aggressive Behaviour*	*Bullying*	*Non-Compliance*
Physical Abuse	-.028	-.012	-.005	-.057	.111**	.109**	.089**
Psychological Abuse	-.083*	-.079*	-.051	-.108**	.069*	.082*	.074*
Sexual Abuse	-.004	-.028	-.018	-.101**	.148**	.201**	.131**
Physical Neglect	-.028	-.042	-.036	-.123**	.095**	.170**	.151**
Emotional Neglect	-.090**	-.070*	-.066*	-.142**	.087**	.129**	.104**
Educational Neglect	-.076*	-.061	-.052	-.132**	.090**	.122**	.076*
Child Abuse (as a whole)	-.069*	-.056	-.044	-.137**	.121**	.159**	.121**

*P< 0.05, **P < 0.01.

Correlation results (Table 3.37) indicate that child abuse was found closely linked with various behaviour patterns of students.

Specifically, physical abuse was found positively associated with aggressive behaviour, bullying and non-compliance. Psychological abuse was found negatively related with social interaction, helping behaviour and study behaviour but positively linked with aggressive behaviour, bullying and non-compliance. Sexual abuse was negatively linked with study behaviour but positively related with aggressive behaviour, bullying and non-compliance. Physical neglect was found negatively associated with study behaviour but positively related with aggressive behaviour, bullying and non-compliance. Further, emotional neglect was found negatively related with social interaction, helping behaviour, discipline and study behaviour, but positively linked with aggressive behaviour bullying and non-compliance. Educational neglect was found negatively correlated with social interaction and study behaviour but positively related with aggressive behaviour, bullying and non -compliance. Finally, child abuse as a whole was found negatively related with social interaction and study behaviour. However, aggressive behaviour, bullying and non-compliance were found positively linked with child abuse (as a whole).

C. Stepwise Multiple Regression Analysis

The correlations, reported in earlier section of the results showed that forms of child abuse were found significantly correlated with cognitive, motivational, affective and behavioural functioning of children. Hence, it was considered relevant to go for stepwise multiple regression (SMRA) analysis to determine the relative contributions of forms of child abuse to criterion variables. Regression results are displayed in Tables and interpreted in the following section.

1. Prediction of Cognitive Processes from Child Abuse

Based on the perusal of correlation results, it was considered to go for stepwise multiple regression analysis (SMRA) to determine the relative contributions of child abuse to verbal abilities, working memory and memory span. The findings of this analysis are in order:

Table 3.38: Stepwise Multiple Regression Analysis for Verbal Ability and its Domains on the Child Abuse

(Predictors) Dimensions of Child Abuse	*R*	R^2	R^2 *Change*	*Beta* β	*F Value*
	(Criterion Variable)				
	Word Analogy				
Sexual Abuse	.159	.025	.025	-.159	25.66*
Opposite Word					
Physical Abuse	.134	.018	.018	-.134	18.037**
Educational Neglect	.148	.022	.004	.098	11.01**
Sexual Abuse	.169	.028	.007	-.102	9.57**
Word Similarity					
Sexual Abuse	.129	.017	.017	-.089	16.625**
Physical Abuse	.149	.022	.005	-.084	11.08**
Word Classification					
Sexual Abuse	.126	.016	.016	-.173	15.847**
Psychological Abuse	.143	.021	.005	.083	10.33**
Sentence Completion					
Sexual Abuse	.153	.023	.023	-.205	23.480**
Emotional Neglect	.173	.030	.007	.096	15.15**
Verbal Ability (as a whole)					
Sexual Abuse	.187	.035	.035	-.187	35.69**

**P<0.01, *P<0.05.

Prediction of Verbal Ability

(i) Word Analogy: As Table 3.38 denotes, verbal ability (word analogy) was predicted by sexual abuse. Sexual abuse has contributed negatively ($\beta = -.159$, $R^2 = .025$) and it explained 2.5 per cent of variance to word analogy.

(ii) Opposite Word: Results (Table 3.38) further indicate that verbal ability (opposite word) was negatively explained by three factors; physical abuse was found the strongest predictor of opposite word, which contributed maximum negatively ($\beta = -.134$, $R^2 = .018$) followed by educational neglect ($\beta = -.098$, $R^2 = .004$) and sexual abuse ($\beta = -.102$, $R^2 = .007$). Though independently, physical abuse explained 1.8 per cent of variance followed by sexual abuse and educational neglect, i.e. 0.7 per cent and

0.4 per cent variance to criterion variable respectively. But the composite contribution of physical, sexual abuse and educational neglect was 2.8 per cent variance in opposite word.

(iii) Word Similarity: Results (Table 3.38) further indicate that word similarity was negatively predicted by sexual abuse ($\beta = .089, R^2 = .017$) and physical abuse ($\beta = -.084, R^2 = .005$). Where, sexual abuse contributed 1.7 per cent variance independently followed by physical abuse 0.5 per cent variance in word similarity but composite contribution was 2.2 per cent variance to criterion variable.

(iv) Word Classification: Table 3.38 further, evinced that sexual abuse ($\beta = -.173, R^2 = .016$) and psychological abuse ($\beta = -.083, R^2 = .005$) have significantly negatively predicted to word classification. Independently sexual abuse contributed 1.6 per cent followed by psychological abuse which contributed 0.5 per cent variance but composite contribution was 2.1 per cent to word classification.

(v) Sentence Completion: Further, regression results evinced (Table 3.38) that sentence completion was significantly explained by sexual abuse ($\beta = -.205, R^2 = .023$) and emotional neglect ($\beta = -.096, R^2 = .007$). Sexual abuse independently contributed 2.3 per cent variance in criterion variable (sentence completion) followed by emotional neglect which explained 0.7 per cent variance but composite contribution was 3.0 per cent to sentence completion.

(vi) Verbal Ability: Table 3.38 again denotes that sexual abuse has significantly predicted verbal ability (as a whole) ($\beta = -.187, R^2 = .035$) and explained 3.5 per cent of variance to criterion variable.

2. Prediction of Affective Processes from Child Abuse

Again Regression analysis was done to determine contribution of child abuse to affective process i.e., depression and anxiety.

As Table 3.39 denotes, depression was predicted by only educational neglect. Educational neglect has contributed positively ($\beta = .115, R^2 = .013$) and explained 1.3 per cent of variance to depression.

It is also clear from regression results (Table 3.39) that anxiety was predicted by emotional neglect. Emotional neglect contributed positively ($\beta = .137, R^2 = .019$) and explained 1.9 per cent of variance to criterion variable.

Table 3.39: Stepwise Multiple Regression Analysis for Depression and Anxiety on to the Child Abuse

(Predictors) Dimensions of Child Abuse	*R*	*R^2*	*R^2 Change*	*Beta β*	*F Value*
	(Criterion Variable)				
	Depression				
Educational Neglect	.115	.013	.013	.115	11.78**
	Anxiety				
Emotional Neglect	.137	.019	.019	.137	16.919**

**P < 0.01.

3. Prediction of Motivational Processes from Child Abuse

Regression results (Table 3.40) denote that motivational factors i.e., academic achievement motivation and aspiration were predicted by sexual and physical abuse.

Table 3.40: Step-wise Multiple Regression Analysis for Academic Achievement Motivation and Aspiration on to the Child Abuse

(Predictors) Dimensions of Child Abuse ↓	*R*	*R^2*	*R^2 Change*	*Beta β*	*F Value*
	(Criterion Variable)				
	Academic Achievement Motivation				
Sexual Abuse	.128	.016	.016	–.128	14.46**
	Aspiration				
Physical Abuse	.122	.015	.015	–.122	13.17**

**P < 0.01.

Results (Table 3.40), indicate that academic achievement motivation was negatively predicted by only sexual abuse ($\beta = -.128$, $R^2 = .016$) which explained 1.6 per cent of variance to academic achievement motivation.

It is also clear from regression results (Table 3.35) that aspiration was predicted by physical abuse, which has contributed negatively ($\beta = -.122$, $R^2 = .015$) and explained 1.5 per cent of variance to aspiration (Table 3.40).

4. Prediction of Behavioural Functioning from Child Abuse

Stepwise multiple regression analysis (SMRA) was done to examine the relative contribution of child abuse to children's behaviour and obtained results are furnished in Table 3.41.

Table 3.41: Stepwise Multiple Regression Analysis for Behavioural Functioning on to the Child Abuse

Predictors	*Criterion Variables*				
Dimensions of Child Abuse	*R*	R^2	R^2 *Change*	*Beta* β	*F Value*
	Social Interaction				
Emotional Neglect	.089	.008	.008	.133	7.394**
Sexual Abuse	.111	.012	.004	-.079	5.69**
Helping Behaviour					
Psychological Abuse	.078	.007	.007	.136	5.640*
Sexual Abuse	.116	.014	.007	-.104	6.31**
Discipline					
Emotional Neglect	.065	.004	.004	.109	3.923*
Sexual Abuse	.092	.008	.004	-.079	3.89*
Study Behaviour					
Emotional Neglect	.142	.020	.020	.142	18.97***
Aggressive Behaviours					
Sexual Abuse	.148	.022	.022	.148	20.530
Bullying Behaviour					
Sexual Abuse	.201	.041	.041	.185	38.960**
Physical Neglect	.214	.046	.005	.118	22.13**
Psychological Abuse	.225	.051	.005	-.087	16.28**
Non-Compliance					
Physical Neglect	.152	.023	.023	.152	21.87**

*P < 0.05, **P < 0.01.

(i) Social Interaction: As Table 3.41 denotes, social interaction was predicted by emotional neglect (β = .133, R^2 = .008) and sexual abuse (β = –.079, R^2 = .004). Though independently, emotional neglect explained 0.8 per cent of variance followed by sexual abuse which explained 0.4 per cent variance but composite contribution was 1.2 per cent variance to criterion variable.

(ii) Helping Behaviour: Results (Table 3.41) indicated that helping behaviour was positively explained by psychological abuse ($\beta = .136, R^2 = .007$) but negatively explained by sexual abuse ($\beta = -.104, R^2 = .007$). Though independently, psychological abuse explained 0.7 per cent of variance followed by sexual abuse that also explained 0.7 per cent but composite contributions of both factors were 1.4 per cent to criterion variable.

(iii) Discipline: Results (Table 3.41) further indicate that discipline was negatively predicted by emotional neglect ($\beta = .109, R^2 = .004$) and sexual abuse ($\beta = -.079, R^2 = .004$). Where, emotional neglect contributed 0.04 per cent followed by sexual abuse (0.04% variance) to discipline, however composite contribution was .08 per cent to discipline.

(iv) Study Behaviour: As Table 3.41 denotes, study behaviour was predicted by emotional neglect ($\beta = .142, R^2 = .02$) which explained 2 per cent of variance in criterion variable.

(v) Aggressive Behaviour: Results (Table 3.41) further indicate that aggressive behaviour in children was predicted by sexual abuse ($\beta = .148, R^2 = .022$), which contributed 2.2 per cent variance to aggressive behaviour.

(vi) Bullying Behaviour: Results (Table 3.41) indicate that bullying behaviour was positively predicted by sexual abuse ($\beta = .185, R^2 = .041$), physical neglect ($\beta = .118, R^2 = .005$) and psychological abuse ($\beta = -.087, R^2 = .005$). Though independently, sexual abuse explained 4.1 per cent of variance followed by physical neglect which explained 0.5 per cent and psychological abuse contributed 0.5 per cent variance to criterion variable but composite contribution of these factors was 5.1 per cent variance.

Non-Compliance: Results (Table 3.41) further indicate that non-compliance was predicted by physical neglect ($\beta = .152, R^2 = .023$) which contributed 2.3 per cent variance to non-compliance behaviour.

Results have proved the adverse impact of child abuse in schools on students' behaviour.

SECTION-5

Impact on Personality and Health Status of Students

Fifth objective of the study is to investigate the impact of child abuse in schools on personality and health status of students. Students' personality and health status were assessed with the help of standardized measures. Firstly, personality related results are reported followed by findings related to health status.

Set A: Impact on Personality

Students' personality was assessed in relation to school setting, school type, grade, gender and level of child abuse. Scores obtained on CPQ and HSPQ (Personality Questionnaires) from different groups of students were transformed into standard scores then, scores were treated statistically in terms of Means and SD. In order to determine the impact of school setting (Rural and Urban) gender and level of abuses, multiple analysis of variance (MANOVA) was computed. Results are displayed in Table 3.42 and 3.43 and figures (Set-A). Similarly, to determine the role of type of school (Government and Private), grade (6-8 Grades and 9-10 Grades) and child abuse on personality pattern of children another set of MANOVA analysis was done (Set-B). Results are displayed in Tables 3.44 and 3.45 and Figures. Results are interpreted in following section.

A. Students' Personality as a Function of School Setting, Gender and Child Abuse in Schools

In order to determine the effect of school setting (Rural-Urban), gender and level of abuses on personality of students Mean, S.D. and Multiple analysis of variance (MANOVA) were computed. Table 3.42 shows Mean and SD of dimensions of personality scores and summary of MANOVA are displayed in Table 3.43.

As Table 3.42 shows, different group of students varied on personality patterns. Further, MANOVA analysis was done to examine the impact of child abuse, school setting and gender. Results are displayed in Table 3.43.

Present results (Table 3.43 and Fig. 3.125) denote a clear-cut variation on most of the dimensions of personality pattern of students. It is clear from the results that students of both school settings differed significantly on ten dimensions of personality (Fig. 3.125). Apart from this, both boys and girls significantly varied on four dimensions of personality (Fig. 3.126).

Table 3.42: Mean and S.D. of Dimensions of Personality by Child Abuse, School Setting and Gender

Dimensions of Personality	*School Setting (Rural/Urban)*		*Boys*		*Girls*	
			Level of Abuse		*Level of Abuse*	
			High	*Low*	*High*	*Low*
A	Urban	Mean (S.D.)	2.89 (1.47)	3.38 (1.50)	3.93 (1.80)	3.85 (1.86)
	Rural	Mean (S.D.)	3.66 (.778)	3.53 (.833)	2.54 (.687)	2.66 (1.35)
B	Urban	Mean (S.D.)	2.76 (1.84)	4.35 (2.32)	2.75 (1.63)	3.11 (2.28)
	Rural	Mean (S.D.)	2.25 (.753)	2.13 (.743)	2.36 (1.12)	2.19 (1.07)
C	Urban	Mean (S.D.)	3.84 (1.96)	4.45 (1.85)	4.04 (1.77)	3.98 (1.99)
	Rural	Mean (S.D.)	4.16 (1.11)	3.33 (1.29)	3.36 (1.56)	3.00 (1.30)
D	Urban	Mean (S.D.)	5.50 (1.98)	6.05 (1.85)	5.11 (1.86)	5.45 (1.81)
	Rural	Mean (S.D.)	5.16 (1.02)	5.13 (1.30)	4.09 (1.81)	3.76 (.995)
E	Urban	Mean (S.D.)	5.20 (1.79)	5.28 (1.80)	4.95 (1.59)	5.54 (1.63)
	Rural	Mean (S.D.)	5.25 (1.54)	4.86 (1.55)	5.18 (1.32)	5.61 (1.35)
F	Urban	Mean (S.D.)	4.05 (1.86)	4.65 (2.43)	4.68 (2.07)	4.27 (2.11)
	Rural	Mean (S.D.)	2.75 (1.48)	3.13 (1.18)	2.45 (.820)	2.66 (1.06)
G	Urban	Mean (S.D.)	3.26 (1.76)	4.45 (2.48)	3.26 (2.28)	3.01 (2.15)
	Rural	Mean (S.D.)	2.75 (1.13)	2.46 (1.50)	1.54 (.934)	`.90 (1.09)
H	Urban	Mean (S.D.)	3.79 (2.18)	4.66 (2.45)	4.57 (2.69)	4.15 (2.30)
	Rural	Mean	2.41	2.40	2.27	1.90
		(S.D.)	(.792)	(1.18)	(1.34)	(1.17)
I	Urban	Mean	3.84	4.56	4.84	4.42
		(S.D.)	(1.70)	(1.95)	(1.99)	(1.75)
	Rural	Mean	5.58	5.53	3.45	4.38
		(S.D.)	(1.08)	(.915)	(1.63)	(1.59)

(Contd.)

J	Urban	Mean	5.10	4.93	4.37	4.61
		(S.D.)	(1.87)	(1.74)	(1.99)	(1.69)
	Rural	Mean	5.66	5.60	4.36	5.52
		(S.D.)	1.72	1.50	1.80	1.69
Q_n	Urban	Mean (S.D.)	5.42 (1.65)	5.46 (1.85)	5.02 (1.69)	5.30 (1.52)
	Rural	Mean (S.D.)	4.91 (1.65)	5.73 (1.85)	5.45 (1.69)	5.23 (1.52)
Q2	Urban	Mean (S.D.)	4.08 (2.65)	4.86 (2.54)	4.22 (2.42)	3.27 (2.07)
	Rural	Mean (S.D.)	3.08 (1.44)	2.80 (1.56)	2.36 (1.43)	2.38 (1.07)
Q3	Urban	Mean (S.D.)	3.13 (2.26)	5.08 (2.38)	4.11 (2.90)	3.50 (2.64)
	Rural	Mean (S.D.)	2.25 (.753)	2.26 (1.33)	1.45 (.934)	1.33 (.864)
Q4	Urban	Mean (S.D.)	5.04 (2.02)	4.76 (1.61)	4.80 (1.53)	4.91 (1.39)
	Rural	Mean (S.D.)	4.75 (1.28)	5.00 (1.25)	4.45 (1.43)	4.38 (1.16)

Table 3.43: Summary of MANOVA of Personality Dimensions by School Setting, Gender and Child Abuse

Dimensions of Personality	*F Values*						
	Setting (A)	*Gender (B)*	*Child Abuse (C)*	*A×B*	*A×C*	*B×C*	*A×B×C*
A	3.15*	.263	.180	13.9**	.203	.107	.761
B	12.6**	.893	2.09	1.54	3.82*	1.25	1.04
C	5.13*	1.65	.355	.652	2.59	.033	1.10
D	13.9**	10.4*	.244	1.87	1.37	.214	.009
E	.005	.489	.525	.455	.380	1.77	.099
F	31.8**	.186	.425	.737	.127	.999	.503
G	19.4**	7.02*	.705	.078	.509	.439	2.98
H	38.7**	.078	.002	.478	.400	1.55	.508
I	1.46	5.29*	1.27	15.5**	.291	.025	4.06
J	3.95*	5.12*	1.18	.099	.919	2.32	.591
O_n	.019	.295	.924	.399	.082	.695	1.72
Q2	18.4**	3.68*	.104	.056	.005	1.11	2.25
Q3	35.2**	2.17	1.20	.368	.701	3.03*	3.82*
Q4	.963	1.11	.000	.732	.125	.005	.558

(N = 900) *p<.05, **p<.01.

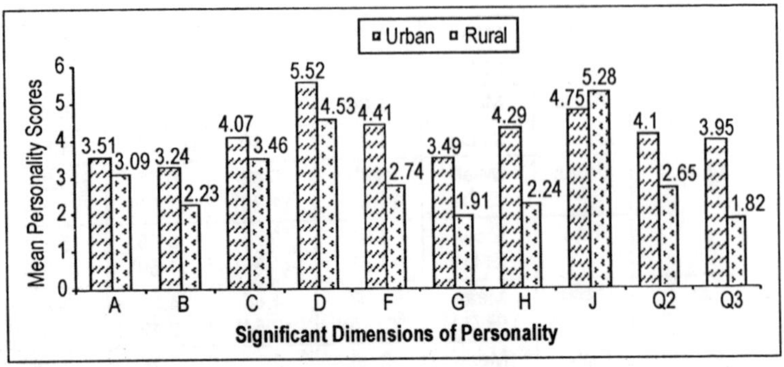

Fig. 3.125: Dimensions of Personality by School Setting.

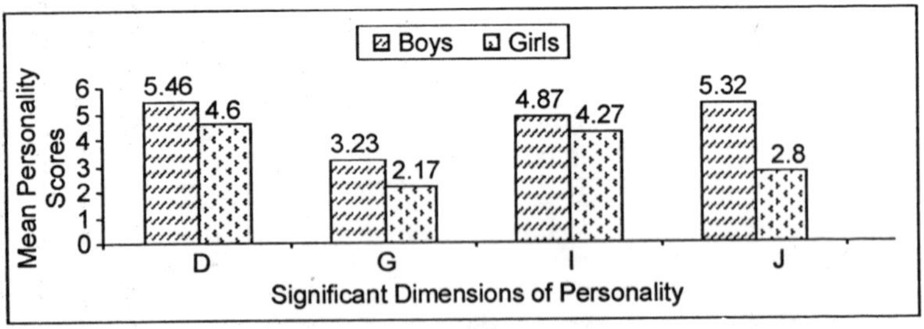

Fig. 3.126: Dimensions of Personality by Gender.

On factor A (Reserved-outgoing), significant main effect of school setting (Rural-Urban) indicated that urban school students were found less reserved (M = 3.51) than rural school children (3.09). Again significant effect of school setting x gender interaction (Fig. 3.127) denotes that urban male students were found more reserved than rural students but reverse pattern was found in case of girls. Urban girl students were found less reserved than their rural counterparts.

On factor B (Less Intelligent-More intelligent) significant main effect of setting indicates that the level of intelligence was found below average level in both groups. Specifically urban school students scored greater on intelligence (M = 3.24) than rural schools children (M = 2.23). Further school setting x child abuse interaction effect was found significant (Fig. 3.125).

As interaction graph (Fig. 3.128) denotes, in case of high abused group, little difference at intelligence level was found between urban school and rural school students but in case of low abused

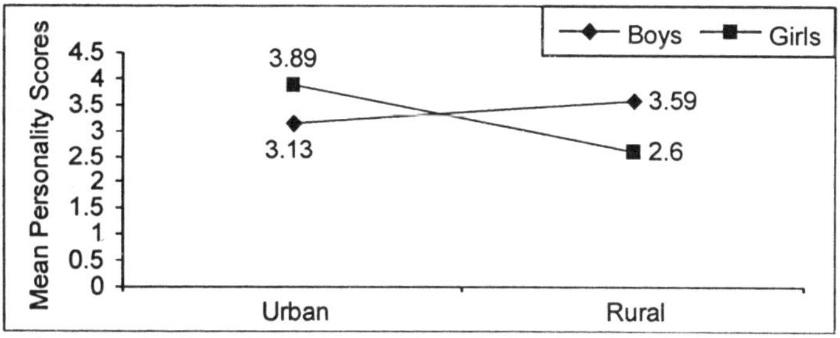

Fig. 3.127: Personality (Reserved Vs. Outgoing) as a Function of Interaction of School Setting and Gender.

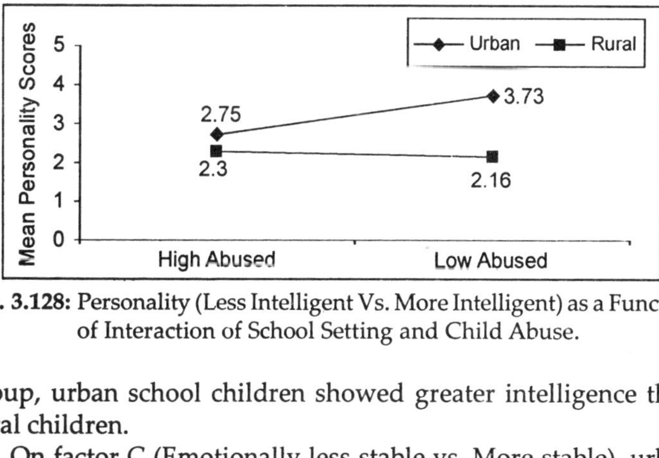

Fig. 3.128: Personality (Less Intelligent Vs. More Intelligent) as a Function of Interaction of School Setting and Child Abuse.

group, urban school children showed greater intelligence than rural children.

On factor C (Emotionally less stable vs. More stable), urban school children were found emotionally more stable (M = 4.07) than rural students (3.46). On factor D (Undemonstrative vs. Excitable Impatient) both genders varied significantly, as F value indicates that boys were found highly excitable and impatient (M = 5.46) than girl students (M = 4.60). Similarly, significant main effect of setting evinced that urban school students were found more excitable, impatient and demanding (M = 5.52) than those of rural schools children (M = 4.53). On factor E (Obedient vs. assertive) none of the main as well as interaction effects were found significant. Further on factor F (Sober vs. Enthusiastic) students of both settings differed significantly. Urban schools children (M = 4.41) were found more enthusiastic and heedless than rural school children (M = 2.74). Further, on Factor G (Expedient vs.

Conscientious) significant main effect of gender indicated that boys were found less expedient (disregard rules) (M = 3.23) than girl students (M=2.17). Furthermore, this tendency varied significantly across two settings. Urban students were found less disregarding (M = 3.49) than rural students (M = 1.91). Students of different settings also differed significantly on Factor H (Shy vs. Adventures). Urban students were found less shy (M=4.29) than rural children (M=2.24). Boys and girls also differed significantly on Factor I (Tough-Minded vs. Tender-Minded), although they scored at average level (Boys: M = 4.87; Girls: M = 4.27). Further school setting x gender interaction effect was found significant (Fig. 3.129).

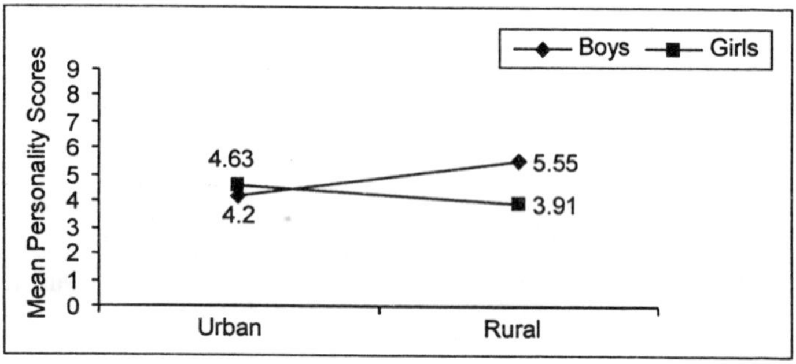

Fig. 3.129: Personality (Tough Minded Vs. Tender Minded) as a Function of Interaction of Setting and Gender.

It is clear from interaction graph (Fig. 3.129), urban girls were found less tough-minded than rural counterparts. Contrary to this, urban boys were found more tough-minded than their rural counterparts.

On factor J (Vigorous vs. Doubting) students scored at average level. The significant main effect of setting indicated that urban children were found more vigorous (M=4.75) than rural students (M=5.28). Further, significant main effect of gender indicates that boys were found less vigorous (M=5.32) than Girl students (M = 4.71). However, effects of setting and gender on factor O were found non-significant. On Factor Q_2 (Group Dependent vs. Self-Sufficient), Significant main effect of setting indicated that Group dependency was greater in rural students (M = 2.65) than urban students (M = 4.10). Both genders (Boys and Girls) varied significantly on this factor. More specifically, boys were found less group dependent and sound followers (M = 3.70) than girl students (M = 3.05).

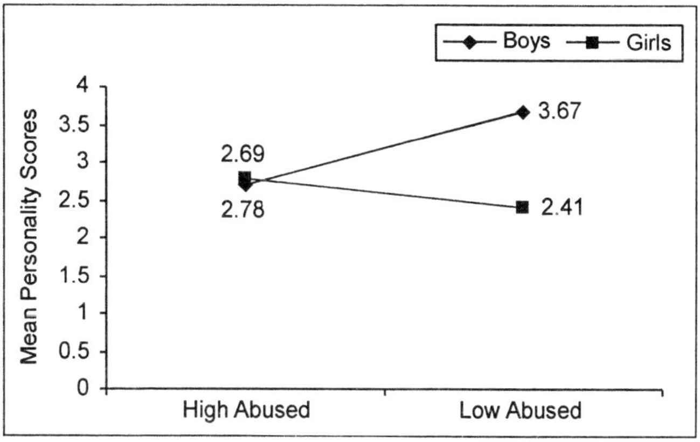

Fig. 3.130: Personality (Uncontrolled Vs. Controlled) as a Function of Interaction of Gender and Child Abuse.

Again, on Q_3 (Uncontrolled vs. Controlled), students of different setting varied significantly (Fig. 3.125). Specifically, Urban school students were found more controlled (M = 3.95) whereas, rural school children were found uncontrolled and less disciplined (M = 1.82). Further on factor Q_3, school setting × gender × child abuse interaction effect was found significant. As interaction graph (Fig. 3.130) indicates that in case of abused group, urban school boys were found less uncontrolled than rural students, whereas urban girl students were found controlled than their rural counterparts whereas, in the case of low abused group, urban school boys were found more controlled than rural school counterparts. Similarly, girl students of urban setting were found controlled, but rural school girl students were found uncontrolled. However on Q_4 (relaxed vs. tense) none of the main effects were found significant.

Effect of Type of School, Grade and Child Abuse on Personality (Set B)

Further, in order to determine the effect of type of school

(Government and Private), grade (6-8 and 9-10) and level of abuses (High and Low) on personality of students, Mean, S.D. and Multiple analysis of variance (MANOVA) were computed. Table 3.44 shows Mean and SD of dimensions of personality scores and summary of MANOVA are furnished in Table 3.45.

Table 3.44: Mean and S.D. of Dimensions of Personality by Type of School, Grade and Child Abuse

Dimensions of Personality		*Government Schools*				*Private Schools*			
		6-8 Grade Students		*9-10 Grade Students*		*6-8 Grade Students*		*9-10 Grade Students*	
		High Abused	*Low Abused*	*High Abused*	*Low Abused*	*High Abused*	*Low Abused*	*High Abused*	*Low Abused*
A	Mean	4.03	4.31	3.66	3.53	4.03	4.31	2.63	2.68
	(S.D.)	(1.87)	(1.81)	(.778)	(.833)	(1.87)	(1.81)	(1.12)	(1.12)
B	Mean	3.62	4.92	2.25	2.13	3.62	4.92	2.04	2.01
	(S.D.)	(2.00)	(2.28)	(.753)	(.743)	(2.00)	(2.28)	1.04	1.08
C	Mean	5.14	5.23	4.16	3.33	5.14	5.23	2.90	2.81
	(S.D.)	(1.76)	(1.73)	(1.11)	(1.29)	(1.76)	(1.73)	(1.26)	(1.17)
D	Mean	6.25	6.52	5.16	5.13	6.25	4.46	4.46	4.37
	(S.D.)	(2.12)	(1.70)	(1.02)	(1.30)	(2.12)	(1.70)	(1.42)	(1.38)
E	Mean	5.48	5.63	5.25	4.86	5.48	5.63	4.83	5.26
	(S.D.)	(1.94)	(1.88)	(4.86)	(1.55)	(1.94)	(1.88)	(1.41)	(1.41)
F	Mean	5.81	5.68	2.75	3.13	5.81	5.68	2.87	2.69
	(S.D.)	(1.30)	(2.04)	(1.48)	(1.18)	(1.30)	(2.04)	(1.33)	(1.13)
G	Mean	4.48	5.05	2.75	2.46	4.48	5.05	2.07	1.78
	(S.D.)	(1.96)	(2.14)	(1.13	(1.50)	(1.96)	(2.14)	(1.18)	(1.10)
H	Mean	6.11	5.81	2.41	2.40	6.11	5.81	2.29	2.25
	(S.D.)	(1.78)	(1.92)	(.792)	(1.18)	(1.78)	(1.92)	(1.19)	(1.24)
I	Mean	4.77	5.02	5.58	5.53	4.77	5.02	3.70	3.92
	(S.D.)	(1.84)	(1.77)	(1.08)	(.915)	(1.84)	(1.77)	(1.77)	(1.68)
J	Mean	5.03	4.78	5.66	5.60	5.03	4.78	4.57	4.94
	(S.D.)	(2.17)	(1.78)	(1.72)	(1.50)	(2.17)	(1.78)	(1.73)	(1.69)
O_N	Mean	5.55	5.68	4.91	5.73	5.55	5.68	5.07	5.02
	(S.D.)	(1.71)	(1.86)	(1.16)	(1.38)	(1.71)	(1.86)	(1.56)	(1.30)
Q2	Mean	5.92	5.21	3.08	2.80	5.92	5.21	2.50	2.33
	(S.D.)	(2.38)	(2.31)	(1.44)	(1.56)	(2.38)	(2.31)	(1.40)	(1.27)
Q3	Mean	5.44	5.92	2.25	2.26	5.44	5.92	1.73	1.78
	(S.D.)	(2.42)	(2.03)	(.753)	(1.33)	(2.42)	(2.03)	(.999)	(1.06)
Q4	Mean	5.59	5.13	4.75	5.00	5.59	5.13	4.38	4.42
	(S.D.)	(2.11)	(1.64)	(1.28)	(1.25)	(2.11)	(1.64)	(1.35)	(1.16

Further, to assess the effect of type of school, grade and child abuse on personality development of students multiple analysis of variance (MANOVA) was computed. Results are displayed in Table 3.45.

Table 3.45: Summary of MANOVA of Personality Dimensions by School Type, Grade and Child Abuse

Variables	*F Values*						
Dimensions of Personality	*School Type (A)*	*Grade (B)*	*Child Abuse (C)*	*A × B*	*A × C*	*B × C*	*A × B × C*
A	5.55*	27.4**	.345	5.55*	.050	.649	.050
B	.135	94.2**	7.46*	.135	.010	9.35*	.010
C	4.86*	87.1**	.845	4.86*	.848	1.84	.848
D	2.69	52.2**	.212	2.69	.004	.548	.004
E	.000	4.86*	.149	.000	.805	.074	.805
F	.147	195.9**	.005	.147	.466	.317	.466
G	2.30	124.7**	.413	2.30	.000	3.65*	.000
H	.102	298.4**	.600	.102	.001	.402	.001
I	13.6**	.842	.492	13.6**	.079	.123	.079
J	3.03*	1.29	.037	3.03*	.190	.636	.190
O_N	.396	3.89*	1.37	.396	.960	.345	.960
Q_2	1.04	128**	3.42*	1.04	.012	.912	.012
Q_3	1.21	262.9**	1.27	1.21	.002	.940	.002
Q_4	1.22	11.5*	.540	1.22	.057	2.04	.057

*P<.05, **P<.01,***P<001.

As results indicate, type of school, grade and child abuse exerted significant effect on various dimensions of personality (Table 3.45) (Figs. 3.131, 3.132 and 3.133).

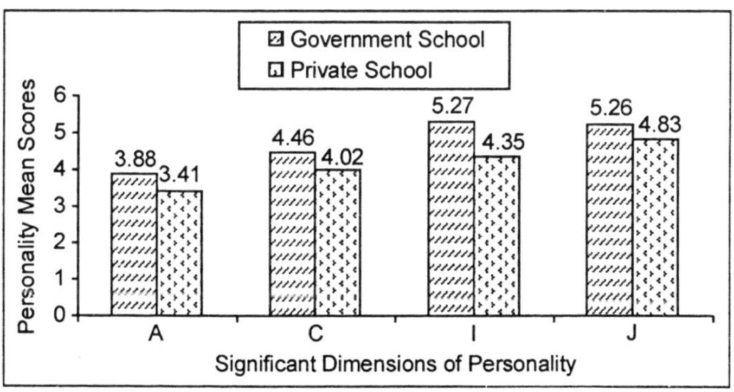

Fig. 3.131: Personality Dimensions by School Type.

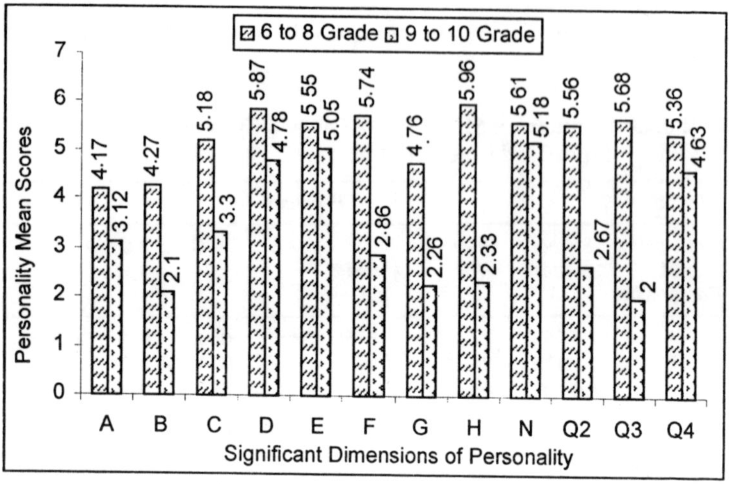

Fig. 3.132: Personality Dimensions by Grade.

Results (Table 3.45 and Fig. 3.131) indicate that on factor A (Reserved vs. outgoing) Government school children and private school children varied significantly. More specifically, government school children were found less reserved (M = 3.88) than private school children (M = 3.41). Furthermore, Junior High school (6-8 grade) students were found less reserved (M = 4.17) than high school (9-10 grade) students. Type of school x grade interaction effect was also found significant. As interaction graph (Fig. 3.133) indicates that Junior High School students of both government and private schools were found equally less reserved. However, High school students of government school were found less reserved than private school students.

On Factor B (Less Intelligent vs. More intelligent) significant main effect of Grade indicated that Junior High school students were found more intelligent (M = 4.27) than high school students (M = 3.12). Main effect of child abuse on factor B was also found significant. As Fig. 3.134 indicates high abused students were found less intelligent (M = 2.88) than low abused students (M = 3.49).

Further, grade x child abuse interaction effect was found significant. As interaction graph (Fig. 3.134) indicates that in case of low abused group, Junior High School students were found more intelligent than their High School counterparts. Whereas, in

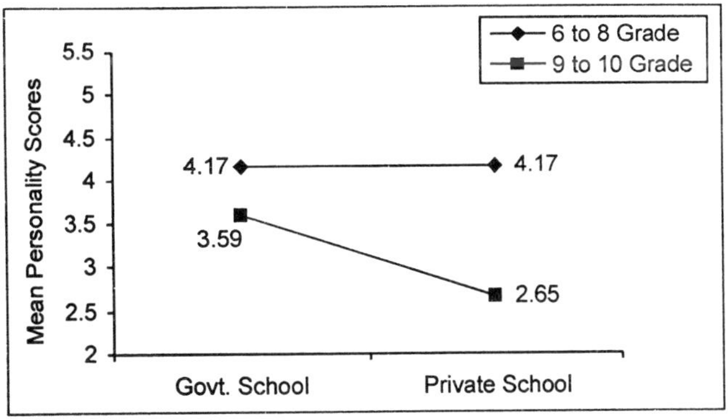

Fig. 3.133: Personality (Reserved vs. Outgoing) as a Function of interaction of Type of School and Gender.

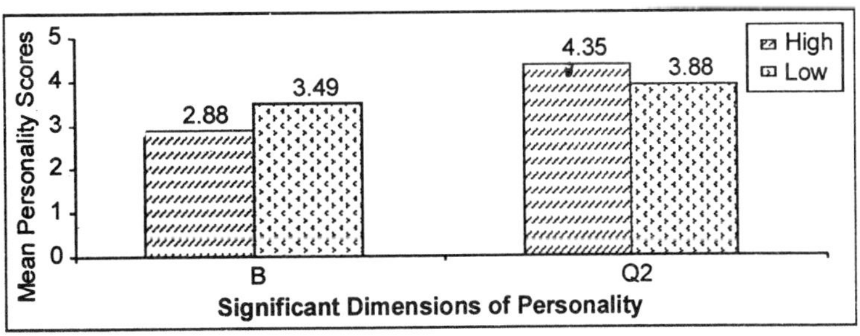

Fig. 3.134: Personality Dimensions by Level of Child Abuse.

case of high abused students, the level of intellect was found low in both grades, though Junior High school students displayed little better than High school students.

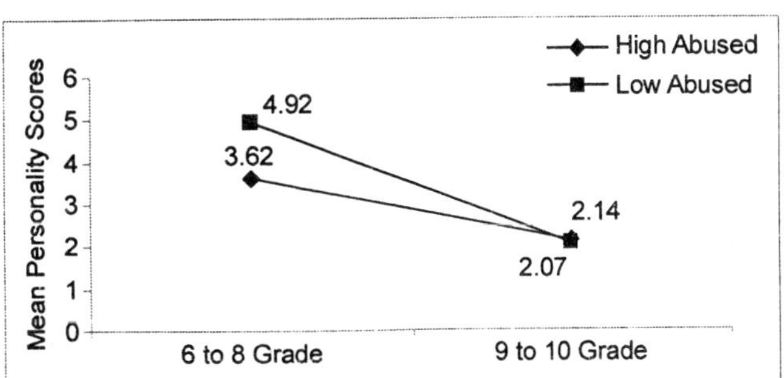

Fig. 3.135: Personality (less intelligent vs. more intelligent) as a Function of Grade and Child Abuse.

On Factor C (Emotionally less stable vs. More stable), government school students were found more emotionally stable (M = 4.46) than private school students (M = 4.02). More specifically, main effect of grade evinced that Junior high school (6-8 grade) students were found more emotionally stable (M = 5.18) than High school (9-10 grade) students (M = 3.3). Again type of school x grade was found significant. Junior High school students of both types of school were found equally more emotionally stable, whereas, High school level students of government school were found more emotionally stable than private school students.

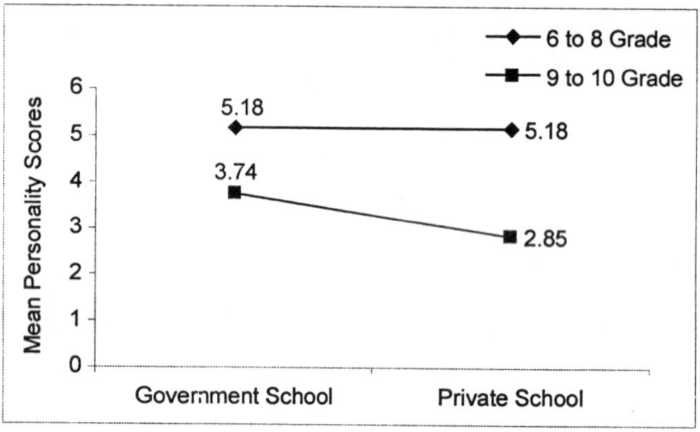

Fig. 3.136: Personality (Emotionally Less Stable vs. Emotionally More Stable) as a Function of Type of School and Grade.

Further, on personality factor D [Phlegmatic (inactive) vs. Excitable Impatient (overactive)] type of school did not vary significantly. Whereas, significant main effect of grade indicated that junior high school (6-8 grade) students were found more excitable (M = 5.87) than high school (9-10 grade) students (M = 4.78).

On factor E (Obedient vs. Assertive), the main effect of school type was found non-significant whereas, grade effect was found significant (Table 3.45). Specifically, Junior High school (6-8 grade) students were found more assertive (M = 5.55) than high school (9-10 grade) students (M = 5.05).

On Factor F (Tacitum vs. Enthusiastic) effect of school type was found non-significant. But significant grade effect showed that Junior High school (6-8 grade) students were found more enthusiastic (M = 5.74) whereas, High school (9-10 grade) students were found more tacitum (M = 2.78).

On factor G (Expedients vs. Conscientious) type of school effect was found non-significant. However, significant main effect of grade indicates that Junior High school (6-8 grade) students were found less expedient (disregard rules) and showed high superego strength (M = 4.92) than high school (9-10 grade) students (M = 2.26).

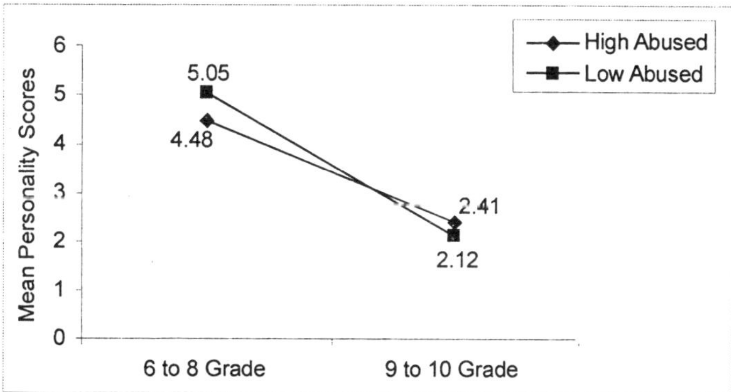

Fig. 3.137: Personality (Expedient vs. Conscientious) as a Function of Grade and Child Abuse.

Further, grade x child abuse interaction effect was found significant. As interaction graph (Fig. 3.137) denotes in case of Junior High school students, low abused children were found more conscientious than high school students. But in case of High school students, low abused children were found little more expedient than high abused children.

As results show (Fig. 3.132), different Grade level of students also differed significantly on Factor H (Shy vs. Adventuresome). Junior high school (6-8 grade) students were found more adventuresome (M = 5.96) than high school (9-10 grade) students (M = 2.33).

On factor I (Tough-minded vs. Tender-Minded) government school students were found more tough minded (M = 5.22) than private school students (M = 4.35), (Fig. 3.131). However, grade did not differ significantly.

Moreover, type of school x grade effect was found significant. As interaction graph (Fig. 3.138) presents that high school students of government schools were found tender minded than private

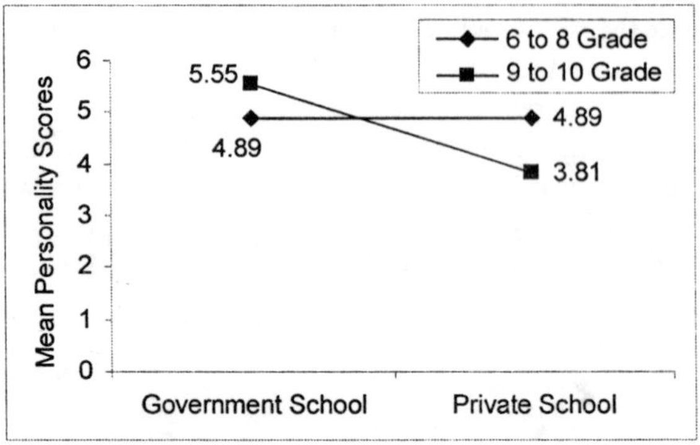

Fig. 3.138: Personality (Tough minded vs. Tender minded) as a Function of Type of School and Grade.

schools counterparts. But Junior High school students of both government and private schools were found equally less tough minded.

Further, on factor J (Vigorous vs. Doubting) government school students were found more doubting (5.26) than private school students (M = 4.83). Again type of school x grade interaction effect was found significant (Table 3.45).

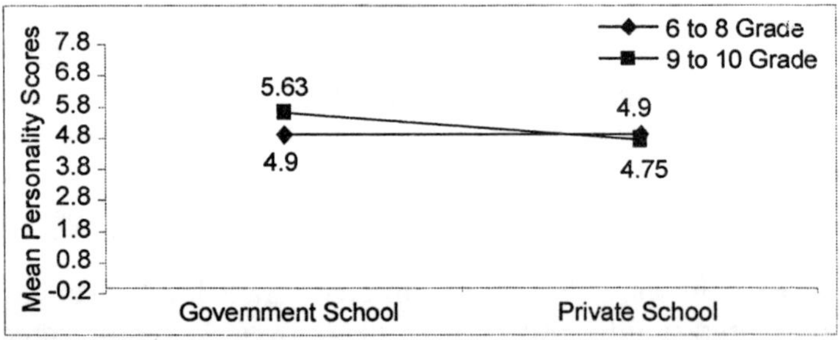

Fig. 3.139: Personality (Vigorous vs. Doubting) as a Function of Type of School and Grade.

As interaction graph (Fig. 3.139) indicates that high school students of government school were found more doubting than their private school counterparts. Whereas, junior high school students of both types of schools scored at average level on this factor.

On factor N (Self-Assured vs. Apprehensive), school type did not differ significantly but significant main effect of grade

(Fig. 3.126) suggested that High school (9-10 grade) students were found less apprehensive (guilt prone) (M = 5.18) than Junior High school (6-8 grade) students (M = 5.61).

On Factor Q_2 (Group Dependent vs. Self-Sufficient) school type did not vary significantly. Yet, grade effect was found significant (Fig. 3.126). Results indicate, Junior High School (6-8th grade) students were found less group dependent (M = 5.56) than high school (9-10th grade) students (2.67). Further, Fig. 3.134 indicates that main effect of child abuse was found significant. High abused children were found less group dependent (M = 4.35) than low abused children (M = 3.88).

On factor Q_3 (Undisciplined vs. Controlled), effect of school type was found Non-significant. But significant grade effect denotes that Junior High school (6-8th grade) students were found more controlled (M = 5.68) than high school (9-10 grade) students (M = 2.00) (Table 3.45).

Similarly on Factor Q_4 (Relaxed vs. Tense) type of school did not differ significantly. Yet, significant grade effect showed that junior high school (6-8th grade) students were found more tense and frustrated (M = 5.36) than high school (9-10th grade) students (M = 4.63) (Fig. 3.132).

Conclusion of Results

Findings of set-1, suggests that personality pattern of students was significantly influenced by school setting (rural and urban) and gender (male and female). The effect of level of abuses (high and low) was partially supported. Specifically urban school children as compared to their rural counterparts were found less reserved, intelligent, emotionally stable, excitable and more assertive, enthusiastic and more conscientious, more adventurous, less tender minded, less apprehensive, less group dependent, and more controlled. Again, male students as compared to female students were found more excitable, less expedient, tender minded and more doubting. Results, thus, indicate that rural-urban setting of schools has exerted strong impact on most of the dimensions of personality. The roles of gender and child abuse in personality (dimensions) are partially supported.

Second set of MANOVA results revealed that government school students as compared to private school counterparts were found less reserved, emotionally more stable, less tough minded and more doubting. Grade effect on personality was found significant. Results suggest that Junior high school (6-8th grade) students as compared to High school (grade 9-10th) students were found less reserved, more intelligent, emotionally stable, excitable, assertive, more enthusiastic, conscientious, more adventurous, little more apprehensive and more self-sufficient. Results also indicated that (Fig. 3.134) high abused children were found less intelligent than low abused children. However, high abused children as compared to low abused group were found less group-dependent. In brief, type of school, grade and level of child abuse have significantly influenced the personality of students.

Set B: Impact on Health Status of Students

Data obtained on health questionnaire were scored and treated statistically in terms of Mean, SD and Analysis of Variance (ANOVA), correlations and Step-wise Multiple Regression Analysis (SMRA). Graphic representation of data was also done. Obtained results are displayed and interpreted in following section.

Univariate Analysis

(i) Effect of type of School, Gender, Grade and Child Abuse on Physical Health—Scores obtained on physical illness were analyzed in terms of Mean, S.D. and ANOVA. Results are shown in Tables 3.46 and 3.47 and figures. Results indicate that students varied on physical health across different groups.

Table 3.46: Mean and S.D. of Physical Health by Type of School, Gender, Grade and Child Abuse

Variables		*Government School*				*Private School*			
		Boys		*Girls*		*Boys*		*Girls*	
		High Abused	*Low Abused*	*High Abused*	*Low Abused*	*High Abused*	*Low Abused*	*High Abused*	*Low Abused*
6-8th Grade	Mean	2.12	2.32	2.29	2.14	2.61	1.77	2.55	1.5
	SD	2.01	1.97	2.07	1.89	2.14	1.90	2.33	1.68
9-10th Grade	Mean	3.71	2	4.2	3.06	3.09	1.6	3.88	2.53
	SD	2.50	1.51	2.58	3.23	2.34	1.56	3.03	2.26
11-12th Grade	Mean	5	3.5	4.74	3.77	2.62	1.6	3.77	3
	SD	4.92	3.11	3.00	2.72	2.72	3.57	3.18	2.41

Table 3.47: Summary of 2x2x2 ANOVA of Physical Health as a Function of Type of School, Gender, Grade and Child Abuse

Source	*Sum of Squares*	*df*	*Mean Square*	*F*
Type of school (A)	57.193	1	57.193	8.86**
Gender (B)	25.366	1	25.366	3.93*
Grade (C)	169.289	2	84.645	13.12**
Child abuse (D)	115.627	1	115.627	17.92**
A×B	4.611	1	4.611	.715
A×C	39.028	2	19.514	3.02*
A×D	1.367	1	1.367	.212
B×C	24.627	2	12.314	1.909
B×D	.715	1	.715	.111
C×D	25.148	2	12.574	1.949
A×B×C	10.346	2	5.173	.802
A×B×D	.268	1	.268	.041
A×C×D	11.250	2	5.625	.872
B×C×D	3.757	2	1.878	.291
A×B×C×D	.589	2	.294	.046

*P<0.05, **P<0.01.

Again, to determine the significant effects of type of school (Government and Private), gender (Boys and Girls), grade (6-8th, 9-10th and 11-12th) and child abuse level (high and low) on physical health, a 2x2x3x2 ANOVA analysis was done. Results displayed in Table 3.47 indicate the significant effects of type of school, gender, grade and child abuse on Physical health status. The significant main effect of Type of school on Physical health is displayed in Fig. 3.140.

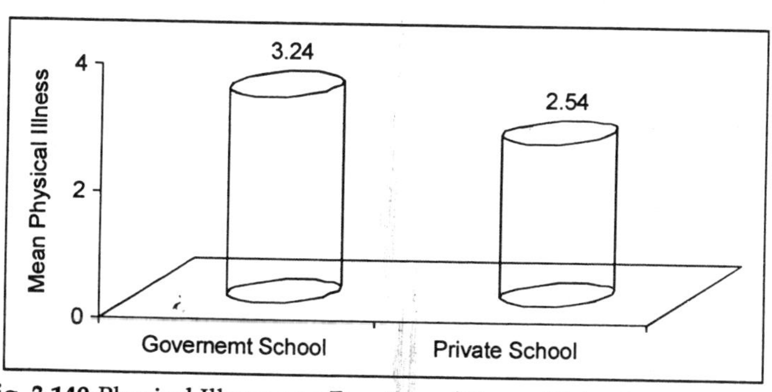

Fig. 3.140: Physical Illness as a Function of Type of School.

As figure indicates the physical health problem was found lesser in students of private school (M = 2.54) as compared to government school students (M = 3.24) Fig. 3.140.

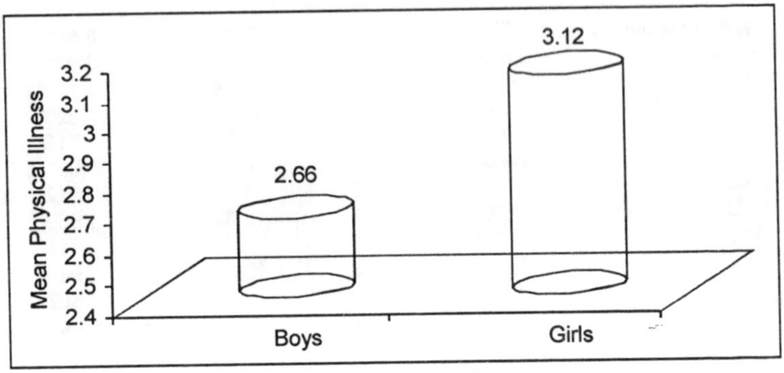

Fig. 3.141: Physical Illness as a Function of Gender.

Similarly, significant main effect of gender on physical health (Fig. 3.141) denotes that girls showed more health problems (M = 3.12) than boys (M = 2.66).

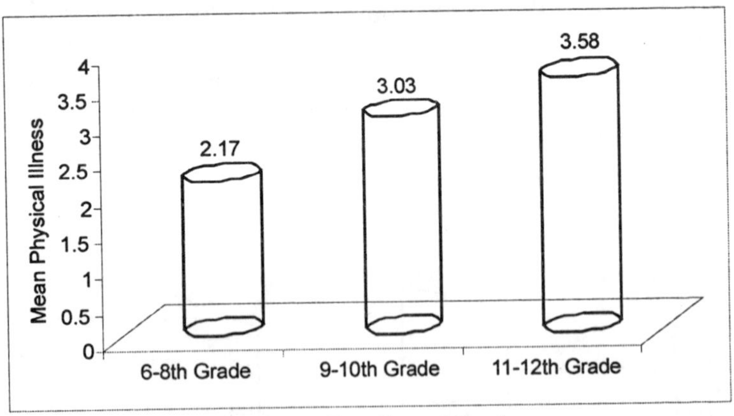

Fig. 3.142: Physical Illness as a Function of Grade.

Further, significant main effect of grade on physical health (Table 3.47 and Fig. 3.142), suggests that Intermediate level (11-12th grade) students showed more health problems (M = 3.58) than High School (9-10th grade) students (M = 3.03) and junior high school (6-8th grade) students (M = 2.17).

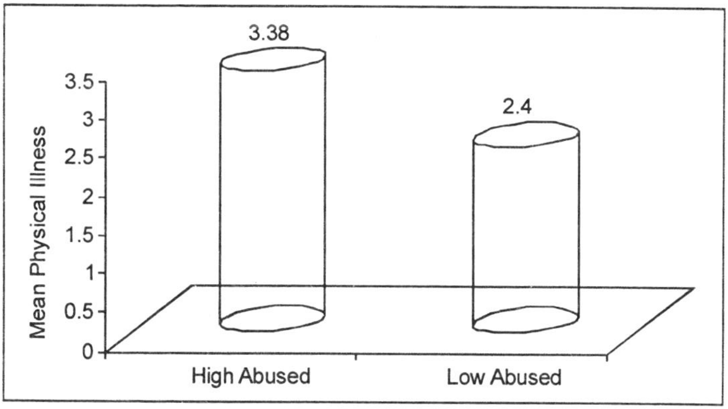

Fig. 3.143: Physical Illness as a Function of Child Abuse.

Further, the main effect of child abuse was also found significant (Table 3.47 and Fig. 3.143) which suggests that high abused group of students showed more physical health problems (M = 3.38) than low abused group of students (M = 2.4). The type of school and grade interaction effect was also found significant.

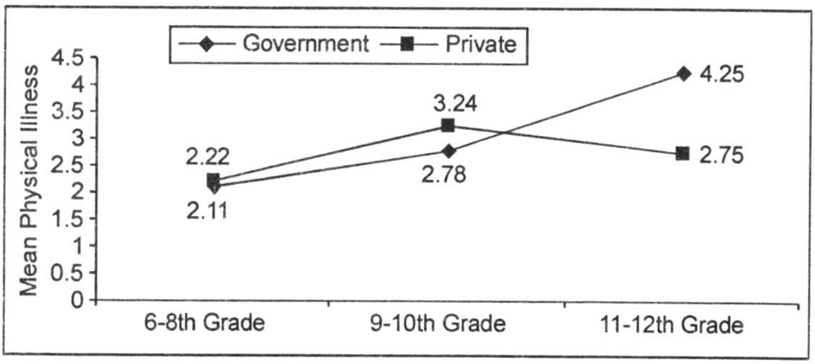

Fig. 3.144: Physical Illness as a Function of Interaction of Type of School and Grade.

As Figure 3.144 indicates that in case of government schools, physical health problems increased with increasing grade level. More health problem was found in Intermediate level students than High school and Junior High school students. However, in case of private school students, high school students showed more health problems than their Intermediate and Junior High school counterparts.

(ii) Psychological (Mental) Health as a function of Type of School, Gender, Grade and Child Abuse

Scores obtained on psychological illness were treated statistically in term of Mean, SD and Analysis of Variance (ANOVA). Results are shown in Table 3.48 and figures.

Table 3.48: Mean and S.D. of Psychological (Mental Health) by Type of School, Gender, Grade and Child Abuse

Variables		Government School				Private School			
		Boys		Girls		Boys		Girls	
		High Abused	Low Abused	High Abused	Low Abused	High Abused	Low Abused	High Abused	Low Abused
6-8th Grade	Mean	3.73	4.52	4.08	4.10	4.8	4.06	4.73	3.58
	SD	2.90	3.15	3.00	3.05	3.47	4.12	2.86	3.56
9-10th Grade	Mean	6.25	4.35	6.6	6.43	6.68	3.47	7.90	6.07
	SD	4.86	4.46	3.50	4.67	4.12	3.05	4.43	4.04
11-12th Grade	Mean	6.96	5.12	7.95	7.13	4.62	3	6.77	5.68
	SD	4.83	4.12	4.07	4.81	3.88	5.65	4.62	4.44

As Table 3.48 denotes, students varied on psychological illness across different groups. Further, to determine the effects of type of school, gender, grade and child abuse on psychological health (Mental illness), a 2 × 2 × 3 × 2 analysis of variance was computed. Results are presented in Table 3.49.

Results displayed in Table 3.49, denotes the significant impact of gender, grade and level of abuse on psychological (mental) health of students.

As Figure 3.145 denotes, girls showed more psychological health problems (M = 5.99) than boys (M = 4.80).

Similarly, grade effect was also found significant. Mental health problems were found far greater in High school and Intermediate level students than Junior High school level students (Fig. 3.146).

Similarly, the main effect of child abuse was also found significant. As Figure 3.147 shows, High abused group of students expressed more psychological health problem (M = 5.92) as compared to low abused group of students (4.79).

Further, the significant interaction effect of gender x grade (Fig. 3.148) revealed that minimum level of mental health problems were reported by Junior High school (6-8th grade) level both male and female students. However, girl students of High school

Table 3.49: Summary of 2x2x3x2 ANOVA of Psychological Health as a Function of Type of School, Gender, Grade, and Child Abuse

Source	*Type III Sum of Squares*	*df*	*Mean Square*	*F*
Type of school (A)	28.774	1	28.774	1.824
Gender (B)	150.259	1	150.259	9.525**
Grade (C)	426.925	2	213.462	13.53**
Child abuse (D)	152.677	1	152.677	9.678**
A×B	6.272	1	6.272	.398
A×C	82.637	2	41.318	2.619
A×D	27.221	1	27.221	1.725
B×C	126.019	2	63.010	3.994**
B×D	10.030	1	10.030	.636
C×D	65.239	2	32.620	2.068
A×B×C	9.453	2	4.726	.300
A×B×D	.197	1	.197	.013
A×C×D	10.487	2	5.243	.332
B×C×D	31.973	2	15.986	1.013
A×B×C×D	1.321	2	.661	.042

**P<0.01.

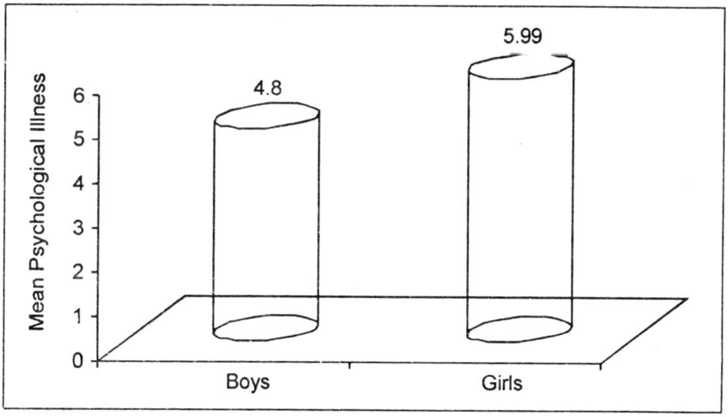

Fig. 3.145: Psychological Illness as a Function of Gender

(9-10th grade) and Intermediate level (11-12th grade) reported more health problems as compared to boys of High school and Intermediate levels.

ANOVA results thus proved that child abuse along with type of school, gender and grade impacted physical and mental health status of students.

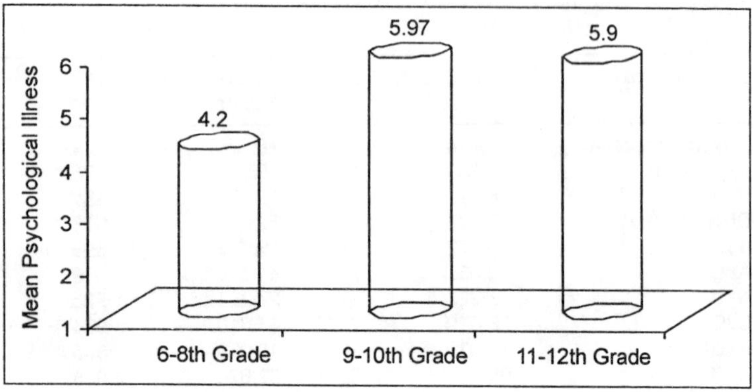

Fig. 3.146: Psychological (Mental) Illness as a Function of Grade.

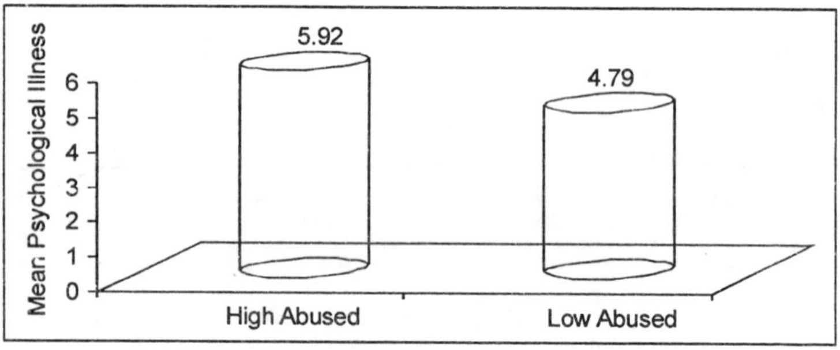

Fig. 3.147: Psychological Illness as a Function of Child Abuse

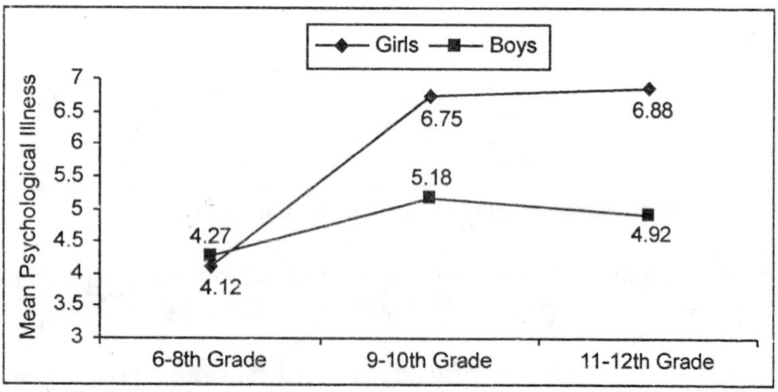

Fig. 3.148: Psychological Illness as a Function of Interaction of Gender and Grade

Correlation Analysis

In order to determine relationship between child abuse and health (Illness), correlations were computed. Specifically, correlational analysis was done to establish the association of forms of school abuse with physical and mental illness of students. Results are shown in Table 3.50 and interpreted in subsequent section.

Table 3.50: Correlations between Child Abuse and Health (Physical and Psychological Illness)

Dimension of Child Abuse	*Physical Illness*	*Psychological Illness*
Physical Abuse	.128**	.081*
Psychological Abuse	.192**	.136**
Sexual Abuse	.141**	.090**
Physical Neglect	.167**	.099**
Emotional Neglect	.234**	.165**
Educational Neglect	.225**	.154**
Child Abuse (as a whole)	.227**	.152**

*P<0.05, **P<0.01.

(i) Relationships between Child Abuse and Physical Health (Illness): As Table 3.50 denotes, all forms of child abuse i.e., physical abuse, psychological abuse, sexual abuse, physical neglect, emotional neglect and educational neglect as well as child abuse as a whole were found highly positively correlated with physical illness in students.

(ii) Relationship between Child Abuse and Psychological (Mental) Illness: It is clear from correlation results (Table 3.50), that child abuse was found positively linked with mental illness. Similarly, positive associations among all forms of child abuse and mental illness were found. Results thus, indicate that abusive experiences lead to more health problems in students.

Multiple Regression Analysis

Prediction of Health Status from Child Abuse

Based on the perusal of significant correlation results, it was viewed to go for stepwise multiple regression analysis (SMRA) to determine the relative contributions of child abuse to health status of students. Results are depicted in Table 3.51, findings of this analysis are in order:

Table 3.51: Stepwise Multiple Regression Analysis of Health on the Child Abuse

(Predictors) Dimensions of Child Abuse	R	R^2	R^2 change	Beta β	F value
			(Criterion Variable) Physical Health		
Emotional Neglect	.234	.055	.055	.147	52.196**
Educational Neglect	.246	.060	.006	.115	28.97**
		Mental Health			
Emotional Neglect	.165	.027	.027	.165	25.3**

*P<0.05, **P<0.01.

Physical Health: As Table 3.51 denotes, physical health was positively predicted by two factors; emotional neglect was found strongest predictor of physical health, which contributed positively (β = .147, R_2 = .055) followed by educational neglect (β = .115, R_2 = .060). Though independently, emotional neglect explained 5.5 per cent of variance followed by educational neglect which contributed 0.6 per cent variance in criterion variable. But composite contribution of both factors was 6 per cent variance to physical illness.

Mental Health: It is also clear from regression results (Table 3.51) that mental health was predicted by only emotional neglect. Emotional neglect has contributed positively (β = .165, R^2 = .027) and explained 2.7 per cent of variance to mental health.

To conclude, present results have proved strong association between child abuse and health. Further, differential role of forms of abuses in physical and psychological health has been proved on the basis of regression results.

4
Discussion

The findings of present study are interpreted and discussed under five major sections. At the outset, major findings of the study based on five objectives have been interpreted. In the subsequent four sections of the chapter, the predictors of child abuse, incidence and forms of abuse witnessed in schools and consequences of child abuse on students have been interpreted and discussed in the light of empirical and theoretical evidences.

Specifically, first section deals with the role of environmental and socio-demographic factors in the origin of child abuse and neglect in schools. In the second section, the demographic and personality characteristics of abusive and non-abusive school personnel are interpreted. In third section of the chapter, the specific forms of abuses witnessed in schools are reported and interpreted. In the fourth section, the impact of child abuse on cognitive, motivational, affective and behavioural functioning of students has been discussed. Finally, personality pattern and health status of students as a function of child abuse is presented and discussed in the light of empirical and theoretical evidences. On the basis of overall findings of the study, a Model has also been developed and displayed, linking antecedent factors, process variables and consequences of child abuse. Lastly, implications of the study, issues for further researches and recommendations/ remediations have been provided in the light of findings of present piece of research.

Major Finding of the Study

Findings of this study proved that the magnitude and forms of child abuse differed in accordance with environmental settings, contextual and socio-demographic features as well as personal characteristics of the students and school personnel. Further, abusive experiences of students caused adverse impact on cognitive, motivational, affective, and behavioural functioning. The personality and health status of students were also affected by abusive treatment of school personnel. Results obtained on Univariate/multivariate analysis, correlation and regression analysis of data for each objective are interpreted in preferential order:

Findings of Objective-I

Interpretation of ANOVA Results

Present findings evinced that various forms of child abuse are witnessed at high rate in schools of Uttar Pradesh. However, the magnitude and forms of abuses varied in accordance with school settings, school environment, and socio-demographic features of victims as well as perpetrators. Present findings report:

The Role of Environment in Child Abuse: The magnitude and forms of abuses differ in rural and urban school settings. Specifically, physical abuse and educational neglect were found more in rural schools whereas, psychological abuse, emotional neglect and abuse as a whole were found greater in urban schools.

- Forms of abuse also varied in accordance with type of schools and medium of education. In government schools, the cases of physical abuse, sexual abuse, physical neglect, emotional neglect, educational neglect and abuse as a whole were found higher than private schools. Contrary to this, psychological abuse was found very high in private schools.
- Child abuse level also differed in Hindi and English Medium schools. Physical abuse, sexual abuse, emotional neglect, educational neglect and abuse as a whole were identified more in Hindi Medium schools than English medium schools, whereas, psychological abuse and physical neglect were found higher in English medium schools than Hindi medium schools.

- The school environment showed link with magnitude and forms of abuses. Positive school environment played significant role to control child victimization whereas, negative dimensions of school environments intensified the incidence of child abuse in schools.

Socio-Demographic Factors and Child Abuse: The incidence of child abuse also varied according to socio-demographic characteristics of students. Specifically:

- Child abuse was found far high in Scheduled Caste students than OBC and General caste students. Specifically, psychological abuse, sexual abuse, emotional neglect, educational neglect were found more in SC students than OBC and General Caste students. But physical neglect was found more in OBC students than SC and General Caste students.
- Boys were found more physically abused than girls. Whereas, girls were identified more physically, emotionally and educationally neglected than boys.
- The level of abuse also differed across education level of children. Specifically, physical abuse and sexual abuse were found more in junior high school students than intermediate and high school students. Contrary to this, psychological abuse, physical neglect, emotional neglect and educational neglect were found higher in intermediate level students than junior high school and high school level students.

Interpretation of Correlation and Regression Results

Despite comparative analysis, correlation and regression analyses were also done. Correlation results are interpreted followed by regression results.

- As correlation results indicate, the setting of school and type of school were found inversely related with forms of child abuse and abuse as a whole. Some forms of abuses are present at higher level in urban and government schools as compared to rural and private schools.
- Further, school environment was found closely linked with child abuse. Positive dimensions of school environment

were found negatively associated with child abuse. Specifically, creative stimulation was found negatively related with sexual abuse. Similarly, cognitive encouragement was found negatively correlated with sexual abuse. Likewise, acceptance domain of school environment was found negatively correlated with physical abuse, psychological abuse, sexual abuse, emotional neglect, educational neglect and child abuse as a whole. Contrary to this, negative dimension of school environment i.e., rejection was found positively correlated with physical abuse, psychological abuse, sexual abuse, physical neglect, emotional neglect, educational neglect and abuse as a whole.

- Demographic characteristics of students were also found related with child abuse. Students' caste was found positively related with sexual abuse, physical neglect, emotional neglect and abuse as a whole, which suggests that abuses are higher in SC students than OBC and General caste students.
- Gender was found negatively correlated with physical abuse, psychological, sexual abuse and abuse as a whole which explains that boys were found more abused than girls on some domains.
- Age was found positively linked with psychological abuse, sexual abuse and physical neglect, emotional neglect and educational neglect and abuse as a whole. Similarly, grade was found positively associated with psychological abuse, physical neglect, emotional neglect, educational neglect and abuse as a whole. These results suggest that with increasing age and grade the incidence of abuses increases.

Regression results have also proved differential role of school setting and school environment in child abuse. Specifically, positive domains of school environment have played buffering role to minimize incidents of abuse whereas, negative dimensions of school environment have worked as intensifier in the occurrence of child abuse in school setting.

Findings of Objective-II

A close perusal of results obtained on objective II, revealed that certain demographic and psychological characteristics of school personnel (teachers) were found associated with each other. Apart from this, certain dimensions of personality were also found linked with their childhood abusive experiences. More specifically, school type was found positively correlated with gender and marital status of teachers whereas, gender was found negatively correlated with age. Caste was found strongly negatively related with agreeableness domain of personality. Marital status was found positively associated with openness. Family type was found negatively related with neuroticism, but positive link was found with extraversion, openness and agreeableness. Extraversion was found positively correlated with openness, agreeableness and consciousness. Similarly openness was found positively correlated with agreeableness and consciousness. The agreeableness was found positively correlated with consciousness.

- The childhood abuses of teachers were found directly associated with five personality domains. More specifically, Childhood Psychological Abuse (CPsyA), Childhood Physical Neglect (CPN) and Childhood Emotional Neglect (CEN) were found negatively related with Agreeableness domain of personality. Again, childhood emotional neglect (CEN) was found negatively related with Conscientiousness and Extraversion. Contrary to this, childhood psychological abuse (CPsy. A) and childhood emotional neglect (CEN) were found positively linked with Neuroticism. Further, childhood psychological abuse (CPsy. A) was found positively related with Openness domain of personality.
- SMRA results evinced that personality factors were explained by certain demographic characteristics of teachers. Neuroticism was predicted by family type. Again openness was predicted by marital status, school type and gender. Caste has predicted to agreeableness and conscientiousness was predicted by district and marital status.
- Results further revealed interesting facts. The forms of abuses as reported by teachers in their schools include—Physical punishment, psychological abuse, emotional neglect, aggressive behaviour, bullying, discrimination and partiality, educational neglect, verbal abuse, sexual

abuse, demoralizing, teasing and unethical behaviour with students.

It is clear on the basis of findings of objective II, certain demographic characteristics, childhood abuses and personality characteristics of school personnel have close link with expression of abusive behaviour with students.

Findings of Objective-III

Third objective of the study was to explore the magnitude and specific forms of abuses in school setting. School personnel/ teachers were interviewed on semi-unstructured interview schedule and data analysis was done using qualitative analysis method. Results are presented here in accordance with responses of teachers on three questions in preferential order.

1. What do You Understand by Child Abuse and Neglect?

Responses obtained on question-1 were recorded and transformed into percentage.

Forms and magnitude of abuses in schools as reported by Government school teachers are: Physical abuse—25 per cent, mental torture—24 per cent, discrimination between students—12 per cent, neglect—21 per cent, demoralization—09 per cent, child abuse as a crime—09 per cent. Whereas, according to Private school teachers, forms and magnitude of child abuse include: Physical abuse—28 per cent, mental torture—22 per cent, discrimination between students—15 per cent, neglect—19 per cent, and demoralization—16 per cent.

2. Which Types of Abuse are Generally Found in Schools?

Responses obtained on question-2 were also recorded and percentage was determined. It is clear from results that both government and private school teachers accepted that child abuse is found in many forms in school setting. Forms of abuses identified in government schools are: Mental torture—37 per cent, physical punishment—27 per cent, neglect—12 per cent, sexual harassment—12 per cent and bullying—12 per cent. Whereas in private schools types of abuse include: Mental torture—41 per cent, physical punishment—27 per cent, neglect—23 per cent and sexual harassment—9 per cent.

3. *Which Types of Abuse have you Witnessed in Your School?*

Responses obtained from teachers on question-3 were recorded and transformed into percentage. As results indicate that government school teachers reported forms of abuses such as—Bullying—50 per cent, physical punishment—30 per cent, verbal abuse—10 per cent and sexual exploitation—10 per cent. Whereas, abuses reported by Private School teachers include: Bullying—25 per cent, Verbal/psychological abuse—35 per cent, physical punishment—30 per cent, and sexual exploitation—10 per cent.

It is clear from the above results that child abuses are present at high rate in schools in many forms. No school setting is immune of happening of abusive treatment by teachers, school personnel, and gangs of students (Bullies).

Findings of Objective-IV

The consequences of child abuse in schools on cognitive, motivational, affective and behavioural functioning of students were examined under section IV. Results are interpreted briefly in following sections.

A. Impact on Cognitive Process

In this part students' cognitive functioning i.e., verbal ability and memory process (memory span and working memory) were assessed as a function of type of school, grade, gender and child abuse in school setting. Results indicate:

- **Verbal ability:** The verbal ability of students was found significantly influenced by abuse level, type of school and grade. Specifically, highly abused students showed poor verbal ability than low abused children. Verbal ability was found inferior in government school students than private school students. Verbal ability was found very poor in high school students. Despite this, Junior high school students expressed superior verbal ability than Intermediate level students.

- **Memory span:** The memory span of students also differed as a function of level of abuse, type of school, gender and grade. Private school students showed superior memory span than government school students. The memory span of high school students was identified far low than intermediate and junior high school students.
- **Working memory:** Working memory (WM) of students also varied as a function of level of abuse, gender and grade. Specifically—Abused children were found inferior on central executive WM and Working memory as a whole. Senior class students scored higher on working memory and its various dimensions than junior class students. Gender difference on working memory is partially supported.

B. Impact on Motivational Process

- The achievement motivation level of students was also examined as a function of school child abuse, type of school, grade and gender. Results report that abused children were found low academic achievers than low/ non abused children. Government school students were found low academic achievers than private school students.
- The level of aspiration was significantly influenced by child abuse, gender and grade. The role of type of school was partially supported. Specifically High abused children showed lower aspiration level than low abused children. The aspiration levels of girls were found higher than boys. Junior high school students showed more aspiration than intermediate and high school level students.

C. Affective Process

The affective process (depression and anxiety) of students was also assessed as a function of school (child) abuse, type of school, grade and gender.

- Results evinced that the depression level was found higher in government school students than private school students. An interaction result denotes that depression level was found higher in high abused children than low abused children. The roles of gender and grade were partially supported.

- Results further revealed the significant role of child abuse and grade in anxiety level of students. Specifically: High abused children displayed more anxiety than low abused children. Anxiety level was found far high in high school students than intermediate level students and junior high school level students.

D. Impact on Behavioural Process

The behavioural functioning (Positive and Negative behaviour) of students was also assessed as a function of school child abuse, type of school, grade and gender. Results obtained for positive and negative behaviour are briefly hereunder.

I. Positive Behaviours

Social Interaction: High abused children were found far inferior on social interaction (positive behaviour) than low abused children. Further high school students showed lesser social interaction than intermediate level and junior high school level students.

Helping Behaviour: Helping behaviour was jointly influenced by child abuse, type of school, gender and grade. But none of the main effects was found significant.

Disciplinary Behaviour: Girls were found more disciplined than boys. Interaction results indicate that child abuse along with type of school, gender and grade exerted impact on disciplinary behaviour. High abused children displayed less disciplinary behaviour than low abused children.

Study Behaviour: High abused children displayed poor study behaviour than low abused children. Study behaviour was found superior in intermediate level students than junior and high school level students.

II. Negative Behaviours

Aggressive Behaviour: High abused children displayed

heightened aggressive behaviour as compared to low abused children. Rest of the main effects were found non-significant.

Bullying: High abused children displayed heightened bullying behaviour as compared to low abused children. Rest of the main effects were found non-significant on bullying.

Non-Compliance: High abused children displayed higher level of non-compliance behaviour as compared to low abused children. Non-compliance was found maximum in intermediate level students. High school level students displayed more non-compliance than junior high school level students.

Interpretation of Correlation Results

Data were also analyzed in terms of Bivariate and Stepwise Multiple Regression analysis. First correlation results are interpreted followed by regression results in nutshell:

- Child abuse and its forms were found to be negatively correlated with verbal ability and its dimensions. Child abuse and its forms were also found negatively correlated with memory span and working memory.
- Correlation results also indicate that forms of child abuse and abuse as a whole were found negatively correlated with academic achievement and aspiration level of students.
- Positive association between child abuse and affective process was found. Specifically, child abuse and its forms were found positively correlated with depression and anxiety.
- Child abuse and its forms were found negatively associated with positive dimensions of behavioural functioning. Positive behaviours i.e., social interaction, helping behaviour, discipline and study behaviour were found inversely related with forms of child abuse. Contrary to this, negative dimensions of behaviour such as aggression, bullying and non-compliance were found positively linked with child abuse and its forms.

Interpretation of Règression Results: The psychological consequences of child abuse on students were predicted on the basis of Stepwise Multiple Regression analysis. Results are interpreted in following section.

A. Prediction of Cognitive Process: Child abuse and its forms have predicted negatively to verbal ability and memory process of children. Specifically:

- Verbal ability as a whole was strongly predicted by sexual abuse. The dimensions of verbal ability were also predicted by different forms of abuses. Word analogy was predicted by sexual abuse. Whereas, opposite word was predicted by physical abuse, educational neglect and sexual abuse. Again, word similarity was predicted by sexual abuse and physical abuse. Word classification was predicted by sexual abuse and physical abuse. Sentence completion was predicted by sexual abuse and emotional neglect.
- Memory span was negatively predicted by child abuse and its forms. Similarly, working memory and its domains were inversely explained by child abuse. Specifically, phonological working memory was negatively predicted by emotional abuse and abuse as a whole. Further, psychological abuse and sexual abuse contributed negatively to visuo-spatial working memory and central executive working memory. Likewise, overall working memory was predicted by psychological abuse, sexual abuse and educational neglect.

B. Prediction of Affective Process: Child abuse and its forms predicted positively to depression and anxiety level of children. Specifically, depression was positively predicted by child educational neglect and anxiety was positively predicted by child emotional neglect.

C. Prediction of Motivational Process: Child abuse and its forms have predicted negatively to academic achievement motivation and aspiration. Specifically: Academic achievement motivation was negatively predicted by child sexual abuse, and aspiration was negatively predicted by child physical abuse.

D. Prediction of Behavioural Functioning: Children's behaviours (Positive/Negative) were predicted by forms of child abuse. Specifically, social interaction was negatively predicted by emotional neglect and sexual abuse. Helping behaviour was negatively predicted by emotional neglect and sexual abuse. Students' study behaviour was negatively explained by emotional neglect. Contrary to this, negative behaviours were found positively predicted by forms of child abuse. More specifically, Aggressive behaviour was positively predicted by sexual abuse. Again, child sexual abuse, physical neglect and psychological abuse have positively contributed to bullying behaviour of children. Similarly, physical neglect has contributed positively to Non-compliance behaviour of children.

Findings of Objective-V

The personality and health status of students were examined in relation to child abuse and other factors. Section-V deals with interpretation of results obtained on Univariate, Bivariate and Multivariate analyses. Results are presented in the following section.

A. Impact of Child Abuse on Personality: The personality pattern of children was assessed as a function of environmental setting, gender and child abuse. Further, the role of type of school, grade and child abuse in personality development of children was also examined. Results are reported briefly:

- The rural-urban environmental setting of school exerted significant influence on ten dimensions of personality. Urban school students were found less reserved, more intelligent, emotionally stable, excitable, enthusiastic, conscientious, more adventurous, less doubting, self-sufficient and highly controlled than rural school students. Boys and girls differed significantly on some dimensions of personality. Boys were found more excitable, less expedient, less tender minded and more doubting.
- Type of school exerted significant influence on four dimensions of personality. Government and private school students differed significantly on some dimensions of personality. Government school students were found more reserved, emotionally less stable, tough minded and vigorous than private school students.
- Junior class (6 to 8th grade) students and senior class (9 to 10th grade) students differed significantly on some

dimensions of personality. Specifically, junior class (6 to 8th grade) students were found more reserved, more intelligent, emotionally less stable, undemonstrative, obedient, sober, expedient, shy, self-assertive and group dependent than senior class (9 to 10th grade) students. Child abuse adversely impacted some domains of personality. High abused students were found less intelligent and group dependent than low abused children.

B. Impact on Health

- **Impact on Physical Health:** Physical health status of students was significantly influenced by level of abuse, type of school, gender and grade. High abused children displayed more health problems than low abused children. Health status was found poor in government school students as compared to private school students. Girls showed more physical illness than boys. Intermediate level students expressed more physical health problems than high school students and junior high school students.
- **Impact on Mental Health:** The psychological (Mental health) health of students was significantly influenced by child abuse, gender and grade. Specifically, high abused children expressed more psychological health problems than low abused children. Girls displayed greater health problems than boys. High school students expressed more mental health problems than intermediate level and junior high school level students.

Interpretation of Correlation and Regression Results

- Correlation analysis was done to establish the association between school abuse and physical as well as mental illness of students. Results are interpreted briefly. Child abuse as a whole and its dimensions were positively correlated with physical illness. Child abuse as a whole and its dimensions were also found positively associated with mental health.

Prediction of Health Status: Physical health was positively predicted by emotional abuse. Again physical health was positively predicted by emotional abuse. Similarly, mental health was positively predicted by emotional abuse.

In brief, the findings of present study as mentioned earlier have explored numerous causative factors of child maltreatment in schools. Furthermore, results proved the adverse consequences of child abuse on cognitive, motivational, affective and behavioural functioning of children. Apart from this, child abuse has caused detrimental impact on personality and health status of children. The effects of school setting, type of school, gender and grade on students' health were partially proved.

The empirical and theoretical validation of present findings has been presented in the following section.

The Empirical Validation of Present Findings

The findings of the study have strong empirical supports. In this section, results are interpreted and discussed in accordance with objectives of the study.

1. The Influence of Environmental Factors on Child Abuse in Schools

The findings of present study evinced that numerous environmental factors exercised significant role in the incidence of child abuse and neglect in schools. Physical and educational neglect were found higher in rural schools whereas, psychological abuse and emotional neglect and abuse as a whole were found greater in urban schools. Besides this, type of schools (Government and Private) and medium of education in schools (Hindi and English) also played significant role. The school environment also contributed significantly to incidence of child abuse and neglect. So, positive school environment minimizes the occurrence of child abuse whereas negative school environment intensify the cases of maltreatment in school setting. Present findings have ample empirical supports.

Since multiple forces determine the origin of child abuse and neglect at four ecological levels: the individual (ontogenetic), the family (the micro-system), the community (the exo-system) and the culture (the macro-system) in which each level is nested with each other (Belsky, 1984). Findings of the present study evinced that child abuse is present at alarming threshold in rural and urban schools as some forms of abuses were found significantly higher in rural schools whereas, other forms are prevalent in urban schools. It appears that in both settings, children are abused; only dimensions and forms of maltreatment differ. Since the traditional pattern of discipline in schools is highly accepted in rural schools and therefore, teachers/principals of rural schools exercise corporal punishment to discipline/control their students. Whereas, in school of urban setting, students are frequently abused verbally/ psychologically.

Although, with passage of time teacher's attitude towards students and discipline methods are gradually changing. Urban school teachers are more aware with system. Majority are more interactive and co-operative with students and also apply democratic pattern to discipline their students than rural school teachers. Guardians and students of urban environment are more aware. As a matter of fact, physical abuse and educational neglect were found greater in rural schools, whereas, psychological abuse and emotional neglect were found higher in urban schools. Rural school teachers were also found more neglectful and irresponsible. Since less exposure, irresponsibility, lack of awareness and over- or undercrowded classrooms are some of the root causes of high incidence of physical abuse and educational neglect in rural schools. Contrary to this, in urban schools, certain other forms of child abuse i.e., psychological abuse, sexual harassment, discrimination, bullying (gang attack) etc. are found at alarming threshold (Pandey, 2005; 2007, 2017; Baruah, 2003; Gil, 1971).

2. *The Role of Socio-Demographic Characteristics in Child Abuse*

Present results also evinced that numerous social and demographic factors related to students and teachers/school personnel exercised significant role in the origin of child abuse and neglect. Findings have been interpreted and discussed in the light of other researches.

Students' Socio-Demographic Characteristics and Child Abuse: The findings of present study denoted a clear-cut association between certain socio-demographic characteristics of students and child maltreatment.

(i) The Socio-economic Status: Forms of child maltreatment differed across socio-economic status of students. Specifically, physical abuse, sexual abuse, emotional neglect and educational neglect were found higher in SC students than OBC and General category students. However, the physical neglect was found more in OBC than SC and GC students. The socio-economic status of family directly influences the status of students in many ways, including abusive treatment by school personnel. Other studies also confirm present findings.

As National Incidence Study (NIS-III) reports, children of low-income strata were found significantly more victims of child maltreatment however; children of different strata were also found abused and neglected in some or other forms. Studies indicated that a large segment of population, who are socially disadvantaged or sufferers of social-isolation and poverty are found more abusive. Since social isolation is eventually a noted characteristic feature of abusive families, who lack social recognition, adequate care, peer groups, close friends and adequate housing (Coulton *et al.* 1995, Thompson, 1994). Abusive parents often lack social control on others in the family, neighbourhood, community and social agencies, which provide needed support and assistance (Korbin, 1994). Numerous studies support that there are multiple factors responsible for high rate of maltreatment in low status families (Straus *et al.*, 1980). Coulton *et al.* (1995) identified that in low class families' unstable or violent family situation; several disadvantages (Housing, privacy, noise, pollution, crowding etc.) are very common and emerge as major socio-cultural factors exercising impact on high rate of child maltreatment in North America. In a study, Pandey (2012) found that Low SES students as compared to Middle and High SES groups were found highly maltreated in many forms and also showed behavioural problems in schools.

(ii) The Demographic Characteristics: Numberous studies have identified that age and gender are the main demographic characteristics, significantly linked with differential reporting of maltreatment (Pandey, 2005, 2007; Sedlak and Broadhurst, 1996). These studies support present findings.

- ***Student's Gender***: Results denote significant variations on forms of abuses between boys and girls. Girls were found more physically, emotionally, and educationally neglected than boys whereas, boys were found more physically abused than girls. There may be numerous causes of girl child neglects. In our patriarchal society, boys are given priority within the family as well as outside the family including school setup, therefore, discrimination between boys and girls shifts from family to school setting and thus, abuse by school personnel are very natural.

Other studies prove present finding. National Incidence Study (NIS) reported that girls were 25 per cent more likely to be the victims of any form of abuse than boys. However, 80 per cent of the girls become victims of sexual abuse (Finkelhor, 1993). The dynamics of sexual abuse vary for boys and girls. Finkelhor (1995) reported that boys and girls are more likely to be sexually abused by male non-family members. Pandey (2007) identified that girls are more psychologically as well as sexually abused and neglected than boys, whereas boys are identified more physically abused and neglected.

Child's Age/Grade: Present results denote that forms and extent of abuse and neglect differed significantly across varying age and class grade levels of students. Children and preadolescents were found more physically and sexually abused than adolescents. Further, grade level of students was also linked with child maltreatment. Psychological abuse, physical neglect, emotional neglect and educational neglect were found higher in intermediate level students than junior high school and high school level students. Whereas, physical and sexual abuse were found more in junior high school students than intermediate and high school level students. Correlation and regression results also proved that some forms of abuses increased with increasing age level. Age and grade play differential role in child abuse and neglect.

Other studies conducted in family setup also support the role of age in child maltreatment. Pandey (2005, 2007) evinced that Pre-adolescents and children (6-10 yrs.) were found more physically abused than adolescents. However, sexual abuse was identified maximum among adolescents. Other studies also confirm this finding (Sedlakand Broadhurst, 1996). According to National Incidence Study-III reports, toddlers, pre-schoolers and younger adolescents are the most common victims of physical and emotional abuses, which correspond to the origin of greater independence and parent-child conflicts at these developmental stages. However, child physical abuse exercises influence on development of a sizeable number of children of all age groups yet, the main reason of physical injury among older children (12-17 yrs.) is, increasing conflict between parents/teachers and teenagers.

Child's Education: Results also denoted negative association of child education with physical and sexual abuse. Lower class students (6-8th grade) were found more physically and sexually assaulted by school personnel than high school and intermediate level students. Whereas, positive link between education and other forms of abuses were found, as senior class students were found victims of psychological abuse, physical neglect, emotional neglect and educational neglect than junior class students.

Many studies partially support present findings. Pandey (2007) identified that low educated children were found more victims of child maltreatment than high educated children. Education makes children more aware of their rights and responsibilities. They can retaliate or rationalize adults and protect themselves from adult abusive treatments. Educated children can skillfully avoid the circumstances of being victims of sexual abuse and neglects. NIS findings also confirm that low education was positively linked with high rate of child abuse and neglect.

3.Teachers' Demographic Characteristics and Child Maltreatment: A close perusal of results revealed that several demographic characteristics of teachers/adults were found closely associated with child abuse and neglect. Major findings are discussed in the light of other empirical evidences.

(i) Teachers' Age: Results indicated that younger teachers (age below 35 yrs.) were found more abusive than older teachers (40+yrs). The incidence of Child Physical Abuse (CPA), Child Sexual Abuse (CSA) and Child Physical Neglect (CPN) were significantly higher by younger teachers than those of elderly teachers. Since, majority of younger teachers face more challenges, show less tolerance and feel high pressure and stress to cope with home-work interface, which in turn make them abusive than more experienced and mature teachers who enjoy teaching and have better ability to cope with stressful situations.

Since positive support and guidance is essential for proper development of children within a safe environment, although, it may cause early helplessness and dependency, but also encourages the child to differentiate and acquire own identity. Numerous studies (Steele, 1980; Bowlby, 1969, 1973, 1980) suggested that development of attachment dynamics is relevant to provide a secure emotional base in early life, which facilitates to the development of self-esteem, a capacity for autonomous functioning and empathy for other. Pandey (2007) evinced that home-work interface and poor parenting skills are common in younger adults (parents/teachers), they exercise maladaptive coping strategies to face challenges at workplace and deal with children in abusive manner.

(ii) Teacher's Gender: The gender difference of teachers was found linked with child abuse. Child Physical Abuse (CPA), physical neglect and educational neglect were committed more by male teachers than females. Contrary to this, psychological abuse and emotional neglect were done more frequently by female teachers. Other studies also support present results. (NIS-III, 1984; Pandey; 2007; 2010).

(iii) Teachers' Marital Status: Results denote that unmarried teachers were found more abusive than married teachers. Since lifestyle of adults has close link with personal and social adjustment and satisfaction (Pandey, 2008). So, married people can make better adjustment in stressful situations, they are more able to handle challenges and responsibility in schools and classroom setup too. They also have better ability to handle and cope with hassles created by students in classroom situation as compared to unmarried teachers.

To conclude, numerous socio-demographic characteristics of the students and teachers contribute to the origin of child abuse and neglect in school setting.

4. Childhood Abusive Experiences and Personality of Teachers

Present findings indicate close association between childhood abuses of teachers and their personality. Childhood psychological abuse, physical neglect and emotional neglect were found negatively correlated with agreeableness domain of personality. Likewise childhood emotional neglect was found inversely related with conscientious and extraversion. Contrary to this, childhood psychological abuse and emotional neglect were found positively related with neuroticism. Again, childhood psychological abuse was found positively related with openness dimension of personality. Teachers, who scored higher on neuroticism and openness domain of personality, were also identified more abusive.

Other studies identified that personality traits have been associated with childhood abuse and neglect and have also been found to impact the quality and satisfaction of romantic relationship (Holland and Roisman, 2008). In another study, Rosogesh and Cicchetti (2004) found negative association between childhood maltreatment and agreeableness. Other studies have also proved that childhood psychological abuse, emotional neglect and physical neglect have strong impact on personality traits (Holland and Roisman, 2008). These results suggest that childhood abusive experiences damage proper development of personality of individual. Often, they develop abusive personality type. Such adults as a father abuse their children in the family and as a teacher maltreat students in the school. This cycle of abusing continues generation to generation.

5. The Psychological Consequences of Child Abuse on Students

The incidence of child abuse by teachers and consequences on students' psychological functionings were assessed with the help of various measures. Present findings proved the damaging impact of child abuse on students. Findings have been interpreted and discussed in the light of other empirical evidences in this section.

(i) Impact on Cognitive Functioning

Student's cognitive functioning, viz., verbal ability, memory span and working memory as a function of environmental setting of schools, type of schools, gender, grade/age and child abuse were investigated. Findings are discussed for each cognitive process in relation to other studies in the following section.

- **Verbal Ability:** A close perusal of results evinced that child abuse exercised negative impact on verbal ability of students. Highly abused students displayed poor verbal ability than low abused students. Specifically, dimensions of verbal ability, and verbal ability as a whole were found adversely affected by abusive treatment of teachers. Furthermore, verbal ability was found inferior in government school students than private school students. High school level students showed very poor verbal ability than intermediate and junior high-school students. It is also clear from regression results that the child abuse and its various forms contributed negatively to verbal ability.

Present finding has empirical supports. In a study, Pandey, Tamta and Tripathi (2015) examined the role of verbal ability in the development of working memory. They identified that verbal ability correlated positively with working memory and its domains. In another study, Pandey and Tamta (2013) evinced negative association between child maltreatment and verbal ability. Other studies also investigated link between child maltreatment and cognitive development throughout the life span (De Bellis *et al.*, 2005). Studies suggest that chronic abuse and neglect in childhood have damaging effect on brain maturation and organizational processes including verbal ability (Bremner *et al.*, 1999; De Bellis, 2005). Child maltreatment may also be associated with global cognitive deficits including impaired intelligence, poor academic performance, memory and learning disabilities (De Bellis *et al.*, 2009; Goodman *et al.*, 2010).

- **Memory Span:** Results of present study denoted that abused children showed low level of memory span than non/low-abused children. Apart from this, government school students displayed lower memory span than private school students. Memory span was found far inferior in high-school students than intermediate and junior high-school students. However, gender difference was found non-significant. Correlation results proved negative relationship of child maltreatment with memory span. Further, regression results proved that various forms of child abuse contributed negatively to memory span.

Present study can be supported from other research findings, Pandey (2007a, b) evinced the significant impact of child abuse, setting and gender on development of memory span. The abusive experiences of children caused adverse impact on their memory span. Rural children showed lower memory span than urban children. Memory span was found higher in boys than girls. In another study Pandey (2011) examined the role of child maltreatment, age, gender and setting on cognitive functioning i.e., memory span and level of intellect. Results proved that child abuse, age and setting contributed significantly to children's cognitive functioning.

- **Working Memory:** Working memory of students was also measured. Findings revealed that working memory as a whole and central executive dimension of working memory were found far inferior in abused children than low abused children. Further, senior class students scored higher on working memory and its various dimensions than junior class students. However, gender difference on working memory was found partially significant.

Present findings have ample empirical support. In a study, Pandey and Tamta (2013) evinced that child abuse caused detrimental impact on development of working memory in children. High abused group was found inferior on dimensions of working memory i.e., phonological loop, central executive and overall working memory as compared to low abused group. Findings indicated that some forms of abuse i.e., psychological abuse, sexual abuse, and emotional neglect have contributed negatively in the development of working memory and its components.

Other findings have also evinced that children who experience abuse show deficits on central executive memory (Nolin and Ethier, 2007). These studies find associations between childhood abuse and neglect and language deficits, reduced cognitive functioning, and attention deficit disorders (National Research Council, 1993). Due to abusive experience, the frontal lobe, a part of brain damaged (at least left) and working memory capacity impaired (De Prince *et al.*, 2009).

Numerous studies show that children subject to abuse without neurological injury show deficits of central executive functioning, memory, attention, visuo-spatial ability, language and motor speed, in some cases also accompanied by significant cerebral atrophy (Pears and Fisher, 2005; Prasad *et al.*, 2005; Porter *et al.*, 2005). Abuse has also been associated with lower level of intelligence (Nolin and Ethier, 2007; Pandey, 2011). Child maltreatment can lead to specific deficits in short-term verbal memory (Bremner *et al.*, 1995), visual memory (Savitz *et al.*, 2007), executive functions (WM) (Mezzacappa *et al.*, 2001) and sustained attention (Beers and De Bellies, 2002). The exposure to more than one form of maltreatment was analyzed by Nolin and Ethier (2007), who found that abused and neglected children performed worse on cognitive functions test than comparison group. Research findings suggest that exposure to forms of maltreatment may have adverse impact on cognitive functioning, and thus pose a cumulative risk of negative developmental effects (Cicchetti and Toth, 2005; Pandey, 2007; Pandey, Tamta and Tripathi, 2015).

(ii) Impact of Child Abuse on Motivational Process

The academic achievement motivation and level of aspiration in students as a function of child abuse, type of school, grade and gender were also assessed in present study. Results report that abused children expressed lower level of academic achievement motive, and aspiration as compared to non/low abused children. Students of Government schools were found low achievers than private schools. Aspiration level was greater in girls than boys. Further, high school level students showed lower level of aspiration than intermediate and junior high school students. Thus, abusive experiences caused detrimental impact on motivation level of children.

Other studies also support present results. In a comprehensive study, Pandey (2005; 2007) revealed that children abused by parents expressed low levels of achievement and aspiration than non-abused children. Apart from this, motivation level varied across setting, age, gender and socio-economic status of respondents. Children belonging to rural setting, young age and low socio-economic status were found low achievers than their comparison groups. Boys were found high achievers than girls. Findings further denoted that the level of aspiration was poor in abused children as compared to non-abused group of children. Child abuse was found to be negatively related with achievement motivation and level of aspiration (2007). Earlier, Misra and Tripathi (1980) showed that deprived people were found low achievers than low deprived people. A sizeable number of studies denoted that people from low strata of society have low achievement levels than middle and high SES groups (Angelini *et al.*, 1970; Uhr *et al.*, 1969; Nygard, 1969; Srivastava and Tiwari, 1967; Rosen, 1962). It is clear from the results of present study and other research findings, that negative consequences of child abuse on achievement and aspiration level of children are mediated by maltreating experiences during childhood as well as many socio-cultural factors.

(iii) Impact on Affective Process

Depression and Anxiety levels in students were also measured in relation to school child abuse, type of school, grade and gender. Results evinced that Government school students as compared to private school counterparts showed more depression. Depression level was found higher in abused children.

Furthermore, the effects of abuse and grade on anxiety were found significant. Specifically, high abused students showed more anxiety than low abused counterparts. The level of anxiety was found greater in high school students than intermediate and junior high school students. Other studies also support the results.

Depression, severe anxiety, panic attacks and post-traumatic stress disorder (PTSD) are the most common consequences of abuse: the literature suggests that between 30 and 50 per cent of sexually abused children meet the full criteria for a PTSD diagnosis (Widom 1999; Darves-Bornoz *et al.* 1998), and up to 80 per cent experience at least some 'post-traumatic' symptoms (McLeer *et al.*, 1992; Cuffe *et al.*, 1998). These symptoms include hyper-vigilance, intrusive thoughts, and sudden intrusive flashbacks of the abuse experience. Child physical abuse can lead directly to neurological damage, physical injuries, pain and disability or, in extreme cases, death. Emotional abuse has an important impact on a developing child's affective functioning behaviour and self-esteem. It can be especially damaging during the critical period of infancy, and affect children especially during their school years.

(iv) Impact on Behavioural Functioning

The effects of school child abuse, type of school, grade and gender on children's behaviours were also assessed. Results evinced that Positive behaviours i.e., Social interaction and Study behaviour were found very poor in abused group of children. Apart from this, interaction results indicate that along with other factors, abusive experiences diminished Helping behaviour and Disciplinary behaviours in students.

Contrary to this, negative behaviours viz., Aggressive behaviours, Non-compliance and Bullying behaviour were found higher in high abused children. Regression results proved differential roles of forms of abuse in behaviours. The findings of this study also partially proved the significant roles of type of schools, grade and gender in behavioural functioning of children. Present findings have ample empirical supports.

Earlier researches have also explored that abusive treatment by adults (parents/teachers) diminished positive behaviours and increased negative behaviours in children (Pandey *et al.*, 2015). Pandey (2010) studied the impact of the exposure of domestic violence on child behaviour in schools. She found that exposed group of children as compared to non-exposed group were found poor in study behaviour, disciplinary behaviour, and helping behaviour and also displayed lesser school activities and social interaction in school. A number of studies revealed that abused children displayed deficiency in pro-social behaviour and communication and showed physical aggression. They also showed disturbed peer interaction, deficits in pro-social behaviour, social withdrawal and isolation (Prino and Peyrot, 1994; Crittenden, 1992; Hoffman-Plotkin and Twentyman, 1984).

In a recent study, Pandey, Tripathi and Prasad (2015) investigated the role of parenting in shaping children's behaviour. They identified that positive parenting i.e., love, encouragement, acceptance, progressiveness, democratism, independency and dominance played favourable role in developing positive behaviours and controlling negative behaviours in children. Contrary to this, negative parenting exercised detrimental impact in shaping desirable behaviours in children. Earlier, Pandey (2007) identified that child maltreatment was found positively related with aggressive behaviour and abuse contributed favourably to heightened level of aggression in children. Abused children as compared to non-abused children showed more aggression and level of aggression was also found higher in rural and younger age children than their urban and pre-adolescent/adolescent counterparts.

A bulk of studies conducted worldwide, confirms the heightened aggression and related externalizing behaviours in children who are victims of physical abuse (Wolfe *et al.*, 1998; Shields, Cicchetti and Ryan, 1994; National Academy of Sciences, 1993). In a study Dodge *et al.* (1997) reported that the experience of child physical abuse included aggressive behaviour and communicate its appropriateness as a problem solving skill. High aggression and other problems in abused children may be related to the witnessing family violence and other negative life events. High level of family conflicts, including verbal and physical aggression has been found to be associated with emotional problems and diminished social functioning (Fantuzzo *et al.*, 1991). Thus, heightened aggressions in abused children are very natural and can be interpreted on the basis of frustration-aggression theory propounded by Dollard and Miller (1950), which suggests that arousal of aggression, is the outcome of frustration. Children, who are abused, gradually become frustrated as being unable to save themselves or retaliate and develop aggressive tendency.

(v) Impact on Personality Development of Students

Students' personality as a function of child abuse, school setting, type of schools, gender and grade was assessed. Results revealed that abused children were found less intelligent and more group dependent than low abused children. Urban school children as compared to rural counterparts were found more reserved, intelligent, emotionally stable, enthusiastic and, conscientious, less doubting, self-sufficient and more controlled. Gender differences on some dimensions of personality were also found. Boys as compared to girls were found more excitable, lesser expedient and tender minded but more doubting. Furthermore, students of government schools as compared to private school counterparts were found more reserved, emotionally less stable, tough minded and vigorous. Grade-wise variations were also found. Specifically, Junior class students (6-8th grade) as compared to senior class (9-10th grade) students were found more reserved, intelligent, emotionally less stable, undemonstrative, obedient, sober, expedient, shy, self- assessed and group dependent.

Present findings have sound empirical and theoretical supports. Pandey (2007) evinced that child abuse by parents caused damaging impact on personality development of children. The positive domains of personality were found to be negatively correlated with child maltreatment whereas negative domains were found positively associated with child abuse and neglect. Specifically, abused children were found less intelligent, expressed weak ego strength, shyness and group dependency. Apart from this, they were found more excitable, disregarding rules, artless, more tense and frustrated. Contrary to this, non-abused children showed high intelligence, strong ego strength and high patience. They were found more rules bound and circumspect (more practical) and therefore, they showed better leadership capacity, decision-making ability and self-sufficiency, however, were found less tense and frustrated. Fisher *et al.* (1997) also showed many personality disorders in physically abused children. High rates of depression and conduct disorder were found in abused adolescents (Pelcovitz *et al.*, 1994). Child sexual abuse causes severe long-term and short-term consequences on personality development. They showed low self-esteem, guilt and shame (Conte and Schuerman, 1987; De Francis, 1969). Other studies report high rates of depression, withdrawal and suicidal tendencies (Gladstone *et al.*, 1999; Kolko *et al.*, 1988; Friedrich *et al.*, 1986). Researches observed more common symptoms of fearfulness in sexually abused children (Browne and Finkelhor, 1986). A sizeable number of studies indicated that psychologically maltreated children showed lower level of social competence and adjustment problems and high level of insecurity (Egeland, 1991; Vissing *et al.*, 1991). Other studies also confirmed the presence of low self-esteem, anxiety, depression, dissociation and interpersonal sensitivity in adults who were psychologically abused as a child (Downs and Miller, 1998; Kent and Waller, 1998; Briere and Runtz, 1988, 1990).

Thus, unfavourable family environment, teacher (Adult)-student relationship, poor parenting skills, unfavourable school environment and classroom setting and inputs from community etc. positively contribute to the origin of child maltreatment in family and schools.

(vi) Impact on Health Status

The health status of students as a function of child abuse, type of schools, gender and grade/age was investigated. Findings are discussed in relation to other empirical evidences.

The physical health status of students was significantly influenced by level of abuse, type of school, gender and grade. High abused children displayed more health problems than low abused children. Health status was found poor in government school students as compared to private school students. Girls showed more physical illness than boys. Intermediate level students expressed more physical health problems than high school students and junior high school students. Physical neglect and psychological abuse contributed positively to physical illness.

Similarly, students' mental health was significantly influenced by child abuse, gender and grade. Specifically, high abused children expressed more mental health problems than low abused children. Girls displayed greater health problems than boys. High school students expressed more mental health problems than intermediate level and junior high school level students. Forms of abuses correlated positively to psychological illnesses. Psychological abuse and emotional neglect predicted positively to mental illness. Present results have been supported by a sizeable number of researches.

A study evinced that child abuse was found associated with numerous physical and mental health problems like; central nervous system damage, physical defects, growth and mental retardation, and speech problems (Chester, 2006). Other study also found an association between childhood abuse and hormonal disruption, manifesting in a deregulation of the HPA (hypothalamic pituitary adrenal) axis (Cicchetti and Rogosch, 2001). In addition, childhood abuse also has strong links to later health problems, including heart disease, liver disease, cancer and chronic lung disease (Felitti *et al.*, 1998).

Child abuse and neglect have been shown to cause important regions of the brain to fail to form or grow properly, resulting in impaired development. These alterations in brain maturation have long-term consequences for cognitive, language, and academic abilities and are connected with mental health disorders. Adults who experienced abuse or neglect during childhood are more likely to suffer from cardiovascular disease, lung and liver disease, hypertension, diabetes, asthma, and obesity (Felitti and Anda, 2009). One study showed that children who experienced neglect were at increased risk for diabetes and poorer lung functioning, while physical abuse was shown to increase the risk for diabetes and malnutrition (Widom, Czaja, Bentley, and Johnson, 2012). Additionally, child maltreatment has been shown to increase adolescent obesity. A longitudinal study found that children who experienced neglect had body mass indexes that grew at significantly faster rates compared to children who had not experienced neglect (Shin and Miller, 2012). Many health problems, including panic or post-traumatic stress disorder, chronic fatigue syndrome, fibromyalgia, depression, some auto-immune disorders, suicidal tendencies, abnormal fear responses, preterm labour, chronic pain syndromes, and ovarian dysfunction can be understood, in some cases, as manifestations of childhood maltreatment (Kendall-Tackett, 2000; De Bellis, 2005).

Apart from empirical validations, present findings require theoretical interpretations to achieve sound conceptual base to understand the phenomenon of child abuse and its consequences on students.

Theoretical Interpretations of Findings

Researchers have propounded numerous macro level (sociological) and micro level (psychological) theories to explain the nature and origin of child abuse within the family and outside the family (in schools etc.). Findings of the present study can also be interpreted on the basis of theories mentioned below.

1. Sociological Perspectives of Child Abuse

(i) Cultural Explanations: Present results report that incidence of child abuse witnessed at high rate in schools of Uttar Pradesh. However, forms of abuse differed in accordance with type of schools and settings. The findings are supported by Cultural Explanation approach, which suggests that violence is an accepted and encouraged form of cultural expression in our society. The acceptance of violence in the culture contributes to criminal violence in the family, schools or in the society (Tolan and Guerra, 1988; Straus, 1977). The aggression and violence in the home reflects the society's tolerance for aggression (Wyatt, 1994). Apart from this, the family/social norms also influences at certain extent of family or societal aggression. Discipline, from social scientists perspective, is the cost and the implantation of cost also ranges from legitimate to illegitimate dimensions.

(ii) Strain Theory: In present study, cases of child abuse and neglect were found maximum in low caste (SC/ST), low socio-economic status and low occupation family status students. This finding receives support from "Strain Theory" which suggests that high rates of child maltreatments are found in low income families, unemployed families and families receiving aids (Limber and

Nation, 1998). The unequal distribution of opportunities along with the stressors associated with poverty (financial worries, ill-health and crowded living conditions), produces high level of stress and frustration in lower income families (Farrington, 1980; Straus, 1980). Pandey (2007) reported positive association between child abuse and parental stress. As stress and frustration become overwhelming, adults'/teacher's aggression may be directed to innocent children in the form of abusive acts.

(iii) Social Bonding Theory: Another finding of the present study is that teachers with certain demographic and socio-psychological characteristics were found highly abusive and this result can be explained on the basis of "Social Bonding Theory". The theory attempted to answer the questions that in a given cultural and social context, which factors encourage family/school violence? Why some people are more violent than others? Since, Social Bonding Theory explains that most people are sufficiently motivated to commit deviant act (Child abuse and neglect) yet what social forces prevent certain people from committing abusive acts? People do not commit deviant acts when they have a stake in conformity. Three components of Social Bonds determine the possibility of child maltreatment, viz., low levels of Commitment, Attachment and Belief (Travis, 1993; Hirschi, 1969). Present results, along with numerous researches on child maltreatment are also supported by Social bonding theory.

(iv) Deterrence Theory: The findings of present study are also supported by the Deterrence/Control Theory (Gibbs, 1975) which focuses on the influence of formal social controls. Gelles and Straus (1988) suggest that parents/teachers abuse their children/students when there are insufficient legal structures to keep them from losing control. The cultural acceptances of parent-to-child or teacher-to-student violence blur the line between legitimate discipline and child maltreatment. However, the mandatory reporting laws and public awareness are increasing pressure to save children from abusive families, parents and teachers in school setting (Besharov, 1996).

2. Psychological Perspective of Child Abuse and Neglect

Although sociological theories successfully explain why child abuse exists in a society but they fail to explain why individual family member or school teacher is violent? Primarily, these theories interpret child abuse in structural terms, but do not explain variation in individual's cognitions and behaviours. Explaining the behaviour of individual is more difficult than explaining structural pattern of maltreatment, hence certain psychological theories have made effort to identify risk factors that make maltreatment more understandable and predictable. Thus, interpretation of present results, in relation to psychological perspectives has also been made in the following sections.

(i) Biological Factors: Present study identified that younger and low IQ school personnel were found more abusive than their comparison group. Researches indicate that biological characteristics of abusers are found to be associated with child abuse and neglect. Abusers show hyper responsive physiological activity to both positive and negative child stimuli. Such activity might make the abuser more physiologically reactive in stressful situation with children and lead to abuse (Milner and Chilamkurti, 1991). Other biological factors, i.e. I.Q. neuropsychological deficiencies, deficit disorders, physical disabilities and disorder and health problems were found closely linked with child maltreatment (Pandey, 2007; Milner, 1998; Crittenden, 1992).

(ii) Psychological Characteristics: The findings of the present study denoted that abusive teachers expressed high level of negative personality traits i.e. neuroticism and openness. Apart from this, close positive association between childhood maltreatment and neuroticism and openness was reported. In addition, these teachers were found more abusive towards students. A sizeable number of researches also identified that maltreating adults showed higher level of cognitive distortions, depressive symptoms, stress, low self-esteem, more substance abuse or dependence as compared with non-maltreating adults (Milner *et al.*, 1995; Ethier *et al.*, 1995., Chan, 1994). Certain other studies reported that abusive adults (parents/teachers) display more anger control problems, hostility and low frustration tolerance than non-abusive counterparts (Milner *et al.*, 1995; Bauer and Twentyman, 1985). It appears that certain psychological and behavioural factors lead to child maltreatment.

(iii) interaction Theories: The results of present study are also supported by the reciprocal nature of the Teacher-Student relationship. This theory suggests that difficult child behaviours

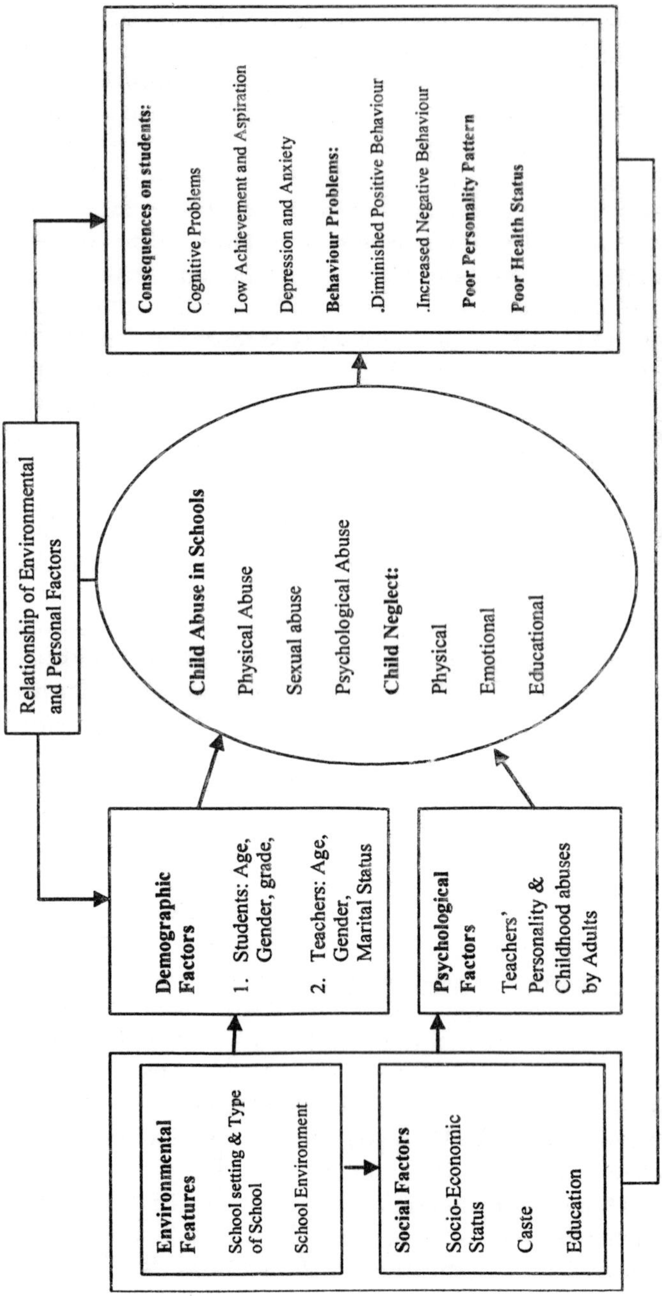

Fig. 4.1: Psycho-Social Dynamics of Child Abuse in Schools and its Consequences.

interact with behavioural problems and deficits of parents/teachers i.e., poor skills or anger control problems (Pandey, 2004; Milner, 1993). Attachment theory (Bowlby, 1969) suggests that attachment is an enduring emotional bond that develops during the first year of infant's life. Failure to form a secure attachment in early life may contribute to problems in school age and adulthood in the form of inability to develop close personal relationship (Ainsworth and Bowlby, 1991). The insecure pattern of attachment was found in abused, neglected and psychologically abused children (Pandey, 2004; Crittenden, 1998). Researchers stressed that insecure attachments are caused by parental unresponsiveness to the physical and psychological needs of the child. Poor bond between parent/teacher-child relations may lead to difficult child behaviours and increased challenges for parents as the child develops, resulting in an inverse escalation of abusive parent-child interactions (Crittenden, 1998; Cerezo, 1997; Hurlock, 1984). Similarly, poor bond in family continues and shifts outside the family in the form of abusive pattern of student-teacher relationship.

(iv) Role of Social Learning Theory: Findings of the study has also been successfully analyzed on the basis of Social Learning Theory. Bandura (1971) emphasized the process of modeling which individual learns social and cognitive behaviour by simply observing and imitating model's behaviour. Children exposed to violence acquire that violence is an acceptable way to resolving conflicts in family or schools and expressing emotions. Thus, observation and reinforcement of violence within a social context teach children how to perform abusive acts.

Evaluation of Current Theoretical Status of Child Abuse and its Impact on Students: In the light of the present study and other researches, some issues have been raised, which are unresolved in given theories. The macro level sociological theories emphasize very well the structural roots of child maltreatment but lack to explain the processes involved in the origin of abuses. Therefore, micro level psychological theories have been applied to explain the processes involved in abusive behaviour. However, biological and personality traits mainly emphasize the root causes of problems within the person, whereas, the social learning theory and the interaction theories focus on major psychological processes in relation to social context (viz., family and school agents) in the origin of child maltreatment.

Moreover, there is a need to develop a wide range theory of child abuse outside the family (in schools) which can better explain, what is child abuse? And why does child abuse occur in schools? Hence, it is essential to emphasize the role of certain mediating and moderating factors in between the antecedent and consequences of child abuse. Present researcher has endeavoured to incorporate these factors in the relationships of antecedents and consequences of child abuse in the school context. Therefore, on the basis of present findings, a model has been devised to show the social and psychological dynamics of abuse, in schools and its consequences on students as well as to discuss the relationship between environmental, mediating and outcome variables (Fig. 4.1).

The first level of the model includes environmental and social factors. The environmental features include: environmental setting of schools, type of school and school environment. The social factors involve socio-economic status, income, caste and education. These factors showed clear-cut linkage with child abuse and its consequences.

The second level of model includes the demographic and psychological factors. The demographic features involve students' age, gender, education and grade as well as Teachers' age, gender, marital status and education. Psychological characteristics involve Teachers' personality, and their childhood abuses. These factors were found connected with child abuse and its consequences. In school setting, the child (victim) has focal place confronting any sort of interaction with teachers or school personnel, who may be found as perpetrators and the nature of interaction between students and teachers determine the frequency and intensity of child maltreatment.

Third level of the model indicates different forms of child abuse and neglect which are originated and shaped by environmental/contextual, demographic and psychological factors and interrelationships of these factors. Within and outside the family (in schools), child abuse/neglect may take place as a whole or in any forms i.e., Child physical abuse (CPA), Child psychological Abuse (C Psy. A), Child sexual abuse (CSA) and Child Neglect, viz., Physical, emotional and educational neglects, which in turn exercise damaging impact on development of children. As Fig. 4.1 indicates child abuses in schools along with interrelationships of environmental, socio-demographic and personal factors have damaging consequences on development of cognitive, motivational, affective and behavioural functioning as well as personality and health status of students.

Implications of the Present Study

The present piece of research is not merely a theoretical exercise, but also is based on empirical data from a large number of participants (Teachers and Students) of different schools of Uttar Pradesh. It is an intensive school based research study; hence obtained results have empirical, theoretical and professional significance.

Child abuse in school setting is considered one of the most serious psycho-social issues not only in India, but also around the globe. The cases of child abuse in schools are witnessed in plenty but it is either ignored or unnoticed. Therefore, present researcher endeavoured to study psycho-social dynamics of child abuse in schools and its psychological consequences on students. It was seriously felt that without understanding the potential etiological factors of child abuse by school personnel/teachers, this problem would not be prevented. Firstly, for the sake of identification of cases, a systematic screening was done by using multiple strategies. To identify the predictors of child abuse and its consequences on students numerous standardized measures were exercised on students and teachers. Findings have uncovered various antecedents, mediating factors and outcomes of school abuse on students.

- Present research has proved that many forms of child abuse are present in schools of Uttar Pradesh at high rate and no school is immune of abusive activities. The pervasive roles of environmental, demographic, social and psychological factors were identified in the incidence of abuses in school setting. This finding would be instrumental to understand the ingredients of child abuse in school setting.
- Results also evidenced the adverse consequences of school abuse on cognitive, motivational, affective and behavioural functioning of students. Apart from this, personality and health status of students were also adversely affected by abusive treatments by adults/teachers. These findings

would be helpful to guide teachers, guardians, school authorities as well as students to understand the causes of child abuse in schools and its damaging consequences on students.

- Since the study intended to provide conceptual clarity and theoretical base for understanding the ingredients of child abuse in school setting and exploring its consequences on school children. Therefore, on the basis of findings of present study, a number of remediation programmes and preventive interventions can be developed which would serve the purpose of National interest. Therefore, this research has proved its practical and theoretical significance.

Suggestions for the Further Study

A critical analysis of the findings of the present study pointed out some of the issues which led to fresh views for further investigation.

1. Although, child abuse within the family is widely studied issue, therefore in the present study effort was made to investigate child abuse outside the family i.e. in the school setting. Children directly or indirectly experience different forms of abusive treatments outside the family by school-teachers, peer groups, relatives and/or any adults, significant to the child. Apart from school/institutional abuses, ritualistic abuse, organized sexual exploitation, and child pornography are certain serious forms of child maltreatments. Thus, these issues should also be focused in further researches.

2. Present study has mainly focused on ecological, socio-demographic and personal factors as root causes of child maltreatment in school setting. However, it is also essential to highlight the role of certain biological and cultural factors in the origin and sustenance of child abuse and neglect in schools and society. Despite this, the nature and gravity of child abuse vary from culture to culture but conceptualization and classification of child abuse and neglect are primarily done by western researchers. Thus, there is a need to provide more comprehensive definition of child abuse, emphasizing cross-cultural perspectives.

3. The study of child abuse by school personnel is a sensitive issue and such researches suffer from under or false reporting of

cases. During data collection, it was realized that respondents and school administrators tried to fake or hide the correct reporting of abusive activities in schools. They twisted their responses on structured measures. So, there is need to apply multiple strategies (both quantitative and qualitative) to identify the actual nature, frequency and intensity of child maltreatment in school setting. These considerations will be taken in further researches.

4. In this research, certain forms of abuse and neglect in schools were reported by school teachers on an open-ended interview schedule (reported in result section). However, the cases of bullying were observed in plenty and such abuses were committed by classmates, seniors and other school personnel. The victims of abuses differed in accordance with socio-demographic characteristics and setting of schools. Thus, intervention programme at school level should be implemented to aware victimized students, their parents, teachers and other school personnel including other students about causative factors and detrimental consequences of abusive acts on students.

5. In the present study, the consequences of school abuse on cognitive, motivational, affective, and behavioural functions as well as personality and health status of students have been thoroughly investigated. Further, teachers' childhood abusive experiences, demographic and personality patterns were assessed. Therefore, to understand the predictors of school abuses, other mediating/ moderating factors (coping, skills, self-esteem etc.) should be thoroughly investigated. Despite this, nationwide study should be conducted to find out the magnitude and actual forms of abuses in schools.

Conclusion and Recommendations

Findings of the study, clearly stressed that many forms of child abuse are present in schools of Uttar Pradesh at high rate and no school is immune of abusive activities. The pervasive roles of environmental, demographic, social and psychological factors were identified in the incidence of abuses in school setting. Furthermore, results evidenced the ill consequences of school abuse on cognitive, motivational, affective and behavioural functioning of students. Apart from this, personality and health status of students are also adversely affected by abusive treatments by teachers.

A cursory glance at findings of present study reveal that although child abuse in schools is present at high level in many forms, but unfortunately it is unnoticed and unreported. A large segment of child community is in the direct trap of this evil. Thus, preventive efforts (both short-term and long-term) are urgently needed. Therefore, innovative school based preventive/promotive interventions should be designed and implemented to support abused children and improve their career and quality of life. Thus, certain recommendations/remediation to control child abuse in schools and its adverse impact on students are suggested:

1. Develop Systematic Understanding of the Ingredients of Child Abuse in Schools

Prior to designing any intervention programme, it is essential to systematically scrutinize the causative roots of child abuse in schools from multidimensional approaches. Belsky (1980) has proposed four ecological roots of etiology of child abuses viz., ontogenetic level (personal factors), micro system (family factors), macro system (social factors, school setting) and exo-system (cultural factors) levels respectively. So based on Belsky's model, numerous preventive programmes can be developed and implemented in schools. Therefore, it is essential to explore causative factors; personal and situational/social causes of abuses in schools, then plan innovative intervention programmes to counteract the prevalence of child abuse in general and school abuse in particular.

2. Generate Knowledge Through Awareness Programme

Present results suggest for sensitizing the public and victimized group and their parents about issues related to school (child) abuse. People should be made aware of existing legal efforts to protect child abuse or any other crimes against children. Regular workshops, conferences, meetings, group discussions and various communication channels should be exercised to cognize students, parents, school authorities/personnel and public. Besides this, it is essential to design and implement intervention programmes at school level to cognize victims about the sign and symptoms of abuses and intensions of abusers and girls should learn the difference between the good touch and bad touch. Simultaneously, public should be sensitized towards gender equality, human rights, and non-violence.

3. Prevent Health Hazards in Abused Victims

In the present study, a large number of students/victims reported poor physical and mental health status and emotional problems. However, in most of the school settings, no adequate facility and counselling centres to help students were observed. So, school personnel should be clearly informed about the links among child abuses, emotional trauma and health hazards. In addition, concerted efforts should be made by school authority, child psychologists, counsellors, health professional and community leaders, to chalk out intervention programmes integrating comprehensive medical and psychological care for abused victims. These efforts will be relevant in rebuilding confidence and maintaining health and well-being of students.

4. Implement School Based Intervention Programmes to Help Students

Every school should have a number of measures in place to help and protect their students including—

- Staff who have been trained to identify signs of abuse.
- A designated teacher or counsellor should be hired for dealing with child protection.
- Procedures for checking on staff before they are allowed to work with children.
- A child protection policy which includes procedures to be followed if a teacher or school personnel is accused of abusing a child.
- Everyone employed in school (administrators, principals, teachers, clerks, peons, school bus drivers or any other staff) should be vetted (criminal record check).

5. Implement Programmes for Academic Enhancement of Abused Children

The study revealed linkages between child abuses and poor

psychological functioning of students. Moreover, abused children showed many cognitive, motivational, affective and behavioural problems. So, intervention programme should be designed for abused children to overcome negative impacts of school abuse. Therefore, remedial programmes for victimized students at school/ institution level should be enforced to promote such students academically. Apart from this, their parents should be made aware of the damaging consequences of school abuse. Moreover, abusive school personnel/teachers should be given proper guidance and counselling to learn skills and effective coping strategies to deal with students. Legal support system should also be strengthened for prevention of abuses in schools.

6. Re-conceptualize School Abuse and Develop Innovative Research Strategy

Since child abuse is considered global psycho-social issue, however, the nature and forms of abuse vary from culture to culture. This problem is extensively studied in western countries and therefore, the conceptualization and theories of child abuse are primarily developed by western researchers, where prevention efforts are proliferated since the last few decades. Although, some forms of abuses are culture-specific. Thus, there is a need to re-conceptualize and make a more comprehensive definition emphasizing contextual and cultural perspectives. The conceptualization of child abuse should be done in glocal manner, combining both global as well as local perspectives. Apart from this, a wide range theory of school abuse should be propounded.

Innovative school based and social action-oriented research strategies should be developed to study the multifaceted dynamics of school abuse and its damaging consequences. More specifically, the intervention programmes should be developed targeting the needs of the victims, and it is also essential to bridge the gap between academic and professional roles. This holistic approach will be instrumental to prevent the incidence and prevalence rates of child abuse in general and school abuse in particular in India and around the globe.

References

Aber, J.L. and Allen, J.P. (1987). Effect of maltreatment on young children's socio-emotional development: An attachment theory perspective. *Development Psychology, 23*(3) 406-414.

Aber, J.L. and Cicchetti, D. (1984). The socio-emotional development of maltreated children: An empirical and theoretical analysis. In H. Fitzgerald, B. Lester, and M. Yogman (Eds.). *Theory and Research in Behavioural Pediatrics.* (Vol. 2, pp. 147-205). New York: Plenum.

Aber, J.L., Allen J.P., Carlson, V. and Cicchetti, D. (1989). The effects of maltreatment on development during early childhood: Recent studies and their theoretical, clinical and policy implications. In D. Cicchetti and V. Carlson (Eds.), *Child Maltreatment: Theory and Research on the Causes and Consequences of Child Abuse and Neglect,* (pp. 597-616), Cambridge, U.K. Cambridge University Press.

Agarwal, A. and Tiwari, S. (1988). Future Orientation: A mediator in temporal coding. *International Journal of Psychology, 23,* 151-163.

Ainsworth, M.D.S. and Bowlby, J. (1991). An ethological approach to personality development. *American Psychologist, 46,* 331-341.

Alessandri, S.M. (1991). Play and social behaviour in maltreated preschoolers. *Development and Psychopathology, 3,* 191-205.

Allen, D.M., and Tarnowski, K.J. (1989). Depressive characteristics of physically abused children. *J. Abnorm. Child Psychology, 17*: 1-11.

American Professional Society on the Abuse of Children (1995). *Psychosocial evaluation of suspected psychological maltreatment in children and adolescents. Practices guidelines.* Chicago, IL: APSAC.

Anderson, C.A., Deuser, W.E. and Deneve, K.M. (1995). Hot temperature, hostile affect, hostile cognition and arousal. Tests of general model of affective aggression. *Personality and Social Psychology Bulletin, 21,* 434-448.

Angelini, A.L., Bitencourt, L., Jose, F. and Rosamilha, N.C. (1970). Motive de realizacao edeseuvolvimento economic. *Reuisto Intermericanade Psychologia, 4,* 33-41.

Atkinson, J.W. (1964). *An Introduction to Motivation.* Pinceton, NJ: Van Nostrand.

Augoustions, M. (1987). Development effect of child abuse: Recent findings. *Child Abuse and Neglect, 11* (1), 15-27.

Averill, J.R. (1983). Studies on anger and aggression. Implications for theories of emotion. *American Psychologist, 38,* 1145-1160.

Azar, S.T. (1997). A cognitive behavioural approach to understanding and treating parents who physically abuse their children. In D. Wholfe, R.J. McMahon, and R.D. Peters (Eds.). *Child Abuse: New Direction in Prevention and Treatment Across the Life Span,* (Vol. 4, pp. 78-101), Thousand Oaks, C.A.; Sage.

Bagley, C., and Young, L. (1987). Juvenile prostitution and child sexual abuse: A controlled study. *Journal of Community Mental Health, 6,* 5-26.

Bandura, A. (1971). *Social Learning Theory:* Morris Town, NJ: Prentice Hall.

Baruah, A. (2003). *Child Abuse.* New Delhi: References Press.

Bauer, W.D. and Tentyman, C.T. (1985). Abusing, neglectful and comparison mothers' responses to child related and non-child related stressors. *Journal of Consulting and Clinical Psychology, 53,* 335-343.

Beeghly, M. and Cicchetti, D. (1994). Child Maltreatment, attachment and the self-system. Emergence of an internal state lexicon in toddlers at high social risk. *Development and Psychopathology, 6,* 5-30.

Beers, S.R., De Bellis M.D. (2002). Neuropsychological function in children with maltreatment-related posttraumatic stress disorder. *Am. J. Psychiatry 159, 483-486 10.1176/appi.ajp*.159.3.483.

Beitchman, J.H., Zucker, K.J., Hood, J.E., De Costa, G.A. and Akman, D. (1991). A review of the short term effects of child sexual abuse. *Child Abuse and Neglect, 15,* 537-556.

Belsky, J. (1980). Child maltreatment: An ecological integration. *American Psychologist, 35,* 320-335.

Belsky, J. (1984). The determinants of parenting: A process model. *Child Development, 55,* 83-96.

Berkowitz, L. (1983). Aversively stimulated aggression: Some parallels and differences in research with animals and humans. *American Psychologist, 38,* 1135-1144.

Bernstein, D.P., Fink, L., Handelsman, L., Foote, J., Lovejay, M., Wengel, K., Sopareto, E. and Ruggiero, J. (1994). Initial reliability and validity of new retrospective measure of child abuse and neglect. *American Journal of Personality. 151,* 1132-1136.

Besharov, D. (1996, December, 1). When home is hell: We are too reluctant to take children from bad parents. *Washington Post,* pp. CI, C5-C6.

Bhattacharya, A.K. (1979). Child in India and nutritionally battered child, In R.T. Helfer and C.H. Kempe (Eds). *Child Abuse and Neglect.* Great Britain: Pergamon Press.

Bilbro, T., Boni, M., Johnson, B. and Roe, S. (1979). The relationship of parental acceptance-rejection, to the development of moral reasoning.

Unpublished manuscript. University of Connecticut, Center for the Study of Parental Acceptance-Rejection.

Bottoms, B.L., and Goodman, G.S. (Eds.). (1996). International perspectives on child abuse and children's testimony: *Psychological research and law*. Thousand Oaks, CA: Sage.

Bottoms, B.L., Shaver, P.R., and Goodman, G.S. (1996). An analysis of ritualistic and religion-related child abuse allegations. *Law and Human Behaviour, 20* (1), 1-34.

Bousha, D.M. and Twentyman, C.T. (1984). Mother-child international style in abuse, neglect and control groups: Naturalistic observations in the home. *Journal of Abnormal Psychology, 93*, 106-114.

Bower, G.H. (1981). Mood and memory. *American Psychologist, 36*, 126-148.

Bowlby, J. (1969). *Attachment and Loss:* Vol. 1. Attachment, New York: Basic Books.

Bowlby, J. (1973). *Attachment and Loss:* Vol. 2, Separation. New York: Basic Books.

Bowlby, J. (1980). *Attachment and Loss:* Vol. 3, Loss, Sadness and Depression, New York: Basic Books.

Bracey, D., (1979). *Baby pros: Preliminary Profiles of Juvenile Prostitutes.* New York: John Jay Press.

Brassard, M.R., Hart, S.N., and Hardy, D. (1991). Psychological and emotional abuse of children. In R.T. Ammerman and M. Hersen (Eds), *Case Studies in Family Violence,* (pp. 255-270). New York: Plenum.

Brassard, M.R., Hart. S.N., Hardy, D.B., (1993). The Psychological maltreatment rating scales. *Science Direct 17* (6), 715-729.

Bremner, J.D., Narayan, M., Staib, L.H., Southwick, S.M., McGlashan, T., Charney, D.S. (1999). Neural correlates of memories of childhood sexual abuse in women with and without posttraumatic stress disorder. *Am. J. Psychiatry, 156*:1787-1795.

Bremner, J.D., Randall, P., Scott, T.M., Capelli, S., Delaney, R., McCarthy, G., Charney, D.S. (1995). Deficits in short-term memory in adult survivors of childhood abuse. *Psychiatry Res. 59*:97-107.

Briere, J. and Runtz, M. (1988). Multivariate correlates of childhood psychological and physical maltreatment among university women. *Child Abuse and Neglect, 12*, 331-341.

Briere, J. and Runtz, M. (1990). Differential adult's symptomatology associated with three types of child abuse histories. *Child Abuse and Neglect, 14*, 357-364.

Broadbent, A. and Bentley, R. (1997). Child abuse and neglect in Australia, 1995-96 (Child Welfare Series, No. 17; AIHW Cat No. CWSI). Canberra: Australian Institute of Health and Welfare.

Bronfenbrenner, U. (1977). Towards an experimental ecology of human development. *American Psychologist, 32*, 513-531.

Bronfenbrenner, U. (1979). *The ecology of human development: experiments by nature and design*. Cambridge, M.A.: Harvard University Press.

Brooks-Gunn, J. and Duncan, G.J. (1997). The effects of poverty on children. *The Future of Children, 7* (2), 55-71.

Brown, J., Cohen, P., Johnson, J.G. and Smailes, E.M. (1999). Childhood abuse and neglect: Specificity of effects on adolescent and young adult depression and suicidality. *Journal of the American Academy of Child and Adolescent Psychiatry, 38*(12), 1490-1496.

Browne, A. and Finkelhor, D. (1986). Impact of child sexual abuse: A review of the research. *Psychological Bulletin, 99*, 66-77.

Burgess, A.W. and Hartman, C.R. (1987). Child abuse aspects of child pornography. *Psychiatric Annals, 17*, 248-253.

Burgess, A.W., and Hartman, C.R., McCausland, M.P. and Powers, P. (1984). Response patterns in children and adolescents exploited through sex rings and pornography. *American Journal of Psychiatry, 141*(5), 656-662.

Burgess, A.W., Groth, A.N. and McCausland, M. (1981). Child sex initiation rings. *American Journal of Orthopsychiatry, 51*, 110-119.

Burgess, R.L. (1985). Social incompetence as a precipitant to and consequences of child maltreatment. *Victomology: An International Journal, 10*, 72-86.

Butchart. A., Harvey, A.P., Milan, M., Furniss, T. and Kahen, T. (2006). Preventing Child Maltreatment: A Guide to Taking Action and Generating Evidence. *World Health Organization and International Society for Prevention of Child Abuse and Neglect*. WHO: Geneva.

Bybee, D., and Mowbary, C.T. (1993a). An analysis of allegations of sexual abuse in a multi-victim day-care center case. *Child Abuse and Neglect, 17*, 767-783.

Carlson, B.E. (1991). Emotionally disturbed children's beliefs and punishment. *Child Abuse and Neglect. 15*, 19-28.

Carlson. B.E. (1986). Children's beliefs about punishment. *American Journal of Orthopsychiatry, 56*, 308-312.

Carter, D.L., Prentky, R.A., Knight, R.A., Vanderveer, P.L., and Boucher, R.J. (1987). Use of pornography in the criminal and developmental histories of sexual offenders. *Journal of International Violence, 2*, 196-211.

Cattell, R.B. (1972). Technical Supplement for the Culture Fair Intelligence Test, Scale 2 and 3. Institute for Personality and Ability Testing. Champaign, Illinois, U.S.A. by The Psycho Center T-22, New Delhi.

Cattell, R.B. (1973). Manual for Measuring Intelligence with the Culture Fair Intelligence Test, Scale 2 and 3. Institute for Personality and Ability Testing. Champaign, Illinois, U.S.A. by The Psycho Center T-22, New Delhi.

Cerezo, M.A. (1997). Abusive Family Interaction: A review. *Aggression and Violent Behaviour*, 2 (3), 215-240.

Chan, J. (1981). Correlates of parent-child interaction and certain psychological variables among adolescents in Hong Kong. In J.L.M. Dawson *et al.* (Eds). *Perspectives in Asian Psychology.* Lisse: Swets and Zeitlinger.

Chan, Y.C. (1994). Parenting stress and social support of mothers who physically abuse their children in Hong Kong. *Child Abuse and Neglect, 18,* 261-269.

Chattoraj, R.N. and Saxena, R. (1990). Victimization of Children: An urgent need for effective measures. *Social Change.* Vol. 20, No. 3, 17 23.

Chester, D.L., Jose R.M., Aldlyami E., King H. and Moiemen N.S. (2006). Non-accidental burns in children are we neglecting neglect? *Burns; 32*: 222-28.

Chiappe, P., Hasher, L. and Siegel, L.S. (2000). Working Memory, inhibitory, control and reading disability. *Memory and Cognition. 28,* 8-17.

Child Welfare Information Gateway (2008). Definitions of Domestic Violence: Summary of State Laws. Retrieved June 2009 from www.childwelfare.gov/systemwide/laws_ policies/statutes/ defdomvio.cfm

Childline (2007). Child Sexual Abuse. Available from: http:// wwwchildlineindiaorgin/Background-to-CSAhtm.

Chopra, A., Mittal, P.R., Chander, J., and Kanta, S. (1990). Perianal hypertrophic dinovanosis. *India Sex Transm Dis. 11,* 29-30.

Christopoulos, C., Bonvillian, J.D. and Crittenden, P.M. (1988). Maternal language input and child maltreatment. *Infant Mental Health Journal, 9,* 272-286.

Cicchetti D., Rogosch, F.A. (2001). Diverse patterns of neuroendocrine activity in maltreated children. *Development and Psychopathology. 13*: 677-694.

Cicchetti, D. and Olsen, K. (1990). The developmental psychopathology of child maltreatment. In M. Lewis and S.M. Miller (Eds), *Handbook of Developmental Psychopathology,* (pp. 261-279). New York: Plenum.

Cicchetti, D. (2004). An odyssey of discovery: Lessons learned through three decades of research on child maltreatment. *American Psychologist, 59,* 1-4.

Cicchetti, D., and Toth, S.L. (2005). Child maltreatment. *Annual Review of Clinical Psychology, 1,* 409-438.

Claussen, A.H. and Crittenden, P.M. (1991). Physical and psychological maltreatment: Relations among the types of maltreatment. *Child Abuse and Neglect, 15,* 15-18.

Conte, J.R. and Schuerman, J.R. (1987). Factors associated with an increase of child sexual abuse. *Child Abuse and Neglect, 11,* 201-211.

Coohey, C. (1996). Child maltreatment: Testing the social isolation hypothesis. *Child Abuse and Neglect, 20,* 241-254.

Cook, A., Spinazzola, J., Ford, J., Lanktree, C., Blaustein, M., Cloitre, M., van der Kolk B. (2005). Complex trauma in children and adolescents. *Psychiatric Annals*. 35:390.

Costa, P.T., Jr., and Mc Crae, R.R. (1978). Revised NEO Personality Inventory (NEO PI-R) Professional manual. *Psychological Assessment Resources*. Odessa, Florida.

Coster, W.J., Gersten, M.S., Beeghly, M. and Cicchetti, D. (1989). Communicative functioning in maltreated toddlers. *Development and Psychopathology, 25, 777-793.*

Coulton, C.J., Korbin, J.E., Su, M, and Chow J. (1995). Community level factors and child maltreatment rates. *Child Development, 66,* 1262-1276.

Creighton, S.J. (1993, December). Organized abuse: NSPCC experience. *Child Abuse Review,* 2, 232-243.

Crittenden, P.M. (1988). Distorted patterns of relationship in maltreating families: The role of internal representation models. *Journal of Reproductive and Infant Psychology,* 6, 183-199.

Crittenden, P.M. (1992). Children's strategies for coping with adverse home environments: An interpretation using attachment theory. *Child Abuse and Neglect, 16* (3), 329-339.

Crittenden, P.M. (1993). Characteristics of neglectful parents: An information processing approach. *Criminal Justice and Behaviour, 20,* 27-48.

Crittenden, P.M. (1998). Dangerous behaviour and dangerous contexts: A 35-year perspective on research on the development effect of child physical abuse. In P.K. Trickett, and C.J. Schelienback (Eds.). *Violence against children in the family and the community* (pp. 11-38). Washington, DC., American Psychological Association.

Crittenden, P.M., Anisworth, M.D.S. (1989). Child maltreatment and attachment theory. In D. Cicchetti and V. Carlson (Eds.) *Child maltreatment: Theory and research on the causes and consequences of child abuse and neglect* (pp. 423-463). New York: Cambridge University Press.

Crittenden, P.M., Claussen, A.H. and Sugarman, D.B. (1994). Physical and Psychological maltreatment in middle childhood and adolescence. *Development and Psychopathology, 6,* 145-164.

Cuffe, S.P., Addy, C.L., Garrison, C.Z., Waller, J.L., Jackson, K.L., McKeown, R.E., *et al.* (1998). Prevalence of PTSD in a community sample of older adolescents. *Journal of the American Academy of Child and Adolescent Psychiatry, 37*:147-154. doi:10.1097/00004583-199802000-00006.

Cummings, E.M., M. Hennessy, K.D., Radideau, G.J. and Cicchetti, D. (1994). Responses of physically abused boys to interadult anger involving their mothers. *Development and Pscyhopathology, 6* (1), 31-41.

Darves-Bornoz, J.M., Lepine, J.P., Choquet, M., Berger, C., Degiovanni, A., Gaillard, P. (1998). Predictive factors of chronic Post-traumatic stress disorder in rape victims. *European Psychiatry*. 12:281-287. doi:10.1016/S0924-9338(98) 80045-X.

De Bellis, M.D. (2005). The psychobiology of neglect. *Child Maltreatment, 10*(2), 150-172.

De Bellis, M.D., Hooper, S.R., and Sapia, J.L. (2005). Early trauma exposure and the brain. In J.J. Vasterling and C.R. Brewin (Eds.), *Neuropsychology of PTSD: Biological, cognitive, and clinical perspectives* (pp. 153-177). New York: Guilford.

De Bellis, M.D., Hooper, S.R., Spratt, E.G., and Woolley, D.P. (2009). Neuropsychological findings in childhood neglect and their relationships to pediatric PTSD. *Journal of the International Neuropsychological Society, 15*(6), 868-878.

De Board, L.W. (1969). The achievement syndrome among Negro and White culturally disadvantaged boys. Unpub. Ph.D. Thesis, Vanderbidt University.

De Francis, V. (1969). *A Research Protecting the Child Victim of Sexual Crimes Committed by Adults*. Project conducted under child welfare research grant. R-222 for the U.S. Children's Bureau. Denver: American Human Association.

De Paul, J., and Arrubarrena, M.I. (1995). Behaviour problem in school aged physically abused and neglected children in Spain. *Child Abuse and Neglect, 19*, 409-418.

DePrince A.P., Weinzierl K.M., Combs, M.D. (2009). Executive function performance and trauma exposure in a community sample of children. *Child Abuse and Neglect, 33*:353-361.

Dodge, K.A., Bates, J.E. and Pettiet, G.S. (1990). Mechanisms in the cycle of violence. *Science, 250*, 1678-1682.

Dodge, K.A., Pettit, G.S. and Bates, J.E. (1997). How the experience of early physical abuse leads children to become chronically aggressive. In *Developmental Perspectives on Trauma: Theory, research and intervention* (Vol. 8, pp. 263-288). Rochester, N.Y.: University of Rochester Press.

Doek, J.E. (1985). Child pornography and legislation in the Netherlands. *Child Abuse and Neglect, 9*, 411-412.

Dollard, J., and Miller, N.E. (1950). *Personality and Psychotherapy*. New York: McGraw-Hill.

Downs, W.R. and Miller, B.A. (1998). Relationship between experiences of parental violence during childhood and women's psychiatric symptomatology. *Journal of Interpersonal Violence, 13* (4), 438-455.

Drake, B. and Pandey, S. (1996). Understanding the relationship between neighbourhood poverty and specific types of child maltreatment. *Child Abuse and Neglect, 20*, 1003-1018.

Durkin, K.F., and Bryant, C.D. (1995). "log on to sex": Some notes on the carnal computer and erotic cyberspace as an emerging research frontier. *Deviant Behaviour: An Interdisciplinary Journal, 16*, 179-200.

Earls, C.M., and Devid, H. (1990, December). Early family and sexual experiences of male and female prostitutes. *Canada's Mental Health,* 7 11.

Eckenrode, J., Laird, M. and Doris, J. (1993). School performance and disciplinary problems among abused and neglected children. *Developmental Psychology, 29*:53-62.

Edleson, J.L. (1999). The overlap between child maltreatment and women battering. *Violence Against Women, 5,* 134-154.

Edleson, J.L., Eisikovits, Z.C., Guttman, E., and Sela-Amit, M. (1991). Coginitive and interpersonal factors in woman abuse. *Journal of Family Violence, 6,* 167-182.

Egeland, B. (1991). From data to definition. *Development and Psychopathology, 3,* 37-43.

Egeland, B. and Erickson, M. (1987). Psychologically unavailable care giving. In M.R. Brassard, R. Germain and S.N. Hart (Eds), *Psychological Maltreatment of Children and Youth* (pp. 110-120). New York: Pergamon.

Egeland, B. and Sroufe, L.A. (1981). Developmental sequel of maltreatment infancy. In B. Rizely and D. Cicchetti (Eds), *New Directions for Child Development: Developmental Perspectives in Child Maltreatment,* 11, (pp. 77-92). San Francisco: Jossey Bass.

Egeland, B., Sroufe, L.A. and Erickson, M.F. (1983). The developmental consequences of different patterns of maltreatment. *Child Abuse and Neglect, 7,* 459-469.

Einbender, A.J., and Friedrich, W.N. (1989). Psychological functioning and behaviour of sexually abused girls. *Journal of Consulting and Clinical Psychology, 57,* 155-157.

Erickson, M.F., Egeland, B. and Pianta, R. (1989). The effect of maltreatment on the development of young children. In D. Cicchetti and V. Carlson, (Eds.). *Child Maltreatment: theory and research on the Causes and consequences of child abuse and neglect,* (pp. 647-684). New York: Cambridge University Press.

Ethier, L.S., Lacharite, C. and Couture, G. (1995). Childhood adversiry, parental stress and depression of negligent mothers. *Child Abuse and Neglect, 19,* 619-632.

Faller, K. (1981). Causes of child abuse and neglect. In Faller K. (Ed.) *Social Work with abused and neglected children: A Manual of Interdisciplinary Practice.* New York: Macmillian.

Faller, K.C. (1988b). The spectrum of sexual abuse in daycare: An exploratory study. *Journal of Family Violence, 3*(4), 283-298.

Famularo, R., Fenton, T. and Kinschereff, R.T. (1992). Medical and developmental histories of maltreated children. *Clinical Pediatrics, 31,* 536-541.

Famularo, R., Kinschereff, R. and Fenton, T. (1991). Post-traumatic stress disorder among children clinically diagnosed as borderline personality disorder. *Journal of Nervous and Mental Diseases, 179,* 428-431.

Fantuzzo, J.W. (1990). Behavioural treatment of the victims of child abuse neglect. *Behavioural Modification, 14,* 316-339.

Fantuzzo, J.W., Depalola, L.M., Lambert, L., Martino, T., Anderson, G., and Sutton, S. (1991). Effects of interparental violence on the psychological adjustment and competencies of young children.

Farrington, K.M. (1980). Stress and Family Violence. In M.A. Straus and G.T. Hotaling (Eds.) *The Social Causes of Husband-to-wife Violence* (pp. 94 114). Minneapolis: University of Minneota Press.

Feldman, R.S. Salzinger, S., Rosario, M., Alvarado, L. and Hammer, M. (1995). Parent, teacher and peer ratings of physically abused and normal treated children's behaviour. *Journal of Abnormal Child Psychology, 23,* 317-343.

Felitti, V.J., and Anda, R. (2009). The relationship of adverse childhood experiences to adult medical disease, psychiatric disorders, and sexual behaviour: Implications for healthcare. In R. Lanius, E. Vermetten, and C. Pain (Eds.), *The hidden epidemic: The impact of early life trauma on health and disease.* Retrieved from http://www.acestudy.org/yahoo_site_admin/assets/docs/LaniusVermetten_FINAL_8-26-09.12892303.

Felitti, V.J., Anda R.F., Nordenberg D., Williamson D.F., Spitz A.M., Edwards V., Koss M.P. and Marks J.S. (1998). Relationship of childhood abuse and household dysfunction to many of the leading causes of death in adults. *American Journal of Preventive Medicine. 14*(4):245-258.

Festinger, L. (1942). A theoretical interpretation of shift in level of aspiration, *Psychological Review, 49,* 235-250.

Finkelhor D. (1993). Epidemiological factors in clinical identification of child sexual abuse: *Child Abuse and Neglect, 17,* 60-70.

Finkelhor, D. (1994-a). Current information on the scope and nature of child sexual abuse. *Future of Children, 4* (2), 31-53.

Finkelhor, D. (1994-b). The International epidemiology of child sexual abuse. *Child Abuse and Neglect, 18,* 409-417.

Finkelhor, D. (1995). The victimization of children: A developmental perspective. *American Journal of Orthopsyhiatry, 65,* 177-193.

Finkelhor, D. (1996). Introduction. In J. Briere, L. Berliner, J.A. Bulkey, C. Jenny and T. Reid (Eds). *The APSAC Handbook on Child Maltreatment* (pp. ix-xiii). Thousand Okas, CA: Sage.

Finkelhor, D. and Browen, A. (1988). Assessing the long term impact of child sexual abuse. A review and conceptualization, in L. Walker (Eds.). *Handbook of Sexual Abuse of Children* (pp. 55-71). New York: Springer.

Finkelhor, D. and Korbin, J. (1988). Child abuse as an international issue. *Child Abuse and Neglect, 17,* 67-70.

Finkelhor, D. and Lewis, I.A. (1988). An epidemiologic approach to the study of child molestation. *Annals of the New York Academy of Sciences, 528*, 64-78.

Fisher, A.J., Kramer, R.A., Hoven, C.W., Greenwald, S., Alegria, M., Bird, H.R., Cannio, G., Connell, R., and Moore R.E. (1997). Psychosocial characteristics of physically abused children and adolescents. *Journal of the American Academy of Child and Adolescent Psychiatry, 36*, 123-131.

Flaherty, E.G., Sege R.D. and Hurley T.P. (2006) Effect of early childhood adversity on health, *Archives of Paediatrics and Adolescent Medicine, 160*: 1232-1238.

Flaherty, M.S., Zavadil, J., Ekas, L.A., Bach, E.A. (2009). Genome-wide expression profiling in the Drosophila eye reveals unexpected repression of notch signaling by the JAK/STAT pathway. *Dev. Dyn. 238*(9): 2235-2253.

Ford, J.D., Racusin, R., Daviss, W.B., Ellis, C., Thomas, J., Rogers, K., Reiser, J., Schiffman, J., and Sengupta, A. (1999). Trauma exposure among children with attention deficit hyperactivity disorder and oppositional defiant disorder. *Journal of Consulting and Clinical Psychology, 67*, 786-789.

Frank, J.D. (1935). Individual differences in certain aspects of the level of aspiration. *American Journal of Psychology, 47*, 119-128.

Frederico, M., Jackson, A., and Black, C. (2008). Understanding the impact of abuse and neglect on children and young people referred to a therapeutic programme. *Journal of Family Studies, 14*, 342-361.

Friedrich *et al.*, W.N. Friedrich, A.J. Urquiza and R.L. Beilke (1986). Behaviour problems in sexually abused young children, *Journal of Pediatric Psychology*, 11, pp. 47-57.

Friedrich, W.N. (1990). *Psychotheraphy of Sexually Abused Children and their Families.* New York, Norton.

Friedrich, W.N., Enbender, A.J., and Luecke, W.J. (1983). Cognitive and Behavioural Characteristics of physical abused children. *Journal of Consulting and Clinical Psychology, 51*, 313-314.

Friedrich, W.N., Urquiza, A.J. and Beilke, R.L. (1986). Behaviour problems in sexually abused young children. *Journal of Pediatric Psychology, 11*, 47-57.

Gaines, R., Sandgrund, A., Green, A.H. and Power, E. (1978). Etiological factors in child maltreatment: A Multivariate study of abusing, neglecting and normal mothers. *Journal of Abnormal Psychology, 87*, 531-540.

Gallup, Orgnaization. (1995). *Discipline Children in America: A Gallup Poll Report*. Princeton, N.J. Author.

Garbarino, J. (1976). A preliminary study of some ecological correlates of child abuse: The impact of socio-economic-stress on mothers. *Child Development, 47*, 178-185.

Garbarino, J. (1997). The role of economic deprivation in the social context of child maltreatment. In M.E. Helfer, R.S. Kempe and R.D. Krugman (Eds.). *The Battered Child,* (5th ed, pp. 49-60). Chicago: University of Chicago Press.

Gelles, R.J. (1983). An exchange social control theory. In. D. Finkelhor, R.J. Gelles, G.T. Hotalling, and M.A. Straus (Eds.) *The Dark Side of Families: Current Family Violence Research,* (pp. 151-165). Beverly Hills, CA: Sage.

Gelles, R.J., and Straus, M.A. (1988). Intimate Violence: The definitive study of the causes and consequences of abuse in the American family. New York: Simon and Schuster.

Gibbs, J. (1975). *Crime, Punishment, and deterrence*. New York: Elsevier.

Gilbert, R., Kemp, A., Thoburn, J., Sidebotham, P., Radford, L., Glaser, D., MacMillan, H.L. (2008). Recognizing and responding to child maltreatment, *The Lancet,* DOI:10.1016/S0140-6736(08)61707-9.

Gilbert, R., Widom, C.S., Browne, K., Fergusson, D.M., Elspeth, W., Janson, S. (2009). Child Maltreatment: Burden and consequences of child maltreatment in high-income countries, *The Lancet, 373*: 68-81.

Gill, D.G. (1970). *Violence Against Children: Physical Abuse in United States.* Cambridge, M.A. Harward University Press.

Gill, D.G. (1971). Violence Against Children. *Journal of Marriage and Family, 33,* 637-648.

Gladestone G., Parker, G., Willhelm, K., Mitchell, P. and Austin, M.P. (1999). Characteristics of depressed patients who report child sexual abuse. *American Journal of Psychiatry,* 156-812.

Gomes-Schwartz, B., Horotwitz, J.M. and Cardarelli, A.P. (1990). *Child Sexual Abuse: The Initial Effects.* Newbury Park, C.A.: Sage.

Goodman, G.S., Bottoms, B.L., and Shaver, P.R. (1994). Characteristics and sources of allegations of ritualistic child abuse (*Executive Summary of final report to the National Center on Child Abuse and Neglect*). Washington, DC: National Center on Child Abuse and Neglect.

Goodman, G.S., Quas, J.A., and Ogle, C.M. (2010). Child maltreatment and memory. *Annual* Review *of Psychology, 61,* 325-351.

Government of India (2011). Ministry of Women and Child Development. Third and Fourth Combined on the Right of the Child. Available From: wcd.nic.in/crc3n4/crc3n4_1r.pdf.

Government of India Census (2011). Office of the Registrar General and Census Commissioner, Ministry of Home Affairs.

Gross, A.B. and Keller, H.R. (1992). Long-term consequences of childhood physical and psychological maltreatment. *Aggressive Behaviour, 18,* 171-185.

Gupta, G.C. (1980). Cognitive Processes. In U. Pareek (Ed). *A survey of research in psychology,* 1971-76, Vol. 1. Bombay: Popular.

Harkness, K., and Lumley, M. (2008). Child abuse and neglect and the development of depression in children and adolescents. In J. Abela and B. Hankin (Eds.), *Handbook of depression in children and adolescents.* New York: The Guildford Press.

Haskett, M. (1990). Social problem solving skill of young physically abused children. *Child Psychiatry and Human Development, 21,* 109-118.

Herrenkohl, E.C., Herrenkohl, R.C. and Egolf, B.P. (1983). Circumstances surrounding the occurrence of child maltreatment. *Journal of Consulting and Clinical Psychology, 51,* 424-431.

Hilton, Z.N. (1992). Battered women's concerns about their children-witnessing wife assault, *Journal of Interpersonal Violence, 7,* 77-86.

Hirschi, T. (1969). *Causes of Delinquency.* Berkeley: University of California Press.

Hoffman, M.L. (1970). Moral Development. In P.H. Mussen (Ed.), *Carmichale's manual of child psychology* (Vol. 2). New York: John Wiley.

Hoffman-Poltkin, D., and Twentyman, C.T. (1984). A multi-model assessment of behavioural and cognitive deficts in abused and neglected preschoolers. *Child Development, 55,* 794-802.

Hoglund, C.L., & Nicholas, K.B. (1995). Shame, guilt and anger in college students exposed to abusive family environment. *Journal of family violence, 10* (2), 141-157.

Holland, A.S., and Roisman, G.I. (2008). Big Five personality traits and relationship quality: Self-reported, observational, and physiological evidence. *Journal of Social and Personal Relationships, 25(5),* 811-829.

Hollowitz, D., and Stulberg, B. (1959). The vicious cycle of parent-child relationship breakdown. *Social Case Work. 40,* 268-275.

Hoppe, F. (1930). Untersuchungenzur handlungs und affect-psychologie. Ix. Erfolg und misserfolg. *Psychologische Forschung 14,* 1-63.

Hotaling, G.T., Straus, M.A. and Lincolin, A.J. (1990). Intra family violence and crime and violence outside the family. In M.A. Straus and R.J. Gelles (Eds.) *Physical violence in American families. Risk factor and adaptation to violence in 8,145 families* (pp. 413-470). New Brunswick. N.J. Transaction Books.

Howe, D. (1995). Pornography and the paedophile: Is it criminogenic ? *British Journal of Medical Psychology, 68(1),* 15-27.

Howes, C., and Espinosa, M.P. (1985). The consequence of child abuse for the formation of relationship with peers. *Child Abuse and Neglect, 9,* 397-404.

Huges, D. (1996). Sex tours via the Internet. Agenda: *Empowering Women foe Equality, 28,* 71-76.

Hughes, H.M. and Graham-Bermann, S.A. (1998). Children of battered women: Impact of emotional abuse on adjustment and development. *Journal of Emotional Abuse, 1,* 75-90.

Hunt, P., and Baired, M. (1990). Children of sex rings. *Child Welfare, 69,* 195-207.

Hunter, J., Goodwin, D.W. and Wilson, R.J. (1992). Attributions of blame in child sexual abuse victims: An analysis of age and gender influences. *Journal of Child Sexual Abuse, 1*, 75-90.

Hunter, W.M., Coulter, M.L., Runyan, D.K. and Everson, M.D. (1990). Determinants of placement for sexually abused children. *Child Abuse and Neglect, 14*, 407-418.

Hurlock, E.B. (1984). *Child Development*. McGraw-Hill series in Psychology.

Hussey, J., Chang, J., and Kotch, J. (2006). Child maltreatment in the United States: Prevalence, risk factors, and adolescent health consequences. *Pediatrics, 118*(3), 933-942.

Ireland, K. (1993). Sexual exploitation of children and international travel tourism. *Child Abuse Review, 2*, 263-271.

Itzin, C. (1997). Pornography and the organization of intra and extra-familial child sexual abuse. In G.K. Kantor and J.L. Jasinski (Eds.), *Out of the Darkness: Contemporary perspectives on family violence* (pp. 58-79). Thousand Oaks, CA: Sage.

Jones, D.P.H., and McGraw, J.M. (1987). Reliable and fictitious accounts of sexual abuse to children. *Journal of Interpersonal Violence, 2*, 27-45.

Jones, T. (1991). Ethical decision making by individual in organization: An issue-contingent model. *Academic of Management Review 16* (2), 366-395.

Jonker, F., and Jonker-Bakker, P. (1991). Experiences with ritualistic child sexual abuses: A case study from the Netherlands. *Child Abuse and Neglect, 15*, 191-196.

Joseph, C. (1995). Scarlet wounding: Issues of child prostitution. *Journal of Psychohistory, 23*(1), 2-17.

Kacker, L., Veradan, S., and Kumar, P. (2007). Study on child abuse: India 2007. New Delhi: Ministry of Woman and Child Development, Government of India.

Kandall, Tackett, K.A., Williams, L.M. and Finkelhor, D. (1993). Impact of sexual abuse on children: A review and synthesis of recent empirical studies. *Psychological Bulitien, 113*, 164-180.

Kaplan, S., Pelcovitz, D., Salzinger, S., Mandel, F.S. and Weiner, M. (1998). Adolescent physical abuse. Risk for adolescents psychiatric disorders. *American Journal of Psychiatry, 155* (7), 954-959.

Kaufman, J. (1991). Depressive disorders in maltreated children. *Journal of American Academy of Child Adolscent Psychiatry, 20*(2), 257-265.

Kaufman, J. and Cicchetti, D. (1989). Effect of maltreatment on school age children's socio-emotional development: Assessment in day camp setting. *Development Psychology, 25*, 516-524.

Kelley, S.J. (1989). Stress responses of children to sexual abuse and ritualistic abuse in day care centers. *Journal of Interpersonal Violence, 4*, 502-513.

Kelley, S.J. (1996). Ritualistic abuse of children. In J. Briere, L. Berliner, J.A. Bulkley, C. Jenny, and T. Reid (Eds.), *The APSAC Handbook of child maltreatment* (pp. 90-99). Thousand Oaks, CA: Sage.

Kelley, S.J., Brant, R., and Waterman, J. (1993). Sexual abuse of children in day care centers. *Child Abuse and Neglect, 17,* 71-89.

Kempe, C., and Helfer, R. (1972). *Helping the battered child and his family.* Philadelpia: J.B. Lippinott.

Kempe, C.H., Silverman, F.N., Steel, B.F., Dorgemueller, W. and Silver, H.K. (1962). The bartered child syndrome. *Journal of the American Medical Association, 17,* 17-24.

Kendall, P.C., Stark, K.D. and Adam, T. (1990). Cognitive deficit or cognitive distortion in childhood depression. *Journal of Abnormal Child Psychology, 18,* 255-270.

Kendall-Tackett, K.A. (2000). The long-term health effects of victimization. *Joining Forces, 5,* 1-4.

Kendall-Tackett, K.A., Wiliams, L.M., & Finkelhor, D. (1993). Impact of Sexual Abuse on Children : A review and Synthesis of recent emperical studies. Psychological Bulletin, *113,* 164-180.

Kent, A. and Waller, G. (1998). The Impact of childhood emotional abuse: An extension of the child abuse and trauma scale. *Child Abuse and Neglect.*

Knuston, J.F. (1978). Child abuse as an area of aggression research. *Journal of Interpersonal Violence, 7,* 244-276.

Kolko, D.J., Moser, J. and Wiedly, S.R. (1988). Behavioural/Emotional indicator of sexual abuse in psychiatric in patients: A controlled comparison with physical abuse. *Child Abuse and Neglect, 12,* 529-541.

Korbin, J. (1987). Child maltreatment in cross-cultural perspective: Vulnerable children and circumstances. In R.J. Gells and J.B. Lancaster (Eds.), *Child Abuse and Neglect, 12,* 529-541.

Korbin, J. (1994). Socio-culture Factor in Child Maltreatment. In G.B., Melton and F.D. Barry (Eds.), *Protecting children from abuse and neglect.* Foundations for a new national strategy, (pp. 182-223) New York: Guildford.

Kurtz, Ph. D., Gaudin, J.M., Howing, P.T. (1993). The consequences of physical abuse and neglect on the school. *Children Abuse and Neglect, 17,* 518-589.

Lanning, K.V., and Burgess, A.W. (1984, January). Child pornography and sex rings. *FBI Law Enforcement Bulletin,* 10-16.

Larrence, D.T., and Twentyman, C.T. (1983). Maternal attribution and child abuse. *Journal of Abnormal Psychology, 92,* 449-457.

Lazarus, R. and Folkman, S. (1984). *Stress, Appraisal and Coping.* New York: Springer Publishing.

Lazarus, R.S. (1981). The Stress and Coping Parading. In C. Eisdoefer, D. Cohen, A. Kleinamn, and P. Maximum (Eds.). *Models for Children Psychopathology,* (pp. 177-214). New York: Spectrum.

Limber, S.P. and Nation, M.A. (1998). Violence within the neighbourhood and community. In P.K. Trickett, C.J. Schellenbach, (Eds)., *Violence Against Children in the Family and the Community* (pp. 171-193).

Washington, DC: American Psychological Association.

Lindberg, F.H. and Distad, L.J. (1985). Post-traumatic stress disorder in women who experience childhood incest, *Child Abuse and Neglect, 9*:329-34.

Maccoby, E.E. and Martin J.A. (1983). Socilization in the context of the family: Parent-child interaction. In P.H. Mussen (Ed), *Handbook of Child Psychology.* (4th Ed., pp. 1-101). New York: John Wiley.

Main, M. and George, C. (1985). Responses of abuse and disadvantaged toddlers to distress in age mates: A study in day care setting. *Developmental Psychology, 21*(3), 404-412.

Main, M. and Goldwyn, R. (1984). Predicting rejection of her infant from mother representation of her own experiences: Implication for the abuse-abusing intergenerational cycle. *Child Abuse and Neglect, 8,* 203-217.

Malamuth, N.M., and Briere, J. (1986). Sexual violence in the media: Indirect effects on aggression against women. *Journal of Social Issues, 42,* 75-92.

Malamuth, N.M., Sockloskie, R.J., Koss, M.P., and Tanaka, J.S. (1991). Characterstics of aggressor against women: Testing a model using a national sample of college students. *Journals of Consulting and Clinical Psychology, 59,* 670-681.

Malhi, P. and Dhillon, K., (2006). Can telephone hiplines play a role in managing child abuse and neglect? Evidence from childline. *Personality Study Group Behave, 26,* 117-131.

Manley, R. (1977). Parental Warmth and hostility as related to sex differences in children's achievement orientation. *Psychology of Women Quarterly, 1,* 129-246.

Manly, J.T., Cicchetti, D. and Barnett, D. (1994). The impact of subtype, frequency, chronicity and severtity of child maltreatment on social competence and behaviour problems. *Developmental and Psychopathology.*

Masten, A.S. and Garmezy, N. (1985). Risk, Valuerability and proactive factors in developmental psychopathology. In B.B. Lahey and A.E. Kazadin (Eds.), *Advances in Clinical Child Psychology.* (Vol. 8, pp. 1-52). New York: Plenum.

McFayden, R.G. and Kitson, W.J.H. (1996). Language comprehension and expression among adolescent who have experienced childhood physical abuse. *Journal of Child Psychology and Psychiatry and Allied Disciplines, 37,* 551-562.

McLeer, S.V., Deblinger, E.B., Henry, D. and Orvaschel, H. (1992). Sexually abused children at high risk for post-traumatic stress disorder. *Journal of the American Academy of Child and Adolescent Psychiatry, 31*:875-879.

McLoyd, V.C. (1998). Social economic disadvantage and child development. *American Psychologist, 53,* 185-204.

Mehta, M. (1979). Kidnapping: A social Evil. In R. Helfer and R. Helfer and C. Kempe (Eds.). *Child Abuse and Neglect*, Vol. 3, 678-682.

Mezzacappa, E., Kindlon, D., Earls, F. (2001). Child abuse and performance task assessments of executive functions in boys. *Journal of Child Psychology and Psychiatry and Allied Disciplines*, 42:1041-1048.

Milner, J.S. (1993). Social information processing and physical child abuse. *Clinical Psychology Review*, 13, 275-294.

Milner, J.S. (1998). Individual and family characteristics associated with interfamilial child physical and sexual abuse. In P.K. Trickett and C.J. Schellenbach (Eds). *Violence Against Children in the Family and Community* (pp. 141-170). Washington, DC., American Psychological Association.

Milner, J.S. and Chilamkurti, C. (1991). Physical child abuse perpetrator characteristic: A review of the literature. *Journal of Interpersonal Violence*, 6, 336-334.

Milner, J.S. and Wimberly, R.C. (1980). Prediction and explanation of child abuse. *Journal of Clinical Psychology*, 36, 875-884.

Milner, J.S., (1995). Physical child abuse assessment: Perceptual evaluation. In J.C. Campbell (Ed). *Assessing for Dangerousness: Voilence by Sexual Offenders, Batterers, and Child Abusers* (pp. 41-67). Thousand Oaks. CA: Sage.

Milner, J.S., Halsey, L.B. & Fultz. J. (1995) Empathetic responsiveness and affective reactivity to infant in high and low risk for physical child abuse mothers, *Child Abuse and Neglect* 19, 776-780.

Mishra, K.S., (1984). *School Environment Inventory*. Ankur Psychological Agency, Lucknow.

Mishra, R.C. (1999). Research on education in India. In S. Perez and P.R. Dasen (Eds), *Open File: Educational Research, Special Issue of Projects, Quarterly Review of Comparative Educational*, XXIX, 3 (pp. 335-348). Geneva: TBE/UNESCO.

Misra, G. and Tripathi, L.B. (1980). *Psychological Consequences of Prolonged Deprivation*. Agra: National Psychological Corporation.

Misra, R.C. (1992). Fifth survey of educational research volume: *National Council of Educational Research and Training*.

Mulhern, S. (1994). Satanism, ritual abuse, and multiple personality disorder: A socio historical perspective. *International Journal of Clinical and Experimental Hypnosis*, 42(4), 265-288.

Nadon, S.M., Koverola, C., and Schludermann, E.H. (1998). Antecedents to prostitution: Childhood victimization. *Journal of Interpersonal Violence*, 13(2), 206-221.

National Academy of Sciences (1993). *Understanding Child Abuse and Neglect*. Washington, DC: National Academy Press.

National Advisory Mental Health Council (1995). Basic behavioural science research for mental health. *American Psychologist*, 50, 838 845.

National Commision for Women (1997). *The Velvet Blouse. The Sexual*

Exploitation of Children. New Delhi: National Commission for Women, Government of India, pp. 1-15.

National Research Council (1993). *Understanding Child and Neglect*. Washington, DC.: National Academy Press.

Neisser, U. (1967). *Cognitive Psychology*, N.Y.: Appleton Century Crofts.

Newberger, C.M. and Cook, S.J. (1983). Parental awareness and child abuse: A cognitive development analysis of urban and rural samples, *American Journal of Orthopsychiatry, 53*, 512-524.

Nolin, P., Ethier, L. (2007). Using neuropsychological profiles to classify neglected children with or without physical abuse. *Child Abuse and Neglect; 31*:631-643.

Nygard, R. (1969). Motive to approach success and motive to avoid failure in boys from different social groups. *Scandinavian Journal of Educational Research, 4*, 222-232.

O'Hagan, K. (1995). Emotional and psychological abuse: Problems of definition. *Child Abuse and Neglect, 19*, 449-461.

Okun, A., Parker, J.C., and Levendosky, A.A. (1994). Distinct and interactive contribution of physical abuse, socio-economic disadvantage, and negative life events to children's social, cognitive and affective adjustment. *Development and Psychopathology, 6*(1), 77-98.

Otto, R.K., Mental, G.B. (1990). Trends in legislation and case law on child abuse and neglect. In R.T. Ammerman and M. Hersen (Eds.), *Children at Risk: An evaluation of factors contributing to child abuse and neglect*. (pp. 55-83). New York: Plenum.

Pagare, D., Meena, G.S., Singh, M.M., Sahu, R. (2004). Risk factors of substance use among street children from Delhi. *Indian Pediatr. 41*, 221-225.

Pandey S. (2017) Understanding Child Abuse in School Setting: Psycho-social Perspective. Project Report submitted to ICSSR, New Delhi.

Pandey, S. (2004). Preventing Child Maltreatment: Ecological Perspective. Unpublished research project report, under D.S.A. programme. Department of Psychology, D.S.A., D.D.U. Gorakhpur University, Gorakhpur.

Pandey, S. (2005). "Social Dynamics of Child Abuse and its Psychological Consequences in Eastern Districts of U.P." Unpublished U.G.C. Research Project. Department of Psychology, D.S.A., D.D.U. Gorkhpur University, Gorkhpur.

Pandey, S. (2007). Does child abuse impair the cognitive development in children? *Psychological Studies, 52*, 4, 357-359.

Pandey, S. (2008). Leadership style and conflict management at Railway Training Centre, Gorakhpur.

Pandey, S. (2010). Domestic violence and child behaviour in school. *Indian Journal of Social and Psychological Studies, 3*, 2, 15-24, 0974-634X.

Pandey, S. (2011). Cognitive functioning in children: The role of child abuse, setting and gender. *Journal of the Indian Academy of Applied*

Psychology, 37, 1, 98-105, 0019-4247.

Pandey, S. (2012). *Child Abuse Checklist*. Rupa Psychological Corporation, Varanasi.

Pandey, S. (2012). Domestic violence and status of women in India. *Indian Journal of Social and Psychological Studies, 5*, 2, 53-63, 0974-634X.

Pandey, S. (2012). *Domestic Violence Checklist*. Rupa Psychological Corporation, Varanasi.

Pandey, S. (2012). *Marital Conflict Questionnaire*. Rupa Psychological Cooperation, Varanasi.

Pandey, S. (2013). Does child abuse impede development of working memory in children? *Indian Journal of Psychological Issues, 21*, 1 and 2, 16-31, 0972-4427.

Pandey, S. and Singh, M. (2008). Women empowerment and personal values as predictors of reproductive health. *Journal of the Indian Academy of Applied Psychology, 34*, 2, 309-316, 0019-4247.

Pandey, S. and Srivastva, S. (2004). Role of coping in work stress-health relationship: A study on career women. Akbar Husain and Tabassum Rashid (Eds). *Stress Behaviour: The Coping Strategies*, Vol. 2.

Pandey, S. and Tamta, P. (2013). Does child abuse impede development of working memory in children. *Indian Journal of Psychological Issues*, Vol. 21, No. (1 and 2) 16-31.

Pandey, S., (2015). Aspiration Scale (modified version by S. Pandey 2007). *First annual report submitted to ICSSR.*

Pandey, S., (2015). Child abuse in school checklist. *First annual report submitted to ICSSR.*

Pandey, S., (2015). Depression Scale (modified version by S. Pandey 2015). *First annual report submitted to ICSSR.*

Pandey, S., (2015). Personal Data Sheet. *First annual report submitted to ICSSR.*

Pandey, S., (2015). Sate Trait Anxiety Inventory for Children (modified version by S. Pandey 2015). *First annual report submitted to ICSSR.*

Pandey, S., Tamta, P. and Tripathi, N. (2015). Does verbal ability facilitate the development of working memory? *Journal of Psychological Researches: An International Journal, 59*, 2, 12-22, 0022-3972.

Pandey, S., Tripathi, N. and Prasad, A. (2015). The role of parenting in shaping children's behaviour. *Asian Academic Research Journal of Social Science and Humanities, 2*, 6: 301-317, 2278-859X.

Pandhi, R.K., Khanna, N., and Sekhri, R. (1995). Sexually transmitted diseases in children. *Indian Pediatr.* 32, 27-30.

Patel, V., Andrew, G. (2001). Gender, sexual abuse and risk behaviours in adolescents: a cross-sectional survey in school in Goa. *Natl. Med. J. India. 14*, 263-267.

Pears, K., Fisher, P.A. (2005). Developmental, cognitive, and neuropsychological functioning in preschool-aged foster children: Associations with prior maltreatment and placement history.

Developmental and Behavioural Pediatrics; 26(2):112-122.

Pelcovitz, D., Kaplan, S., Goldenberg, B., and Mandel, F. (1994). Post-traumatic Stress disorder in physically abused adolescents. *Journal of American Academy of Child and Adolcents Psychiatry, 33* (3), 305-312.

Pelton, L. (1978). Child abuse and neglect: The myth of class lessens, *American Journal of Orthopsychiatry, 48*(4), 608-617.

Pierce, R.L. (1984). Child pornography: A hidden dimension of child abuse. *Child Abuse and Neglect, 8,* 483-493.

Pinheiro, P.S. (2006). *World Report on Violence against Children. United Nations Secretary-General's Study on Violence against Children.* New York: United Nations.

Porter, M.E., Schwab, K. and Lopez-Claros, A. (eds.) (2005). *The Global Competitiveness Report 2005-06: Policies Underpinning Rising Prosperity,* Palgrave Macmillan: New York.

Prasad M.R., Kramer L.A., Ewing-Cobbs L. (2005). Cognitive and neuroimaging findings in physically abused preschoolers. *Arch. Dis. Child, 90,* 82-85 10.1136/adc.2003.045583.

Prino, C.T. and Peyrot, M. (1994). The effect of child physical abuse and neglect on aggressive, withdrawn, and pro-social behaviour. *Child Abuse and Neglect, 18,* 871-884.

Puttman, F.W. (1991). The satanic ritual abuse controversy. *Child Abuse and Neglect, 15,* 175-179.

Ray, M., and Lyer, A.N. (2006). Abuse among Child Domestic Workers. A Research Study in West Bengal. Available from: http://www.cccindia.co/corecenter/Database/Does/DocFile/research_bengal pdf.

Reider, C. and Cicchetti, D. (1989). Organizational perspective on cognitive control functioning and cognitive affective balance in maltreated children. *Developmental Psychology, 25,* 382-393.

Rindfleisch, N. & Nunno, M. (1992). Progress and issues in the implementation of the 1984 out-of-home care protection amendment. Child Abuse & Neglect, 16, 693-708.

Rindfleisch, N., and Nunno, M. (1992). Progress and issues in the implementation of the 1984 out-of-home care protection amendment. *Child Abuse and Neglect, 16,* 693-708.

Rohner, R.P. and Rohner, E.C. (1980). Antecedents and consequences of parental rejection: A theory of emotional abuse. *Child Abuse and Neglect, 4,* 189-198.

Rosen, B.C. (1962). Race, Socialization and the achievement motivation in Brazil. *American Sociological Review, 27,* 612-624.

Rush, F. (1980). *The best kept secret: Sexual abuse of children.* Englewood Cliffs, NJ: Prentice Hall.

Russel, D.E.H. (1986). *The Secret Trauma: Incest in the Lives of Girls and Women.* New York: Basic Books.

Russel, D.E.H. (1988). Pornography and rape: A causal model. *Political*

Psychology, 9, 41-73.

Rust. J.D. and Troup, P.A. (1991). Relationship of treatment of child sexual abuse with school achievement and self-concept. *Journal of Early Adolescence, 11*, 420-429.

Salzinger, S., Kaplan, S., Pelcoviz, D., Samit, C. and Krieger, R. (1984). Parent and teacher assessment of children's behaviour in child maltreating families. *Journal of the American Academy of Child Psychiatry.*

Savitz, J., vander Merwe, L., Stein, D. J., Solms, M., and Ramesar, R. (2007). Genotype and childhood sexual trauma moderate neurocognitive performance: A possible role for brain-derived neurotrophic factor and apolipoprotein E variants. *Biological Psychiatry, 62*(5), 391-399.

Schore, A.N. (2003). Early relational trauma, disorganized attachment, and the development of a predisposition to violence. In M.F. Solomon and D.J. Siegel (Eds.), *Healing Trauma: Attachment, mind, body, and brain.* New York, NY: Norton.

Schteingart, J.S. Molnar, J., Klein, T.P., Lowe, C.B. and Hartman, A.H. (1995). Homelessness and child functioning in the context of risk and protective factors moderating child outcomes. *Journal of Clinical Child Psychology, 24*, 320-331.

Sedlak, A.J. and Broadhurst, D.D. (1996). Executive Summary of the Third National Incidence Study of Child Abuse and Neglect. (DHHS Pub. No. ACF 105-94-1840). Washington, D.C.: Government Parenting Office.

Sharma, T.R., (1984). *Academic Achievement Motivation Test.* National Psychological Corporation, Agra.

Sheintuch, G., and Lewin, G. (1981). Parents' attitudes and children's deprivation: Child-rearing attitudes of parents as a key to the advantaged-disadvantaged distinction in pre-school children. *International Journal of Behavioural Development,* Netherlands, 4, pp. 125-142.

Shields, A.M., Cicchetti, D. and Ryan, R.M. (1994). The development of emotional and behavioural self-regulation and social competence among maltreated school age children. *Development and Psychopathology, 6*, 57-75.

Shin, S., and Miller, D. (2012). A longitudinal examination of childhood maltreatment and adolescent obesity: Results from the National Longitudinal Study of Adolescent Health (Add Health) Study. *Child Abuse and Neglect, 36*(2), 84-94.

Silbert, M. (1982). Prostitution and sexual assault: Summary of results. *International Journal for Biosocial Research, 3*, 69-71.

Silbert, M., and Pines, A.M. (1983). Early sexual exploitation as an influence in prostitution. *Social Work, 28*, 285-289.

Slade, B.B., Steward, M.S., Morrison, T.L., 7 Abramowitz. S.I. (1984). Locus of control. Persistence and use of contingency information in physically abused children. *Child Abuse and Neglect, 8,* 447-457.

Snow, B., and Sorenson, T. (1990). Ritualistic child abuse in a neighbourhood setting. *Journal of Interpersonal Violence, 5*(4), 474-487.

Spielberger, C.D. (1973). The State-Trait Anxiety Inventory for Children (STAIC). *The Psychological Corporation,* San Antonio.

Spinetta, J.J and Rigler, D. (1972). The child-abusing parent: A psychological review. *Psychological Bulletin, 77,* 296-304.

Srivastava, P.K. and Tiwari, M.L. (1967). Socio-economic stratification of need achievement. Psychological Studies, 12, 9-16.

Steele, B. (1980). Psychodynamic Factors in Child Abuse. In C.H. Kempe and R.E. Helfer (Eds). *The Battered Child,* 3rd ed., Chicago: University of Chicago Press.

Strakey, S.L. (1980). The relationship between parental acceptance rejection and the academic performance of fourth and fifth graders. *Behaviour Science Research,* 15, 67-80.

Stratus, M. (1980). Stress and physical abuse. *Child Abuse and Neglect, 4,* 75-88.

Straus, M.A. (1977). Societal morphogenesis and interfamily violence in cross-cultural perspective. *Annals of the New York Academy of Sciences, 285,* 717-730.

Straus, M.A. and Kantor, G.K. (1994). Corporal punishment of adolescents by parents: A risk factors in the epidemiology of depression, suicide, alcohol abuse, child abuse and wife beating. *Adolescence,* 29, 543 561.

Straus, M.A., and Gelles, R.J. (Eds), (1990). *Physical Violence in American Families.* New Brunswick. N.J.: Transaction Books.

Straus, M.A., and Gelles, R.J. and Steinmetz, S.K. (1980). *Behind Closed Doors.* Beverly Hills, C.A.: Sage.

Streeck-Fischer, A., and van der Kolk, B.A. (2000). Down will come baby, cradle and all: Diagnostic and therapeutic implications of chronic trauma on child development. *Australian and New Zealand Journal of Psychiatry, 34*(6), 903-918.

Suri, I.S. (1989). An investigation in to the structure of reasoning ability of 18-year-old students belonging to rural and urban areas Ph.D., Edu. Jamia Millia Islamia.

Taylor, R.P., and Stone, L.E. (1985). Child pornography: Perpetuating the sexual victimization of children. *Child Abuse and Neglect, 9,* 313-318.

Taylor, S.E. (1991). *Health Psychology* (2nd ed) New York. McGraw-Hill.

Thibaunt, J.W. and Kelly, H.H. (1959). *The Social Psychology of Groups.* New York: Wiley.

Thompson, R.A. (1994). Social support and the prevention of child maltreatment. In G.B. Metton and Barry (Eds). *Protecting Children from Abuse and Neglect: Foundations for new National Strategy* (pp. 40-130). New York: Guilford.

Tolan, P.H. and Guerra, N.(1988). Societal causes of violence against children. In P.K. Trickett and C.J. Schellenbach (Eds.), *Violence Against*

Children in the Family and the Community, (pp, 195-209). Washington DC.: American Psychological Association.

Travis, C. (1993, January). Beware the incest-survivor machine. *New York Times*, p. 1.

Triandis, H.C. (1995). *Individualism and Collectivism*. Boulder, Co: Westview Press.

Trickett, P.K., and Susman, E.J. (1988). Parental perceptions of child-raising practices in physically abusive and non-abusive families. *Development Psychology, 24*, 270-276.

Tripathi, L.B. (1988). Higher mental process. In J. Pandey (Ed). *Psychology in India: The State of the Art*, Vol-1, New Delhi: Sage.

Trommsdorff, G. (1998). Social and psychological aspects of ongoing changes in Japan: Introduction. In G. Trommsdorff, W. Friedlmeier, and H.J. Kornadt (Eds.), *Japan in Transition: Social and psychological aspects* (pp. 11-21). Lengerich, Germany: Pabst Science.

Turner, M.L. and Engle, R.W. (1989). Is working memory capacity task dependent? *Journal of Memory and Language, 28*, 127-154.

Uhr, R., Thamas, H. and Becker, J. (1969). Entwich-lungsverlanfe in kindes and Jugenalter. *Zeischrift furent wicklungs psychology and padagogische psychologie*.

UNICEF (2012). *The State of World's Children*. Available from: www.unicef.org/sow2012.

Verma, S.K., Wig N.N. and Pershad, D. (1985). PGI Health Questionnaire. *India National Psychological Corporation*.

Vissing, Y.M., Straus, M.A., Gelles, R.J. and Harrop, J.W. (1991). Verbal aggression by parents and psychosocial problems of children. *Child Abuse and Neglect, 15*, 223-238.

Vondra, J.I., Barnett, D. and Cicchetti, D. (1990) 'Self-Concept, Motivation, and Competence Among Maltreating and Comparison Families'. *Child Abuse and Neglect, 14*: 525-40.

Wage, C.T., and Daro, D. (1998). *Current trends in child abuse reporting and fatalities: The results of the 1997 annual fifty state survey*. Chicago: National Center on Child Abuse Prevention Research.

Waterman, J., Kelly, R.J., Oliveri, M.K., and McCord, J. (1993). *Behind the playground walls: Sexual Abuse in Preschools*, New York: Guilford.

Whitmore, E.A.W., Kramer, J.R. and Knustson, J.F. (1993). The association between punitive childhood experiences and hyperactivity. *Child Abuse and Neglect, 17*, 357-366.

Widom, C., Czaja, S., Bentley, T., and Johnson, M. (2012). A prospective investigation of physical health outcomes in abused and neglected children: New findings from a 30 year follow-up. *American Journal of Public Health, 102*(6), 1, 135-1, 144.

Widom, C.S. (1989). Does violence beget violence? A critical examination of the literature. *Psychological Bulletin, 106*, 3-28.

Widom, C.S. (1999). Post-traumatic stress disorder in abused and neglected children grown up. *The American Journal of Psychiatry, 156*: 1223 1229.

Williams, L.M., and Finkelhor, D. (1990). The characteristics of incestuous fathers: A review of recent studies. In W.L. Marshall, D.R. Laws and H.E. Barbaree (Eds.), *Handbook of Sexual Assault: Issues, theories, and treatment of the offender* (pp. 231-255): New Yark: Plenum.

Wodarski, J.S., Kurtz, P.D., Gaudin, J.M., and Howing, P.T. (1990). Maltreatment and the school age child: Major academic, socio-emotional and adaptive outcomes. *Social Work, 35*, 506-513.

Wolfe, D. (1985). Child abusive parents. An empirical review and analysis. *Psychological Bulletin, 97*, 462-482.

Wolfe, D. (1987). *Child Abuse: Implications for Child Development and Psychopathology*, Newbury Park, CA: Sage.

Wolfe, D. (1988). *In QSO Absorption Lines: Probing the Universe*, J.C. Blades *et al.* Cambridge University Press.

Wolfe, D. (1999). *Child Abuse: Implications for Child Development and Psychopathology* (2nd ed.) Thousand Oaks, CA: Sage.

Wolfe, D., Werkele, C., Reitzel-Jaffe, D. and Lefebvere, L. (1998). Factors associated with abusive relationship among maltreated and non-maltreated youth. *Development and Psychopathology, 10*, 61-85.

Wolfe, D.A., Jaffe, P.J., Wilson, S.K. and Zak, I. (1985). Children of battered women: The relation of child behaviour to family violence and maternal stress. *Journal of Consulting and Clinical Psychology, 53*, 657-665.

Wolfgang, M.E. and Ferracuti, F. (1972). *Delinquency in a Birth Cohort*. London: Tavistock.

World Health Orgnization (1997, March). Child Abuse and Neglect. *http://www.who.inf-fs/en/fact. 150.html.*

Wuttele, S.K. and Miller-Perrin, C.L. (1992). *Preventing child sexual abuse: Sharing the responsibility*. Lincoln: University of Nebraska Press.

Wyatt, G.E. (1994). Socio-cultural and epidemiological issues in the assessment of domestic violence. *Journal of Social Distress and the Homeless, 3*, 7-21.

Zahn-Waxler, C, Cole, P.M., Welsh, J.D., and Fox, N.A. (1995). Psychophysiological correlates of empathy and pro-social behaviours in preschool children with behaviour problems. *Development and Psychopathology, 1*, 27-48.

Zillman, D. (1979). *Hostility and Aggression*, Hillsdale, NJ: Earlbaum.

Index